Selma Zaetz's
Favorite
Ethnic
Recipes

The New England Press
P. O. Box 575
Shelburne, Vermont 05482

Library of Congress Catalog Card Number: 82-61686
ISBN: 0-933050-15-1

Design: David Robinson
Cover and illustrations: Elizabeth Cotten Hemingway

PRINTED IN THE UNITED STATES OF AMERICA

Contents

Foreword

The recipes in this book offer varied and delightful trips to the tables of many lands. They offer you as well the opportunity to set before your family, friends, and guests foods that are superb in taste and attractive in appearance. My interest in ethnic cooking began many years ago as I was growing up in an Israeli-Jewish household and continued into later life as I became acquainted with people from many different countries. I welcomed the opportunity to join my friends and acquaintances in their kitchens and invited them into mine so that I could learn firsthand how to prepare their traditional foods. These have been some of my happiest hours.

As is so often the case, the traditional recipes in this cookbook have been handed down by word of mouth from one generation to the next. More often than not, the preparation of the foods had become a matter of habit and standard measurements were almost nonexistent. In writing these recipes for you I have spent many hours kitchen-testing each one so as to translate my mother-in-law's handfuls and pinches and my Chinese friend's dashes and tads into conventional measurements and directions. It is my hope that you will get to know these recipes well and that they will become standards in your repertory of recipes.

Most of the ingredients in my recipes can be purchased in your local supermarket. They can also be found in department stores with gourmet food sections and are certainly available in ethnic grocery shops. Fortunately, these ingredients keep well, whether on the shelf or in the freezer, and can therefore be used over a long period of time. Once you become familiar with these new foods and spices, you will find using them a pleasure. And what fun it can be to visit stores where people of different ethnic backgrounds buy their staples. Store owners and the people who work in these specialty food shops usually offer a warm welcome and are quite willing to discuss recipes and taste treats with customers who are sincere about experimenting with foreign foods. A visit to an Armenian, Chinese and Polynesian, German, Greek, Italian, Israeli, Spanish, or Mexican food shop will fill your cupboard and freezer with interesting foods and be a rewarding experience as well.

I always enjoy serving ethnic foods to my dinner guests. One of the special pleasures in doing this is the sense of adventure you have in deciding on the menu. You may prepare a Mexican meal, for example, selecting only dishes from that section in this cookbook, or you may prefer, as I do, to prepare dishes from several different countries, choosing not only what pleases you most but also creating a fascinating menu in the process. By all means use you own judgment and make the dinner your individual adventure. You will be happy in knowing that you are a good cook and are also widening the culinary tastes of those around you to a more cosmopolitan and worldly view.

The recipes in this book serve eight people unless otherwise indicated. If you are having four or five people for dinner, divide the measurements in half. If you are having six or seven, use three-fourths of each measurement. For larger parties, multiply the ingredients accordingly, being very careful of your arithmetic. You should, however, use only three-fourths of the multiplied figures for salt, herbs, and spices and then adjust for taste.

In selecting recipes for this book I have not been guided by their ethnic value alone but have as well sought recipes that meet a personal standard of excellence. Most of these recipes can be frozen without fear of losing any appeal or be made ahead with excellent results.

If you are planning a dinner party, start well in advance. Learn to utilize time when you have it. Practice your culinary attempts first on your family—they are most understanding. Once mastered, offer your triumphs to your guests. First, select your menu and make up your shopping list. The actual cooking and preparation for a special occasion should never be haphazard. Make and freeze a week or two in advance if possible; prepare whatever you can a day or two before if it will keep. Never plan a menu that will include more than one dish that will need last-minute doing.

Select the linen, silver, and china you wish to use and make sure, a week ahead, that they are looking their best. Plan your seating arrangements, decide on the accessories you will use, and make sure that you haven't overlooked anything.

I always like to write out the steps for heating and serving, listing the steps in the sequence I will do them. Of course, don't leave too much to be done on "The Day." Above all, see that you are relaxed so that you can truly enjoy your guests and they, in turn, can enjoy your company. Good luck, good appetite, and happy entertaining.

Among the many friends I am indebted to for recipes from their native lands are Anooshig Abajian, Mel Abajian, Frances Bloomenthal, Betty and Lot Cheng, Patricia Chow, Tina Diatlove, Shira Hackel Fisher, Francesca German, Rose M. Hackel, Sonya Zaetz Hackel, Bernadine Lerman, Judith Lerman, Lilian Lisman, Mariafranca Morselli, Sara Pappas, Gail Perazzini, Maria Pizzagalli, Mary Spencer, Marian Terrian, Maria Yherri, and Jennie Zaetz.

Selma Zaetz
Tucson, Arizona
June, 1983

ABOUT THE AUTHOR

Selma Bloomenthal Zaetz is a native Vermonter and a graduate of Burlington High School and the University of Vermont, class of 1933. She married Saul Zaetz in 1931 and is the mother of two children and the grandmother of seven.

Over the years Selma has gained a reputation for ethnic cooking and entertaining and is well known for the many cooking courses that she offered through the Burlington YWCA and the University of Vermont. In addition, she gave lecture demonstrations to such organizations as the New England Medical Association Auxiliary, The Klifa Club, The Women of UVM, the Sara Frank Chapter of Hadassah, and other women's clubs throughout the northeast. During this time Selma was busy writing and refining the original native recipes she had collected from her many ethnic friends. The YWCA published her first collection of recipes in 1974 under the title *Gourmet International,* and it was an immediate success. Copies of this book are used regularly and are still very much cherished by those who own them. Shortly after her cookbook appeared, Selma gave a demonstration of ethnic hors d'oeuvres on Boston's "Good Morning New England" where she appeared with Dr. Joyce Brothers and Myron Floren of the Lawrence Welk Show.

Because of the continuing demand for her original cookbook, Selma has updated, revised and expanded it, and *Selma Zaetz's Favorite Ethnic Recipes* is the result. Of particular interest is the new section on Mexican cookery, a cuisine Selma has come to love, living as she does now in Tucson, Arizona. She continues to teach ethnic cooking classes at the YWCA in Tucson and is busy writing another book, not on ethnic recipes, but in the field of ethnic living, hoping that this, too, will find an enthusiastic audience.

Armenian

Delicious Homemade Yogurt (Madzoon)

½ cup Madzoon or ½ pint
    commercial yogurt
    starter
1 quart milk

A starter of a half cup of Madzoon obtained from a friend or Armenian or Greek restaurant is best. However, if such a starter is not available one may use commercial yogurt with good results. With Madzoon starter: Bring 1 quart of homogenized milk to a boil and pour immediately into a pottery or Pyrex bowl. Allow to cool to lukewarm, 125°. Dissolve the starter with a little of the lukewarm milk and add, mix well. Cover and wrap the bowl in a large Turkish towel. Allow to stand at room temperature for 3-4 hours or until Madzoon gets thick as custard. When right consistency, place in refrigerator and set for an hour or so before using. With commercial starter: Use the method above, using 1 quart of milk to ½ pint commerical yogurt as starter. Repeat process 2 or 3 times to get right consistency. Always save ½ cup of the Madzoon for a starter for the next batch. A starter may be frozen by pouring water to ½ inch deep in top of the saved starter. When ready to use, defrost and pour off water. Madzoon is eaten by itself as a flavorful dish, is used in cooking, is combined with other foods for salads, soups, etc. and is the basis for the refreshing drink, Tahn.

Tahn: Dilute Madzoon with water to a thin drinking consistency, mixing well. Taste and add lemon juice if not tart enough. Chill.

Jajik: A delicious salad served in sauce dishes. Add quartered slices of cucumber to Madzoon. Thin out by adding just a little water, mixing well. Add salt and a touch of crushed garlic to taste for flavor. Allow to blend for half hour in refrigerator before using.

Armenian Bread

Armenian bread, while very tasty, is quite different from the breads most Americans know. It is a dry, flat bread and is served wet or dry, depending on the individuals preference. If it is served wet, the bread is simply broken in pieces and held under running water for a few seconds before serving; this is done to soften the bread just a bit on the outside and still keep it crisp when bitten into. When eaten dry, the bread is particularly delicous spread with butter or hors d' oeuvres. While the bread can be made at home, it is most often bought at Armenian stores. An excellent Armenian bread which can be purchased at almost any grocery store is called Euphrates Bread Waferettes, with sesame seeds.

3

Butter Yeast Cakes, Tea Biscuits (Cherag)

½ cup warm water
2 yeast cakes
2 cup milk, lukewarm
1 pound butter, melted
½ cup sugar
9½ cups flour
4 teaspoons baking powder
1 tablespoon salt
4 eggs, beaten
1 tablespoon black Russian
   caraway seeds (optional)
   Sesame seeds

Crumble yeast cakes in warm water and add 1 tablespoon of the sugar. Heat milk to lukewarm, melt butter and combine. Sift flour, sugar, baking powder and salt together. Make a well in dry ingredients and put in beaten eggs; combine milk and butter mixture and yeast mixture. Mix well adding caraway seeds, if you are using them. Turn out on a lightly floured surface and knead for a few minutes; adding flour if sticky but be sure to keep dough on the soft side. Put dough in a large greased bowl; lightly grease top of dough; cover. Place in a warm, draftless place and allow to rise until double in size or make in evening and allow to raise overnight. Punch down and divide the dough into 3 pieces. Roll out each piece on a lightly floured surface to about ¾ inch thick. Cut in diamond shapes, approximately 1½ x 2½ inches or roll in thin strips and take 3 inch pieces and braid 3 together making small braided cakes. Place on cookie sheets and brush each tea cake with a little of an egg which has been beaten with a tablespoon of milk. Sprinkle tops with sesame seeds. Cover and allow to rise in a draftless place for ½ hour. Bake in 375° oven for about 15 minutes or until golden brown. Makes about 3½ dozen. (Freezes well.)

Stuffed Grape Leaves No. 1 (Derevi Sarma)

4 cups onions, diced
1 cup long grained rice,
   washed
1 cup olive oil
1 teaspoon crushed dried
   mint leaves
2 teaspoons salt
3 teaspoons dill weed or
   ¼ cup fresh dill, chopped
2 tablespoons lemon juice
¼ cup currants (optional)
¼ cup pine nuts (optional)
   Grape leaves, fresh or
   canned

Saute onions in olive oil in a large frying pan until lightly golden. Add rice and rest of ingredients except grape leaves and mix well. Remove from heat and cool. If grape leaves are fresh soak them in boiling water for about 5 minutes; drain; squeeze dry and cut off stems. If canned leaves are used; taste the brine and if very salty, rinse the leaves in warm water and drain and squeeze dry. To fill, place a leaf on a small plate, dull side up, with the stem end toward you; cut off stems. Place a teaspoon of the rice mixture near the stem end and fold over the sides of the leaf and start rolling away from you. They will look rather like the size of a thumb. Arrange a few leaves on the bottom of a large kettle and arrange the rolled, filled leaves in layers on top. Add 2 cups water and place a plate on top of the rolls so that it will hold them tightly in place. Cover and cook over low heat for 1½ hours, or bake in 350° oven for the same length of time; testing one to make sure rice is soft. After they are cooked, allow them to remain covered until cool. Remove from kettle and place in dish that has a tightly fitting cover. Sprinkle with a little olive oil and lemon juice and refrigerate. Serve cold. To be eaten with the fingers. (Will keep up to a month in refrigerator after cooking.)

Cheese-Filled Puff Pastries (Berag)

4 cups flour
½ teaspoon baking powder
     (optional)
¼ pound butter
1 tablespoon olive oil
1 tablespoon lemon juice
1 cup ice water
2 egg yolks, beaten
¾ pound butter

Sift flour and baking powder. Cut the ¼ pound butter into the flour to consistency of small peas. Mix olive oil, lemon juice, ice water and beaten egg yolks well. Add to dry ingredients, forming pastry ball with as little handling as possible. Roll out on lightly floured surface in a rectangle about ½ inch thick. Place ¾ pound firm, cool butter in small chunks all over dough. Roll up as for a jelly roll; wrap in waxed paper and chill in refrigerator for about 15 minutes. Take out and roll out again. Roll up as for a jelly roll, in alternating direction, and replace in refrigerator. Repeat this about 5 times. The last time roll the dough out to about ¾ inch thick and cut into 1 inch squares. Place the pieces on a greased cookie sheet and cover with waxed paper and then a wrung-out damp cloth. Return to refrigerator and allow to rest several hours or overnight. Roll each piece to about ¼ inch thick, rolling out a few pieces at a time, leaving the rest in the refrigerator. Follow directions below for filling and baking.

Filling:

2 pounds Muenster cheese,
     grated
⅛ pound Cheddar cheese,
     grated
⅛ pound Blue cheese,
     crumbled
½ cup chopped parsley
2 eggs, beaten
2 teaspoons black Russian
     caraway or Dill weed
     Salt and pepper to taste

Mix all ingredients well by tossing lightly with a fork. Place a teaspoon of the mixture in the center of each piece of rolled out pastry. Dampen edges with a mixture of:

½ cup water   1 tablespoon cornstarch

Fold over dough to make a triangle, pinching edges together. Prick tops lightly with tines of a fork and brush with an egg beaten with 2 tablespoons water. Bake in 400° oven for 15 minutes or until golden brown. Serve hot. (Freezes well and to reheat, place frozen Berags on cookie sheets in 350° oven for 10-15 minutes.)

Stuffed Grape Leaves No. 2 (Derevi Sarma)

3 cups chopped onions
1 cup olive oil
1 cup rice
2 teaspoons salt
3 cups boiling water
2 teaspoons dill weed
¼ teaspoon cinnamon
½ teaspoon allspice
1 teaspoon paprika
¼ teaspoon pepper
2 large lemons
¼ cup currants (optional)
¼ cup pine nuts (optional)
Grape leaves, fresh or canned

Saute onions in olive oil in the largest size frying pan until lightly golden. Add rice and salt and mix well. Add boiling water and cook, covered, on medium heat until water is absorbed. Remove from heat and allow to cool about 10 minutes. Add seasonings, juice of 1 lemon, currants and pine nuts. Allow to fully cool. If the grape leaves are fresh, soak them in boiling water for about 5 minutes; drain; squeeze dry; and cut off stems. If canned leaves are used, taste the brine and if very salty rinse the leaves in warm water and drain and squeeze dry; cut off stems. To fill, place a leaf on a small plate, dull side up, with the stem end toward you. Place a teaspoon of the rice mixture near the stem end and fold over the sides of the leaf and start rolling away from you. They will look rather like the size of a thumb. Arrange a few leaves on the bottom of a large kettle and arrange the rolled, filled leaves in layers on top. Add 2 cups water and place a plate on top of the rolls so that it will hold them tightly in place. Cover and cook over low heat for 1 hour or bake in 350° oven for the same length of time. After they are cooked, allow them to remain covered until cool. Remove from kettle and place in dish that has a tightly fitting cover. Sprinkle with olive oil and the juice of the other lemon. To be eaten cold with fingers. (Does not freeze well but will keep up to a month perfectly in refrigerator.)

Stuffed Clams or Mussels (Clam or Mussel Dolma)

3 pounds good-sized clams or mussels
3 cups chopped onion
½ cup olive oil
1 teaspoon salt
½ teaspoon allspice
½ teaspoon pepper
¼ cup chopped currants
⅒ cup pine nuts or slivered almonds
½ cup rice

If using mussels, soak in salted water several hours first; if using clams, soak in water to cover with 2 tablespoons corn meal for several hours. Wash the shells of the mussels or clams with a good stiff brush. Open the mussels slightly and cut off the pieces of fuzz in the inside and wash well in fresh water. Loosen the joint of the clams or mussels a little so that they will open easily and close tightly. Saute onion in hot olive oil until golden. Add rest of ingredients and mix well. Put a teaspoon of rice mixture in empty side of the shells, not too full, allowing room for the rice to swell; close the shells and arrange in a large kettle side by side on top of one another. Cover with a plate directly on the clams or mussels; add 2 cups of water. Put on the cover and cook on low heat for 1½ hours or bake in 350° oven for the same length of time. Serve cold with lemon wedges. (Does not freeze but may be made several days ahead of planned use.)

Thin Pastries with Delicious Meat Covering (Lachmajoon)

2   yeast cakes
¼   cup warm water
4¾   cup flour
½   cup butter, melted
1   egg, well beaten
1   tablespoon salt
1   cup water

1   pound meat from lamb
      shoulder, lean
1   cup chopped onion
1   cup chopped green pepper
1   cup chopped parsley
3   cloves garlic, crushed
1   cup canned tomatoes,
      drained
¼   cup tomato sauce
1¼   teaspoons salt
¼   teaspoon pepper
      Dash of red pepper

Crumble yeast in ¼ cup warm water and set aside. Combine flour and salt. Add beaten egg and melted butter to 1 cup water and mix well; add dissolved yeast and water. Make a well in dry ingredients and add all liquid, mixing to a soft dough. Knead for a few minutes and allow to rest while making the topping.

Topping:

Grind the first 4 ingredients through meat grinder twice, or put in food processor until finely chopped. Add rest of ingredients and mix well. Divide dough into about 2 dozen small pieces. Set aside and cover with dish towel. Take each piece of dough and roll to a circle about the size of a saucer and quite thin. Spread thinly with a layer of the meat preparation; covering entire surface to about ⅛ inch of the outer edge. Place on large greased cookie sheet and bake in 425° oven for 15-20 minutes, until meat mixture is cooked and dough is thoroughly done. These are eaten hot and may be served as a main dish along with a vegetable and salad for lunch. The proper way to eat them is to roll them up almost like a cigar. (They freeze beautifully and should be piled with the meat sides facing one another with paper in between and wrapped tightly in aluminum foil for freezing.) Separate while frozen and put in 350° oven to reheat.

Rope Cheese

This is a special cheese found only at food specialty stores or Armenian grocery stores. Taste it, and if too salty, soak covered in hot water for a few minutes. Taste again and dry. It is excellent as an hors d'ouvre, served with Armenian bread or Cherag, black (ripe) pickled olives and Armenian salami (Soujuk). (See pages 3, 7 and 9.)

Black or Purple (Ripe) Pickled Olives

1   pound black or purple
      (ripe) olives
1   cup olive oil
⅓   cup wine vinegar
      Juice of 1 lemon
2-3   cloves garlic, sliced

Put olives in a quart jar. Combine rest of ingredients; shake well and pour over olives, making sure that olives are covered by marinade. Allow to stand 24 hours before using, keeps indefinitely. Marinade may be used several times.

Meat-Filled Pastry Boats (Manti)

4¾ cups flour
1 tablespoon salt
1 teaspoon baking powder
¼ pound butter, melted
1 egg, well beaten
1¼ cups water

Sift dry ingredients together. Combine melted butter, beaten egg and water. Make a well in dry ingredients and add all liquid; mixing with hands to make a soft dough. Knead with well greased hands on a lightly floured surface for just a few minutes. Set aside while making the filling.

Filling:

1½ pounds lamb or chuck, ground twice
1½ cups chopped onion
½ cup chopped parsley
2 cloves garlic, crushed
1 teaspoon salt
½ teaspoon pepper
1 teaspoon crushed dried mint

Mix all ingredients well. Knead dough a few more minutes, adding whatever flour dough takes up to make it workable. Roll out to about ⅛ inch thick and cut into squares about 1½ inches. Put a dab of the meat mixture on each square and pinch the parallel corners together, shaping like a canoe. Grease cookie sheet lightly and arrange Manti close together, open side up. Bake in 375° oven until lightly golden brown. (Freezes well.) Excellent hors d'oeuvres. Serve hot.

Manti may be used for a soup course or luncheon dish also. Heat 10 cups of chicken broth and blend in 2 tablespoons tomato sauce, salt to taste. Pour the hot broth over the hot Manti. To use as a main course for luncheon; serve in soup plates with just a little hot broth and top with several tablespoons of Madzoon.

Soup with Dumplings (Blor Soup)

2 cups oatmeal
¾ cup fine bulghour, cracked wheat
¾ teaspoon salt
¾ cup water

Mix all ingredients very well. Shape into balls the size of marbles.

Broth:

8 cups beef broth
1 cup canned tomatoes
2 tablespoons butter
½ cup chopped onion
1 pound spinach, stems removed
Salt and pepper to taste

Bring broth to a boil; add dumplings and continue boiling 20 minutes. Fry onions in butter until lightly brown. Add onions, tomatoes and spinach to soup. Season and boil 8-10 minutes. Serve hot. (Make a day ahead of planned use.)

Delicious Dried Beef Salami (Soujuk)

Make this in the fall or early spring in the North, in the winter in the South. The first time Soujuk is made it involves a great deal of work because bags must be made in which to cure the Soujuk. However, it is definitely worth the trouble as the Soujuk keeps indefinitely and make an especially delicious hot d'oeuvres. One may also fry thin slices in a little butter, add beaten eggs and cook as an omelet to serve for a delightful luncheon dish.

To make bags, sew smooth, loosely woven cotton material, not cheesecloth, so as to make 3 bags approximately 8 x 15 inches, leaving one of the narrow ends open. These may be used again and again.

6 pounds meat from leg of lamb, ground twice
6 pounds very lean beef, ground twice
2 bulbs garlic, blended with ¼ cup water in electric blender
4 tablespoons black pepper
⅓ cup plus 2 tablespoons salt
½ cup paprika
1 tablespoon mace
4 tablespoons allspice
2½ teaspoons cinnamon
½ teaspoon red pepper
½ cup Cumin (Kimion), plus 1 tablespoon
¾ cup water

Soujuk Mixture:

Put all ingredients, except water, in a large size roaster and mix very, very thoroughly with hands, adding water as you mix when consistency becomes hard to handle. Mixing well cannot be overemphasized. Leaving the seams on the outside, pack the Soujuk mixture into the 3 bags. Push mixture into corners with your hands and flatten. Using a rolling pin on the outside of the bags, flatten each one to about 2 inches thick. Hang on man's suit hangers, folding open end over enough to pin with 3 spaced safety pins. Hang Soujuk on something high in a sunny, airy, dry cool place, such as a porch, garage or basement window, leaving the window open. Allow to hang for 6-8 weeks, until cured, dry and no longer soft or pink inside. When cured, remove from bags, cut each slab in half, wrap in aluminum foil and keep in refrigerator or freezer indefinitely. Soujuk is eaten thinly sliced cold or slightly heated.

Pink Lentil Soup (Vosp Soup)

1¼ cup pink lentils (Vosp), thoroughly washed
¾ cup medium cracked wheat (bulghour)
12 cups water or broth
1½ tablespoons salt or to taste
¼ teaspoon pepper
4 tablespoons butter
1 large onion, diced
4 teaspoons dried mint, crushed with palms of hands

Cook lentils, cracked wheat, salt and pepper in water or broth for 1½ hours, simmering gently. In a small frying pan, melt butter and saute diced onion until lightly browned; add crushed mint. Add all to soup; mix well; serve hot. (Freezes well.)

This is a delicious soup, hearty enough to make a good main dish for lunch or soup course with a light dinner. (Freezes well.)

1 ½ pounds very fat shoulder of lamb, ground twice
3 cups chopped onion
½ cup chopped green pepper
½ teaspoon allspice
¼ teaspoon dried basil
½ teaspoon paprika
1 teaspoon salt
1 cup finely chopped fresh parsley or ½ cup dry parsley
⅛ teaspoon cinnamon
1 teaspoon dried mint leaves, crushed between palms of hands
¼ teaspoon pepper
⅛ cup pine nuts

Filling Inside Ball: (This can be prepared the day before.)

Fry meat over a medium heat until fat is tried out, stirring occasionally. Add onions and cook on a slow heat for 30 minutes; stirring frequently. Add green pepper and cook 10 more minutes. Add rest of ingredients and cook 5 minutes; stirring all the while. Chill in refrigerator. Shape chilled filling into balls the size of large marbles.

1 ½ pounds lean shoulder or leg of lamb, ground twice
1 ½ cups fine bulghour, cracked wheat
1 medium onion, grated
2 tablespoons chopped parsley (optional)
1 ½ teaspoons salt
¼ teaspoon pepper
About ½ cup water

Outside Layer of Meat Balls or Kuftas:

Mix meat, bughour and rest of ingredients together, adding a little water at a time, kneading like dough. Add enough water to make mixture the texture of medium soft dough. Knead for 2 minutes. Make into balls the circumference of about 1 ½ inches. Now take one of the larger outside balls and press your thumb into the middle; work your thumb around to make a round opening for the inside ball. Seal together by smoothing the outside dough with wet fingers. Flatten the roundness of the Kuftas slightly by pressing gently between the palms of your hands. This will make about 2 dozen Kuftas.

Broth:

Make a good strong broth by boiling the bones from the shoulder, leg or chicken bones in about 10 cups of salted water. Boil for 2 hours; skim and strain. Add ½ cup canned tomatoes or tomato sauce; season to taste. Bring to a boil and drop a few Kuftas at a time into boiling broth using all the balls. Cover and cook for 8-10 minutes. Serve hot. (To store or freeze, take Kuftas from broth and keep separately. To heat, drop the Kuftas again into boiling broth and simmer for about 5 minutes.) The Kuftas also may be used for a luncheon dish by dipping cold slices of Kuftas into beaten eggs and frying in hot oil to a golden brown.

Egg Sauce for Soup

2   eggs
     Lemon juice
     Hot soup stock

Beat 2 eggs well; add juice of a lemon and beat again. Blend very, very slowly with hot soup stock by pouring over a fork and stirring constantly so that the egg will not curdle. Delicious added to clear lamb, beef, or chicken broth.

Yogurt (Madzoon) and Noodle Soup (Tutmah Soup)

4   cups Madzoon or yogurt
1   egg, beaten
1¼   teaspoons salt
6   cups water
1   cup wide noodles, broken
       in 1 inch pieces
4   tablespoons butter, melted
1   medium onion, diced fine
4   teaspoons crushed
       dried mint

Mix Madzoon or yogurt with egg and salt. Beat well, add water and mix again. Cook on high heat. stirring vigorously until it boils. Add noodles, lower heat and cook until noodles are tender. Saute onions in butter, add crushed mint. Add to soup, taste for seasonings and cook for another minute. Serve hot. (May be made several days ahead of planned use.)

Tripe Soup (Ishkembeth Soup)

4   pounds fresh beef tripe
4   cups beef broth
4   cups tripe broth
2   medium onions
3   cloves garlic in cheese-
       cloth bag
2   eggs and juice of 2 lemons
       for egg sauce
1½   teaspoons salt
½   teaspoon pepper
     Paprika

Wash tripe well and cover with water in a large kettle. Simmer for 3 hours. Take out tripe and strain broth. Put tripe through meat grinder or food processor. Combine broths and ground tripe, onions and garlic tied in cheesecloth. Simmer over low heat 3 hours, adding beef broth if too much liquid cooks away. Remove onions and garlic bag. Make Egg Sauce as directed in recipe and gradually add to soup. simmer for 10 more minutes. Taste and adjust seasonings. Sprinkle with paprika and serve hot. (Freezes well.)

11

Chopped Raw Sirloin Steak with Vegetables (Chee Kufta)

½ cup fine bulghour, ground
    wheat
1½ pounds lean sirloin beef,
    ground 3 times
⅓ cup finely chopped onion
4 tablespoons finely chopped
    parsley
1½ teaspoons salt or to taste
⅛ teaspoon red pepper
½ teaspoon black pepper
4 teaspoons dried mint,
    crumbled between palms
    of hands
    Tomato juice, about
    ¾ cup
1 large tomato, skinned, seeded,
    and chopped finely
1 green pepper, finely
    chopped
6 tablespoons chopped parsley
3-4 scallions, finely sliced

Cover bulghour with cold water and set aside. Mix next 7 ingredients well, preferably with hands. Squeeze water out of bulghour and add to meat mixture. Mix and gradually add enough tomato juice to make mixture just moist. Shape into individual size patties or pat into serving dish. Mix the chopped tomato, chopped pepper, parsley and scallions well and spread thickly over meat. Delicious eaten uncooked. Fry for those people who are squeamish about eating raw meat.

Stuffed Squash, Zucchini, Tomatoes and Green Pepper (Varied Dolma)

3 medium summer squash
3 medium zucchini squash
3 firm medium tomatoes
3 large green peppers
3 pounds lamb or beef,
    ground
¾ cup rice
2 medium onions, grated
    Pulp from tomatoes
½ green pepper, grated
2 cloves garlic, crushed
½ teaspoon oregano
2½ teaspoons salt
½ teaspoon pepper
1 large can (16 ounce)
    tomato sauce

Wash and clean vegetables; cut squash in thirds and scoop out inside seeds and pulp, leaving ½ inch of the vegetable for a bottom layer. Cut off tops of tomatoes and scoop out pulp and save; cut tops off green peppers; remove seeds and wash. Combine next 9 ingredients; mix well, preferably with hands. Stuff vegetables and arrange in a large kettle. Combine tomato sauce with enough water to bring liquid up ⅓ way on vegetables. Cover and cook over medium heat for 1 hour. Add water as juices cook away. Serve with sauce and pilaf. (Freezes well.)

6-8 pound leg of lamb
¾ cup oil
  Juice of 3 lemons
4 large onions, sliced in eighths lengthwise
¼ teaspoon coarse black pepper
4 cloves garlic, crushed (optional)
½ -1 teaspoon oregano
1 dozen medium tomatoes
6 large green peppers, cut in thirds
2 teaspoons salt

Famous and delicious; fun to make.

Cut lamb into pieces of about 1¾ inch square; removing most of the fat, but leaving a little on, and place in a large bowl. Mix oil and lemon juice well and pour over meat. Add sliced onion, pepper, garlic, if using it, and oregano and toss together lightly. Allow to marinate overnight or at least 6-8 hours in refrigerator. (May be frozen without adding onions. Defrost, add onions and proceed.)

Family Style: (Preferred by most because the flavors blend and mellow.) The meat and vegetables for this style of presentation are broiled separately, allowing for the varied cooking time as well as easier handling. The meat and vegetables are strung separately on large size skewers, stringing loosely, barely touching. The marinade and onions are gathered together in a saucepan, first brushing some of the marinade over the vegetables. Broil meat over a hot charcoal fire or under the stove broiler, about 6 inches away from the fire, turning frequently, until lightly browned all around. When meat has reached this stage, place the skewers of tomatoes and green peppers also over the fire and cook, turning frequently, until nicely broiled and tender. In the meantime simmer the marinade gently on top of the stove until onions are barely cooked, still crisp. When the meat is charred on the outside and still nicely pink on the inside, and the vegetables are done, remove from skewers, pressing all off with a large meat fork onto a deep serving dish. Break tomatoes and peppers into smaller pieces; add cooked marinade and onions; season well with salt. Serve with pilaf. (See recipe using the bones from the leg of lamb for broth for the pilaf.)

Individual Skewers: (More glamorous to serve.) The individual skewers are strung loosely with alternating pieces of meat and veg-tables. Also string the pieces of onions from the marinade (pearl onions are lovely for this), quartering the tomatoes or using the cocktail tomatoes and cutting the green peppers to about the same size as the meat. Pieces of bacon and mushroom caps may also be alternated with meat. While broiling, brush with marinade fre-quently, turning every few minutes. Broil over hot charcoal fire or under a broiler about 6 inches away from fire. Broil to lightly browned on all sides. Simmer the rest of the marinade in a sauce-pan on top of stove for just a few minutes. To serve, pour cooked marinade over pilaf, slip all off the skewers on top of individual servings of pilaf, being careful not to break the alignment. Garnish with parsley.

Grape Leaves Filled with Meat (Dervi Dolma)

Fresh or canned grape leaves
½ pound ground lamb
½ pound ground beef
1 cup finely chopped onion
¼ cup rice
¼ cup chopped parsley
2 teaspoons crushed dried mint
1¼ teaspoons salt
¼ teaspoon pepper
¼ cup tomato sauce
Juice of 1 lemon
Water, beef or lamb broth

If fresh leaves are used, cut off stems and soak leaves in boiling water about 3 minutes; rinse canned leaves under warm running water, drain and squeeze dry. Combine next 8 ingredients, mixing well. To fill, place leaf on a small plate, dull side up, with stem end toward you; cut off stem. Put teaspoon of meat mixture near stem end; fold over sides of leaf and start rolling away from you. (They will look somewhat like a thumb.) Cover bottom of kettle with leaves. Arrange stuffed rolls side by side and one on top of another. Pour over tomato sauce and lemon juice. Cover with a plate, pressing rolls down. Add water or broth to top of plate. Cover and bring to boil, simmer gently for 1 hour. Serve with pilaf. Freezes well.

Yogurt Soup (Tanabour Soup)

½ cup pearl barley
4 cups meat broth, skimmed of fat
3 cups yogurt (Madzoon)
1 egg
1 teaspoon salt
¼ teaspoon pepper
4 tablespoons butter
1 large onion, diced
3 teaspoons dried mint, crushed with palms of hands

Soak barley overnight. Drain and add to broth and cook, simmering, until barley is tender. Beat yogurt together with egg well and add slowly to soup. Add salt and pepper, taste and adjust. In a small frying pan, melt butter and saute onion until lightly browned, add mint, add all to soup. Serve hot or cold garnished with a little chopped parsley. (May be made several days before planned use.)

Hamburg Treat (Luleh Kebab)

1½ pounds lamb, ground, a little fat left
1½ pounds beef hamburg
¾ teaspoon kimion (cumin)
¾ teaspoon curry powder
¾ cup chopped parsley
3 cloves garlic, crushed
1½ teaspoons salt
¼ teaspoon pepper
1 cup tomato juice

Mix all ingredients well, preferably by hand. Shape as short fat sausages. Place over charcoal or in broiler pan and broil, basting frequently with juices. Turn and broil to desired doneness. Delicious done over charcoal. Serve in small Syrian bread, halved, and with a pilaf. (Meat may be prepared for cooking and frozen. Defrost and broil.)

Crown Roast of Lamb with Stuffing (Kabourga)

1   (24 rib) crown roast of
      lamb, as much fat removed
      as possible
½   cup tomato sauce
½   teaspoon thyme
½   teaspoon rosemary
      Salt and pepper

3   cups chopped onions
1   cup chopped green pepper
3   cups hulled wheat or rice
      (do use wheat if possible)
⅔   cup butter
⅓   cup chopped parsley
1½ teaspoons allspice
¾   teaspoon pepper
3   teaspoons salt
¼   cup pine nuts
¼   cup currants
3   cups chicken broth

Salt and pepper roast. Mix tomato sauce, thyme and rosemary. Brush tomato mixture all over meat. Cover rib bone ends with aluminum foil. Roast in 450° oven on rack set in roasting pan, 30 minutes. Meanwhile, prepare stuffing.

Stuffing:

Saute onion and green pepper in butter until golden. Add rest of ingredients; mix well. Cover and simmer gently until broth is absorbed. Remove from heat. After roast has been in oven 30 minutes, remove. Pour off drippings and place a piece of aluminum foil under it. Stuff center; cover stuffing with aluminum foil. Roast in 350° oven for 2½ to 3 hours. Remove aluminum foil and dress rib ends with frills. Slide onto serving platter and garnish. Carve at the table. (May be frozen before stuffing; defrost and proceed as above. Stuffing may be frozen separately.)

Eggplant and Hamburg (Taste Duezmeh)

3   large, long eggplants
3   pounds lamb, ground
      with a little fat
¼   cup chopped parsley
1   medium green pepper,
      chopped fine
2   large onions, grated
¼   teaspoon black pepper
½   teaspoon allspice
2½ teaspoons salt
2   cloves garlic, crushed
1   large can (16 ounce)
      tomatoes
1   green pepper, cut in
      1 inch strips
½   teaspoon oregano

Slice eggplants lengthwise, cutting into about 2 inch slices. Fry in olive oil until golden brown; drain and dry on paper towels. Mix lamb, parsley, green pepper, onions, pepper, allspice, salt and garlic well, preferably with hands. Make a pattie out of the hamburg mixture and place between 2 pieces of eggplant. Place in a large kettle, side by side. Separate layers with strips of green pepper; sprinkle with oregano. Pour tomatoes over all; cover and cook over low heat for 1 hour. Place uncovered in 350° oven for 15-20 minutes, basting frequently. Serve with pilaf. (Freezes well.)

Stuffed Lamb Brisket (Kabourga)

2 whole lamb briskets
¼ pound butter
2 cups chopped onions
1 green pepper, chopped
½ cup chopped parsley
3 cups medium bulghour, cracked wheat
1 teaspoon allspice
½ teaspoon cinnamon
½ teaspoon pepper
3 teaspoons salt
½ cup pine nuts
½ cup currants
2 cups hot water
2 cups tomato sauce
1 teaspoon crushed dried mint

Have butcher cut a pocket in each brisket. Wipe meat with a damp cloth and sprinkle with salt and pepper inside and out. Melt butter and saute onion and green pepper until golden. Add parsley and cracked wheat; add all seasonings except tomato sauce and mint. Add pine nuts and currants and mix well. Add water, stirring all the while, and cook slowly until all water is absorbed. Cool and stuff pockets of brisket loosely. Sew pockets closed. Place in a roasting pan and make gashes in the meat about every 5 inches. Pour tomato sauce over the meat and sprinkle with mint. Roast in 350° oven for 1½ hours covered. Uncover and roast another half hour, basting occasionally. Add water as needed. (Freezes well.)

Stuffed Cabbage Leaves (Cabbage Dolma)

2 pounds lamb, ground with a little fat
¾ cup rice
¾ cup chopped parsley
3 medium onions, grated
1 large size can tomatoes (save ½ cup)
⅛ teaspoon red pepper
¼ teaspoon black pepper
1 teaspoon crushed dried mint
2½ teaspoons salt (save ½ teaspoon)
1 large cabbage
Juice of 1 lemon

Mix first 9 ingredients well, preferably with hands. Cut core out of center of cabbage. Cover with boiling water and allow to steep until leaves loosen and become pliable, or place in large kettle with 2 inches water. Cover and boil for 5 minutes; remove and cool to handle. Peel off leaves of cabbage; cut out tough center veins. Place 1½ tablespoons meat mixture in each leaf; fold sides in and roll so that filling cannot come out. Place in a large pot and sprinkle with saved ½ teaspoon salt; pour over them the saved ½ cup tomatoes and add 1 cup water. Place a plate directly on top of cabbage rolls to press down and keep firm. Cover and bring to a boil; boil 15 minutes; uncover and remove plate. Pour over all the juice of the lemon; cover and cook gently for 1 hour. Push cover back half way on the kettle and allow to rest a few minutes before serving. Serve with a pilaf. (Freezes well.)

Lamb with Parsley and Scallions (Kenara Peyazles)

4 pounds lamb, cut in 1½
   inch cubes
2 teaspoons salt
6 large tomatoes, quartered
2 bunches scallions, chopped
1 cup chopped parsley
½ teaspoon coarse ground
   black pepper
½ teaspoon crushed dried
   mint

Wash meat and cook while still wet, uncovered, over medium heat. When water has cooked away add salt and stir. Cook over low heat, stirring occasionally, until meat is browned all over. Add tomatoes and cook covered for 20 minutes over low heat. Gather all meat in a mound in the center of the pan. Add other vegetables, placing them all around meat. Lightly stir in seasonings with a fork. Cover and take off heat, allow to stand until hot meat warms the vegetables. Serve with a pilaf. (Meat may be cooked and frozen. Defrost and proceed.)

Armenian-Style Hamburgers

3 pounds hamburg
1 large onion, grated
½ green pepper, grated
½ teaspoon oregano
2 teaspoons salt
½ teaspoon coarse ground
   black pepper
3 cloves garlic, crushed
2 medium tomatoes, mashed
2 eggs, beaten

Mix all ingredients well, preferably by hand. Allow to rest a few hours. Shape into patties and broil.

Lamb Chops Armenian Style

2 large onions, sliced
   lengthwise
3 large green peppers, cut in
   1½ inch strips
6 large tomatoes, quartered
16 lamb chops
½ teaspoon oregano
½ teaspoon coarse ground
   black pepper
1½ teaspoons salt
   Salt for chops

Place all vegetables in bottom of broiler pan. Season and place chops on top of vegetables. Broil about 6 inches from heat. Brown on both sides well and season chops with salt when done. Serve chops accompanied by vegetables and drippings with a pilaf.

Lamb and Cracked Wheat (Poreek)

3 pounds lamb, cut in 1½ inch cubes
1½ cups water
1 large onion, diced
⅓ cup chopped parsley
1 tablespoon salt
½ teaspoon coarse ground black pepper
2 tablespoons crushed dried mint
⅓ green pepper, diced
¾ cup tomatoes, cannned or fresh
3 cups medium bulghour, cracked wheat
6 cups water

Place lamb and 1½ cups water in a large kettle and cook over medium heat, stirring occasionally, until water cooks away and lamb browns. Add rest of ingredients and mix well. Cook slowly for ¾ hour, covered. Serve while still a little moist. (Freezes well. Defrost and heat, covered, in 300° oven for 45 minutes.)

Vegetable and Lamb Casserole (Tourlu Guevech)

4 tablespoons butter or margarine
3 pounds lamb, cut in 1½ inch cubes
2 medium eggplants, cut in 1½ inch pieces
2 medium zucchini squash, cut in 1½ inch pieces
2 large green peppers, chopped fine
1½ cups chopped onion
1 pound mushrooms, sliced
4 fresh tomatoes, quartered
1 package frozen okra or ½ pound fresh okra, sliced
2 teaspoons salt
¼ teaspoon black pepper
1 tablespoon paprika

Fry meat in butter until lightly browned. Place in a large earthen casserole, add vegetables and seasonings and mix well. Bake covered in a 300° oven for 2 hours or until all is tender. Serve with Bulghour Pilaf (see page 22). (Freezes well.)

Chicken and Bulghour Pilaf

1 roasting chicken, whole
2 teaspoons salt
½ teaspoon pepper
1 small onion
1 carrot
2 stalks celery
¼ teaspoon dried mint, crushed
Water to cover

Wash and clean chicken. Place in a large kettle with rest of ingredients. When chicken is almost tender, remove and drain. Strain broth and allow to cool. Remove fat from top of cooled broth and baste fat over chicken. Fry chicken in chicken fat, uncovered, over a medium heat, turning to brown on all sides. Make Bulghour Pilaf with chicken broth (see page 22). Dish out on a large platter, cut chicken in serving pieces and place on top of pilaf.

Chick-Pea Salad (Chick-Pea Plaki)

½ cup chopped parsley
1 large sweet onion, diced
2 cans chick-peas, rinsed in cold water, drained
⅓ cup olive oil
½ cup lemon juice or wine vinegar
½ teaspoon salt
⅛ teaspoon coarse ground pepper
2 tomatoes, sliced thinly

Add parsley and dice onion to drained chick-peas. Mix well. Pile into salad bowl. Combine olive oil, lemon juice or wine vinegar, salt and pepper; pour all over salad; toss. Serve in individual salad plates; dress top of each serving with slices of tomato. (May be made ahead with parsley added just before serving.)

Dilled Cucumbers in Yogurt or Madzoon Salad

4 cucumbers, peeled and seeded, sliced very thinly
Lettuce leaves

Dressing:

½ small clove garlic, crushed
2 teaspoons tomato sauce
¼ teaspoon salt
⅛ teaspoon white pepper
1 cup plain yogurt or Madzoon
3 teaspoons dill weed or fresh dill (optional)

Mix well and pour over cucumber slices which have been nicely piled on lettuce leaves just before serving. (Dressing may be made day ahead of planned use.)

Baked Fish (Fish Plaki)

4	pounds sea bass, red snapper, or any thick white fish
⅓	cup olive oil
½	teaspoon white pepper
2	teaspoons salt
	Juices of 2 lemons
2	cloves garlic, crushed
½	teaspoon oregano
½	cup fresh tomatoes, quartered
½	cup tomato sauce
½	cup chopped parsley

Marinate fish in first 6 ingredients for several hours. Place in large baking, serving dish with marinade, tomatoes and tomato sauce. Bake in 350° oven covered for 25 minutes. Uncover, add chopped parsley and baste occasionally. Bake 20 minutes more. Serve with Rice Pilaf (page 22). (Freezes well.)

Baked Eggplant and Vegetables (Imam Bayeldi)

4	medium eggplants

Slice 4 medium eggplants in 1 inch slices, skin on. Bake on dry Teflon-coated cookie sheets or on very lightly greased cookie sheets in 400° oven to brown on bottom, 30 minutes. Turn and bake another 10 minutes. Remove from oven.

Topping:

2	cups chopped green pepper
2	cups onion, cut lengthwise
½	cup chopped parsley
2	teaspoons salt
½	teaspoon pepper
2	cups diced, peeled and seeded tomatoes
4-6	cloves garlic, crushed
2	tablespoons tomato paste
¼	cup olive oil

Fry onion and green pepper in olive oil to golden. Add rest of ingredients and mix well. Cook gently, stirring occasionally, until soft. Pile on top of browned eggplant and bake at 375° for 20 minutes. Serve at room temperature or heated. (Freezes well. Reheat in 350° oven for 15 minutes, putting in frozen.)

Squash Berag

2 medium zucchini, grated,
   combined with 1 teaspoon
   salt, allow to stand 1 hour,
   squeeze dry
1 cup grated Muenster or
   cheddar cheese
4 eggs, beaten
½ teaspoon minced instant
   onion
½ cup flour
2 tablespoons finely chopped
   parsley
   Salt to taste
⅛ teaspoon white pepper
¼ teaspoon dill weed

Mix all ingredients together well. Pour into a buttered 8 x 8 inch baking pan; dot with butter. Bake in 350° oven for 45 minutes. Drain off excess butter if any. Serve as a side dish for dinner or as a main dish for lunch. (Freezes well. Place frozen in 350° oven for 30 minutes to reheat.)

Basic Meat Preparation used for Flavoring Other Things (Khourma)

1 lamb neck bone, split and
   cut at the vertebrae
   by butcher

Wash the pieces of neck bone and allow water to cling to meat. Place in pan, salt very heavily and set over medium heat. Cook, stirring occasionally, until meat is tender, browned well all over and fat has been rendered into pan. Store in refrigerator or freeze and use bits of meat and fat as needed.

Vegetables Plain or with Khourma

3-4 pieces Khourma
3 tablespoons fat from
   Khourma
1 medium onion diced
¼ medium green pepper, diced
2 tomatoes, quartered
2 packages frozen French
   string beans or 1 pound
   fresh beans, Frenched
⅛ teaspoon oregano
¼ teaspoon pepper

Place meat and lamb fat in pan and saute onion and green pepper until onion is golden. (If you do not have Khourma on hand, substitute 3 tablespoons butter.) Add tomatoes and cook, stirring for a few minutes. Add frozen or fresh string beans; cover; lower heat to medium and cook until beans are tender. Season. (All vegetables are delicious cooked this way, particularly summer squash, celery, butter beans, okra or spinach—they may be fresh or frozen.)

Plain or Khourma Cracked Wheat (Bulghour) Pilaf

3-4 pieces Khourma
3 tablespoons fat from Khourma
1 medium onion, diced
2 cups medium cracked wheat, bulghour
4 cups lamb, beef or chicken broth or bouillon, heated
2 teaspoons salt
¼ teaspoon pepper

Place meat and lamb fat in pan and saute onion until golden. Add bulghour and seasonings. Stir until bulghour is coated with fat. (If you do not have Khourma on hand, substitute 3 tablespoons butter.) Add hot broth or bouillon. Cover and cook over medium heat until all broth has been absorbed and bulghour is done. Do not stir while cooking. (There are many ways of preparing this pilaf. Some like to cook the bulghour first in the broth and then fold through the pieces of Khourma and sauteed onion. Another method is to melt butter and coat bulghour, add 2 packages dried onion soup mix and 4 cups water, allowing the onion soup mix to do all the seasoning.) Bulghour needs to cook over medium heat 20-25 minutes.

Rice Pilaf

Vegetable oil or butter
½ cup fine noodles, broken or orzo or slivered almonds
2 cups rice
½ teaspoon pepper
2 teaspoons salt
4 cups lamb or beef broth or bouillon, heated
2 teaspoons butter

Heat enough oil or butter to cover the bottom of a pan to ⅛ inch deep. When hot, add fine noodles, orzo or slivered almonds and cook, stirring constantly, until lightly browned. Add rice, pepper and salt and fry, stirring all the while, until rice is coated with oil or butter. Add broth or bouillon and cook over a medium heat until all liquid is absorbed and rice is pitted on top. Do not stir. Shut off heat and dot rice with butter. Cover with a dish towel and pan cover. Allow butter to melt down the rice. Mix through very gently before serving.

Tomato Pilaf

4 tablespoons butter
3 tomatoes, peeled and quartered
2 teaspoons salt
2 cups rice
3½ cups lamb or beef broth or bouillon, heated

Melt butter and add tomatoes. Cook, covered, stirring frequently, until tomatoes are soft and thick. Add salt and rice, stir until all are coated. Add hot broth or bouillon, cover and cook over medium heat until all liquid is absorbed and rice is done. Do not stir while cooking. When done, shut off heat and dot rice with butter. Cover with a dish towel and pan cover and allow butter to melt down into rice. Mix gently before serving. (If you do not have tomatoes you may use 2 cups of tomato juice and 2 cups lamb or beef broth or bouillon.)

Fancy Pilaf

⅓ pound butter
½ cup chopped onion
2 cups rice
1 chicken liver and chicken heart, sliced fine
4 cups chicken broth or bouillon
3 tablespoons chopped parsley
2¼ teaspoons salt
¼ teaspoon pepper
¾ teaspoon allspice
¼ cup currants
¼ cup pine nuts

Fry onion in butter until golden. Add rice and cook, stirring constantly, until rice is well coated with butter. Add chicken liver and heart; cook stirring for just a few minutes. Add rest of ingredients, mixing well. Cover and cook on low heat until all liquid is absorbed. Do not stir while cooking. When done, shut off heat and dot with little bits of butter, cover and allow butter to melt down into rice. Mix gently before serving.

Wonderful, Different Stuffing:

Follow above recipe except reduce liquid to half. Cook gently until all liquid is absorbed. Cool and stuff very loosely in chicken or medium-size turkey, allowing ample room for rice to swell. One recipe for chicken, double or triple for large turkey, depending on size of bird.

Flaky Pastry and Nut Diamonds (Paklava Dough)

The pastry dough may be purchased at most Armenian stores and is simply called Paklava dough. Greek stores sell the same dough and call it Philo. Some stores sell it as Strudel dough. It is rolled paper thin and comes in sheets tightly packaged together. The packages of dough may be kept up to 2 months in the refrigerator with excellent results. Paklava is a delicious and different dessert, easy to make when the dough is at hand. However, a recipe for making the dough follows for those who find it impossible to purchase.

Dough:

4 cups flour
1 teaspoon baking powder
1 egg, beaten
2 tablespoons yogurt or Madzoon
½ cup water
2 tablespoons olive oil
1 teaspoon salt
Cornstarch

Sift flour and baking powder together. Mix egg, yogurt or Madzoon, water, olive oil and salt together, blending well. Add dry ingredients to liquid, beating well after each addition and blending and working until smooth. Allow to refrigerate for at least 1 hour. Cut off pieces of dough the size of a biscuit. Roll each piece out on a board, coated heavily with cornstarch, to about the size of a medium plate. Pile 4-5 of these together with a lot of cornstarch in between and roll out as one piece. A long, thin rolling pin is best for this. Keep adding cornstarch to prevent sticking. Roll until paper thin, using long pulling motions, rolling away from the center toward the outside. Use about 50 sheets of dough for a batch of Paklava. Package the rest tightly in waxed paper or plastic wrap and aluminum foil for storing in refrigerator.

Paklava Pastry and Nut Diamonds

Filling:

50   sheets Paklava dough

1   pound nutmeats, chopped
     not too fine
1½ pound sweet butter, melted

Butter large-size baking pan well. Stack 5 sheets of dough in pan, brush generously with butter, add another stack of 5 sheets of dough; brush with butter, sprinkle well with chopped nuts. Add another stack of 5 sheets of dough, brush with butter, then 5 more sheets of dough, brush with butter; and sprinkle with nuts, continuing the same until the pan is full to ¼ inch from top of pan and at least 3½ inches thick. The parts of dough cut off may be pieced together and used as layers of dough, too. Be sure to butter every fifth layer and butter and sprinkle nuts on every tenth layer. End Paklava with 10 layers of dough, making sure top layer is smooth and even. Cut whole thing through diagonally first and then in strips, making small diamonds. Pour some of the melted butter over each of the diamonds, about 1 tablespoon, and bake in 350° oven for 15 minutes. Take pan out of oven and pour over the rest of the hot melted butter. Return to oven and bake another 30 minutes, or until top is a pinkish golden. Remove from oven and drain off as much of the butter as possible by removing one small piece in a corner and tilting the pan on something so that the excess butter will drain off into the corner; remove butter with a small spoon. Drain overnight if possible. When well drained, pour lukewarm syrup over it and let it set for a few minutes; then tilt and drain and spoon off all excess syrup. Keeps well about a month without refrigeration or freezing. Serves 16.

Syrup:

2   cups sugar
     Juice of half a lemon
1½ cups water

Simmer gently to make a medium syrup, about 228° on a candy thermometer.

Farina Dessert (Imig Helva)

2   cups farina or wheat hearts
½   cup butter
¼   cup pine nuts
2   cups sugar
1½ cups milk
1½ cups water
⅛   teaspoon salt

Heat farina, butter and pine nuts over low heat, stirring constantly, until nuts are slightly brown. It is better to overcook than not to cook this mixture enough. The mixture will no longer clong to the spoon when it is ready. In the meantime, heat the rest of the ingredients in a second kettle until sugar dissolves and them simmer for 5 minutes. Bring both kettles to the sink to blend together as the mixture bubbles violently when liquid is absorbed. Stir occasionally. When liquid is absorbed, remove from fire and cover pot with a dish towel. Allow to set for 10-15 minutes; then stir lightly with a fork to fluff it up and break all lumps. Serve in dessert dishes and sprinkle with cinnamon if desired. Serve warm.

Orange Preserves

6 large naval oranges
4¼ cups sugar
4¼ cups water
Juice of half a lemon

Lightly peel oranges with vegetables peeler, just barely taking off thin outer skin. Put oranges in pot with water to cover. Bring to boil and drain. Cool and cut oranges into eighths, or place in food processor and coarsely chop. Bring sugar and water to a boil and simmer gently until a few drops form a soft ball in a little cold water (about 1 hour). Add oranges and cook gently for 45-50 minutes, until syrup is heavy. Add juice of half a lemon and cook, stirring, for 1 minute. Keep in covered contrainer. (The oranges and syrup poured over parboiled sweet potatoes, sprinkled with pecan meats, and dotted with butter make a different and delicious candied sweet potato. Bake in 350° oven, covered, until syrup has candied around potatoes.) Delicious served over vanilla ice cream with Simit (recipe follows).

Cake with Sweet Syrup (Shumolly)

½ cup butter, room temp.
4 cups flour
4 teaspoons baking powder
¼ teaspoon salt
1¾ cups milk
2 eggs, beaten
2 tablespoons grated
orange rind
1 cup finely chopped nuts

2 cups sugar
1 cup water
1 tablespoon rum or brandy
flavoring

Stir butter until softened. Sift in dry ingredients. Add milk, eggs and orange rind, which have been mixed together. Add chopped nuts. Beat well and pour into a large, shallow greased baking pan. Bake at 350° for 40-50 minutes or until cake tests done. Cool to lukewarm; cut diagonally into diamond shapes. Pour lukewarm syrup over entire cake. Cool to serve. (Freezes well.)

Syrup:

Boil 10 minutes, cool to lukewarm.

Flaky Pastry and Nut Rolls (Boorma)

An easier type of Paklava (see pages 23-24).

Use same dough as for Paklava, same recipe for filling and syrup. Spread out one sheet at a time; brush well with melted butter. Make a 2-inch-wide line of chopped nuts across the dough about ⅓ of the way down from top of dough. Fold top piece of dough down over nuts. Using a long dowel, about ½ inch in diameter, roll top of folded dough loosely around it, rolling all the way down. Place fingers inside the holes at each end of rolled dough and push dowel off gently, crumbling dough together a little. Place on well-buttered large baking pan, arranging rolls side by side, barely touching one another. Pour over melted sweet butter as for Paklava. Bake as in Paklava recipe. Drain and pour over syrup as in Paklava; drain again. Cut each roll into 4-6 pieces to serve. (Best frozen before syrup is poured on. Defrost and pour over warm syrup and proceed as described above.)

Pastry and Nut Squares (Tell Kadayif: Shredded Pastry)

Kadayif dough may be purchased as one purchases the Philo dough. Greek groceries call this Kadayifa dough.

2	pounds Kadayif dough
¾	pound melted butter
1½	cups chopped nuts
1	tablespoon cinnamon
3	tablespoons sugar

Loosen shreds of dough. Butter a large baking pan and spread half of dough in pan. Mix nuts, cinnamon and sugar and spread over dough. Spread over remaining Kadayif dough evenly. Pour hot melted butter evenly over all. Cover tightly with aluminum foil. Bake at 350° in upper half of oven for 30-40 minutes. Removing foil last 10 minutes, bake until lightly pinkish brown. In the meantime, make syrup and cool.

Syrup:

4	cups sugar
3	cups water
	Juice of half a lemon or
	1 tablespoon Rose Water

Boil sugar and water together for 20 minutes; add lemon juice or Rose Water. Pour cool syrup over hot Kadayif, spooning out carefully and evenly. Cover Kadayif with aluminum foil and allow to stand for half an hour. Turn pan upside down onto a large serving plate, allowing it to drain down. Return pan to upright position and cut into 1½ to 2 inch squares. Serve with extra syrup if desired. (Freezes well without syrup. To defrost, place frozen in top half of 350° oven, covered with aluminum foil, for 20-30 minutes. Pour on cool syrup and follow above instructions. Cool before serving.) Serves 16.

Pastry Sticks (Simit)

½   cup soft vegetable shortening
½   cup butter or margarine
½   cup vegetable oil
½   cup sugar
1   egg, beaten
1   cup lukewarm milk
5   cups flour
2   tablespoons black Russian
    caraway (optional)
2   tablespoons baking powder
⅛   teaspoon salt

Melt shortening, butter or margarine; add oil and sugar and mix well. Add egg and lukewarm milk and stir until blended. Add rest of ingredients and stir to make a soft dough, just stiff enough to handle. Pinch off pieces of dough; roll between palms of hands to about 3 inches long; form small twist of dough, twisting 2 pieces over one another; pinch top and bottom. Brush with beaten egg and 2 tablespoons water blended well and sprinkle with sesame seeds. Place on cookie sheets and bake in 375° oven about 15-20 minutes, until golden. Keeps in a tightly covered container for months.

Grape Juice Pudding

1   quart grape juice
1   cup water
1½   cups fine bulghour,
     cracked wheat
½   cup sugar
6   tablespoons butter
½   cup chopped nuts,
     reserve 2 tablespoons
1   teaspoon cinnamon
½   teaspoon allspice
     Confectioners sugar

Soak cracked wheat in 1 cup water for 10 minutes. Add grape juice and bring to a boil. Lower heat and simmer for 1½ hours, stirring occasionally. Stir in sugar and butter and mix well. Add seasonings and nuts. Pour into individual dessert dishes. Serve warm or cold topped with finely chopped nuts that have been dusted with confectioners sugar.

Chinese

ABALONE

RICE VINEGAR

CHINESE BEAD MOLASSAS

KIMCHE

Barbecued Pork (Char Su)

5   pounds pork tenderloin or
      rib roast section, cut in
      full lengths about 2 inches
      thick
1   bulb garlic, crushed
3   teaspoons brown bean sauce
3   teaspoons Hoisin sauce
2⅓ cups chicken broth
½   teaspoon salt
¾   cup sugar
3   tablespoons light soy sauce
1½ teaspoons 5 spices
2   tablespoons sherry
1½ teaspoons red food coloring
      Light Karo syrup

Mash brown bean sauce and Hoisin sauce; add garlic, broth, salt, sugar and soy sauce. Heat to dissolve and blend. Remove from heat and add 5 spices, sherry and coloring. Pour over meat and marinate overnight or several days. Preheat oven to 375° and place water in lower part of broiler pan; place meat on broiler rack. Roast 45 minutes and then baste with light Karo syrup; roast another 10 minutes; turn and baste other side with Karo syrup; roast 10 minutes more. (Cool and freeze. Defrost; to serve slice in very slin slices.) Best served cold, though can be served hot. Often used as a base for other dishes.

Ginger and Scallion Dipped Chicken or Pork

2-2½ pound broiler chicken
      or
2   pounds pork steak

Place the whole cleaned chicken or port steak on a large plate and place in a larger pot. (Use steamer if you have one.) Put enough water in the pot to steam but not touch the meat. Steam for 1-2 hours or until meat is tender and thoroughly cooked. Cool and salt. Cut into small bite-size pieces with a cleaver or Chinese knife. Serve on toothpicks with the following sauce in which to dip the meat. (May be frozen. Defrost and bring to room temperature to serve.)

Ginger and Scallion Sauce:

1   cup peanut or vegetable
      oil, heat to hot and cool
8   scallions, chopped fine
      Salt and pepper to taste
6-8 inch piece fresh ginger
      root, grated
1   teaspoon Accent (optional)

Mix all ingredients well. Place in bowl and surround with meat. Use 4-6 cloves garlic, crushed, if you do not have fresh ginger root.

Pressed Sherry Chicken

2-2½ pound whole broiler,
dressed and cleaned

Boil enough water to cover chicken. Plunge chicken into the boiling water; cover and bring to a boil again. Shut off heat and allow chicken to stand, covered, 1 hour. Remove chicken, let drip dry for 10 minutes. Sprinkle skin well with salt. Allow to cool. Cut in quarters and marinate in the following Sherry Sauce.

Sherry Sauce:

1 part Sherry
1 part water
½ teaspoon Accent for each
   cup water (optional)

Use enough liquid to cover chicken; marinate for a night and day, turning once. Chop with cheaver or Chinese knife into bite-size pieces and serve cold. (May be prepared several days in advance.)

Fried Fan-Tail Shrimp or Chicken Wings

Shrimp:

3 pounds large shrimp, in
   shells
2 cups flour
2 teaspoons baking powder
½ teaspoon salt
2 eggs, well beaten
1½ cups milk
   Peanut or vegetable oil

Remove shells from shrimp leaving tails on. Open by cutting along the back, removing black line and making shrimp butterfly, cutting to about ⅛ inch from the tail end of shrimp. Pat flat with wood mallet or back of wooden spoon. Make a batter of medium thickness with the flour, baking powder, salt, eggs and milk. Heat oil to 350°. Holding shrimp by the tail, dip into batter; then drop into deep oil, holding shrimp by the tail for just a few seconds before releasing, so that they will be large and full. Fry until golden brown. Drain on paper towels. Serve with the following sauce.

Sweet and Sour Sauce:

1 cup sugar
½ cup vinegar
½ cup water
1 tablespoon minced green
   pepper
1 tablespoon minced
   pimiento
½ teaspoon salt
2 tablespoons cornstarch
   Cold water
1 teaspoon paprika

Mix first 6 ingredients and simmer 5 minutes. Combine cornstarch and enough cold water to make a thin paste. Add to hot mixture, stirring constantly, until sauce thickens and is clear. Cool and strain out the vegetables. Add paprika and mix well.

Chicken Wings:

Make batter as for shrimp adding ½ teaspoon garlic powder. Split wings at center joint; rinse and dry. Dip wings in batter; drip off; deep fry in peanut or vegetable oil at 360° until golden brown. Drain and place in 200° oven to keep warm. Serve with 2 table-spoons Szechuan pepper that has been blended in blender with 1 tablespoon coarse salt. Serve wings with pepper mixture in a small bowl in center of a large platter. Dip wings in pepper mixture to eat.

Egg Rolls (Spring Rolls)

Skins:

Buy skins at Chinese grocery or supermarket. If you wish to use these as hors d'oeuvres use the Won Ton wrappers. Otherwise buy the egg roll size. Wrap tightly in aluminum foil and place in plastic bag to keep up to 6 months in freezer. The following recipe is not too difficult, but it is time consuming. I offer it for those who cannot buy the skins.

2 cups flour
1 teaspoon salt
1 egg, slightly beaten
¼ cup minus 1 tablespoon ice water
1 tablespoon gin or sauterne wine

Combine dry ingredients. Mix egg, ice water, and gin or sauterne; add to dry ingredients, forming pastry ball. Cover with towel and allow to rest 10 minutes. Knead a few times until well blended. Divide dough into 4 pieces and roll each out on a lightly floured surface until paper thin; cut into 4 inch squares. Stack and wrap in aluminum foil until ready to use.

Filling: *(To be made the day before filling and frying.)*

Heat oil to piping hot in largest size frying pan or wok. Add meat and shrimp; cook over highest heat 1 minute, stirring. Add vegetables and cook, stirring 2 minutes. Remove from heat; add seasonings; mix well. Drain in large-size colander (save liquid for soup; freeze to keep), placing large-size plate on top of vegetables and heavy object on top of plate. Best refrigerated until next day.

1 cup finely diced cooked pork, Char Su, beef or chicken
1 cup shrimp, finely diced
2½ cups celery, finely sliced
3 cups bean sprouts, rinsed and well drained
1 cup bamboo shoots, finely diced
1 cup water chestnuts, finely diced
8 large Chinese mushrooms, soaked in water, drained and sliced (optional)
¾ cup scallions, finely sliced
2 teaspoons sugar
2 teaspoons salt
¼ teaspoon pepper
4 tablespoons peanut or vegetable oil

To Wrap: Wrap about 2-3 tablespoons filling in each pastry square, doing 1 at a time, placing filling about 1 inch down from top of square and about ½ inch in from sides. Dampen all edges of pastry with mixture of:

½ cup water   1 tablespoon cornstarch

Brush on lightly with pastry brush. Turn top of pastry over filling; start rolling away from you; press ends together tightly. Makes 60-75 depending on size. Fry in deep fat at 360°, turning so that they will be a uniform golden brown. Drain on paper towels. Serve hot with Sweet and Pungent and Hot Mustard Sauces. (Freezes well; cool and pack in plastic bags. To serve, warm on broiler pan, so excess oil will drain off, in 350° oven for about 25-30 minutes, turning once when top skin has crisped.)

Sweet and Pungent Sauce: See under Cantonese Duckling with Sauce if you wish to make your own, but can be purchased at most grocery stores.

Hot Mustard: Mix Chinese or English dry mustard with water to a thin spreading consistency and it is ready to serve.

Fried Won Ton

Won Ton Skins are available at most Chinese groceries, super-markets or noodle factories. These can be frozen up to 6 months if wrapped tightly in aluminum foil and then placed in a plastic bag. They also re-freeze well after cooking. However, homemade skins are delicious, too, and not too difficult to make if you cannot purchase them.

Skins:

1	egg, well beaten
½	cup ice water
2	cups flour
1	teaspoon salt

Make a stiff dough, adding dry ingredients to egg and water beaten together. Add more flour if dough is not stiff enough to roll. Allow to rest 10 minutes and knead for a minute. Roll out thin on a well-floured surface. Cut dough into 3-inch squares. Wrap tightly in waxed paper with flour between each square; rewrap in aluminum foil until ready to use. Refrigerate or freeze as directed in Egg Roll recipe.

Filling:

Mix all ingredients together well, preferably with hands.

½	pound shrimp, cleaned and chopped in very small pieces, mixed with ½ pound ground pork or chicken, ground twice
3	tablespoons light soy sauce
½	teaspoon sesame oil
1	teaspoon salt
⅛	teaspoon pepper
¼	teaspoon finely minced ginger root
2	tablespoons sherry
½	teaspoon sugar
1	finely chopped scallion
½	cup chopped water chestnuts
½	cup finely chopped bamboo shoots

To Fill: Make a mixture of 1 tablespoon cornstarch dissolved in ½ cup water, use this to seal ends. Turn square of skin around so a corner is pointing toward you. Place about 1 tablespoon filling 1 inch down from corner nearest you. Roll the corner of the dough nearest you over the filling and tuck it under filling; now roll forward about ½ inch. Wet ends of corners on right and left with corn-starch mixture, brushing lightly with pastry brush. Pull both ends towards you; press together, one on top of the other. Fry in deep fat at 350° to golden brown, turning to brown on both sides. Drain on paper toweling and serve hot with a bowl of Sweet and Sour Sauce, the recipe for which is under Fried Fan-Tail Shrimp. (To freeze, cool after frying and freeze in plastic bags. To reheat, place on broiler pan frozen and put in 350° oven for 10 minutes; turn and heat 10-15 minutes more until hot.)

34

Shrimp Toast (Har Too Tzu)

2 pounds cleaned and deveined shrimp, chopped fine
3 tablespoons finely chopped
   onion
½ teaspoon finely grated
   ginger root
¾ teaspoon sugar
1 egg
1½ teaspoons salt
1½ tablespoons cornstarch
3 tablespoons sherry
3 tablespoons vermouth
¼ teaspoon white pepper
18 slices stale white bread,
   crust removed

Combine half of shrimp and half of the rest of the ingredients, except bread, in jar of a blender or food processor. Blend to smooth. Do other half of shrimp and ingredients; combine. Cut crusts off stale bread and then slice into thirds. Spread 1 side of each bread finger with shrimp mixture. Heat deep oil to 375° and deep fry the fingers shrimp side down for 1½ minutes. Turn and brown other side; drain on paper towels. Serve hot. (Prepare for frying in advance. Deep fry just before serving.)

Barbecued Spareribs No. 1

4-5 pounds spareribs, cut be-
    tween ribs
½   cup Chinese bead molasses
½   cup sherry
¼   cup honey
1½ teaspoons salt
4   cloves garlic, crushed

Wipe spareribs with clean cloth; place on rack in shallow baking pan. Combine rest of ingredients and brush over spareribs. Roast in 350° oven for 1 hour, or until done and nicely browned, turning and brushing with sauce approximately every 15 minutes. (Freezes well.)

Barbecued Spareribs No. 2

4-5 pounds spareribs, cut be-
    tween ribs
3½ cups boiling water
4   beef bouillon cubes
4   tablespoons soy sauce
1½ teaspoons salt
4   tablespoons honey
3-4 cloves garlic, crushed

Combine all ingredients listed under spareribs and marinate ribs in them for at least 24 hours. Bake on racks in shallow baking pans in 350° oven for 1 hour, or until nicely browned and well done, turning approximately every 15 minutes.

35

Barbecued Chicken Wings

3-4 pounds chicken wings
¾   cup light Karo Syrup

Clean 3-4 pounds chicken wings; split at center joint; cut off tips and deep fry until golden brown. Drain on paper toweling. (Can be frozen at this point, sauce prepared and kept on shelf.)

Sauce:

¾   cup light Karo syrup
⅓-⅔ cup sugar, depending
     on taste
1   tablespoon Chinese bead
     molasses
5   tablespoons soy sauce
2   tablespoons sherry
2   tablespoons honey
½   teaspoon salt
¼   teaspoon Accent (optional)
⅛   teaspoon Chinese 5 spices,
     if you like the flavor
4   teaspoons flour
5   cloves garlic, crushed
1¼   cups water

Put all ingredients into jar with tight cover. Shake well. Place fried chicken wings in pan and pour sauce to 1 inch deep over them. Cook gently over medium heat, turning frequently, until sauce thickens and wings are well coated. May be done in 350° oven, turning frequently, and basting, baking for 20-30 minutes.

Spareribs are also delicious done with this sauce. Have butcher cut spareribs crosswide into 1 inch widths. Wipe meat and cut between bones to make sparerib bits. Drop into enough water to cover, to which you have added 1½ teaspoon salt. Boil until meat shrinks back and bone tips show. Skim and drain. Cook in above sauce as directed.

Noodle and Lotus Root Soup (Yet-Ca-Mein)

½   pound Chinese Yet-Ca-Mein
     noodles
5   tablespoons peanut or
     vegetable oil
½   cup thinly sliced pork
     or beef, diced
1⅓   cups Chinese dried mush-
     rooms, washed and soaked
     in warm water, drained
8   slices dried Lotus root,
     washed and soaked in
     warm water, cut in ½
     Inch slices and halved
1   tablespoon soy sauce
¼   teaspoon salt
12   cups broth from Egg Roll
     drippings or chicken broth

Boil noodles in boiling water 3 minutes. Drain and pour cold water over them; drain again and set aside. Fry pork or beef in the hot oil until done; pour off oil. Drain mushrooms and Lotus root slices and add to meat aalong with rest of ingredients. Simmer together 5 minutes; taste and adjust seasonings; add noodles and re-heat. (Freezes well.)

36

Vermicelli and Vegetable Soup (Yee Fu Menn)

½   pound flank steak, diced
3   tablespoons peanut oil
1   tablespoon light soy sauce
2   tablespoons sherry
½   teaspoon sugar
1   teaspoon sesame oil
½   cup bamboo shoots, diced
1   cup sliced water chestnuts
8⅓ cups chicken broth
1   small package Chinese or
     Japanese-style instant
     vermicelli

Heat peanut oil to piping hot and add meat; fry until lightly browned. Add seasonings; stir 1 minute and add vegetables; cook tossing for 2 minutes. Add liquid; heat; taste for salt. Remove from heat and add noodles; cover immediately and allow to rest 5 minutes. Serve hot. (May be frozen before adding noodles. Reheat and proceed.)

Sour and Hot Soup (Shuen Lot Tong)

¼   pound diced lean leftover
     pork or fresh pork, fried
     in a little oil
8   cups chicken broth
4   dried mushrooms, soaked,
     drained and cut in 2-inch
     pieces
6   cloud ears, soaked, drained
     and cut in pieces
6   dried tiger lily flowers,
     soaked, drained and cut
     in 2-inch pieces
4   tablespoons minced bamboo
     shoots
4   water chestnuts, diced
4   squares bean curd, about
     8 x 4 inches in all, cut
     in strips
2   tablespoons light soy sauce
½   teaspoon salt
½   teaspoon sugar
2   tablespoons cornstarch
     dissolved in 1 cup water
4   tablespoons rice or white
     wine vinegar, to taste
4-5 dashes Tabasco sauce,
     to taste
2   beaten eggs

Prepare pork and add chicken broth; simmer gently 10 minutes. Add mushrooms, tiger lily flowers, cloud ears, bamboo shoots, water chestnuts and bean curd and simmer 1 minute. Turn down heat. Add soy sauce, salt, sugar and dissolved cornstarch and stir until clear, cooking gently. Add vinegar and Tabasco sauce and taste to adjust seasonings. (If freezing, cool and do so at this point.) Just before serving, heat and very slowly, stirring constantly, add beaten eggs.

37

Chicken Soup with Vegetables and/or Won Ton

1 (5-6 pound) fowl, quartered
12 cups water or chicken broth
2 scallions, chopped
1 clove garlic, crushed
2 tablespoons sherry
1 tablespoons soy sauce
¾ tablespoon salt
2 slices ginger root, if you
can get it

Wash and clean chicken. Cook with all ingredients, just simmering, until chicken is tender. Remove chicken; strain and season to taste.

With Vegetables:

Any or all of these vegetables may be used:

Chinese celery cabbage,
  ½ inch slices
Snow pea pods
Sliced radishes

Thinly sliced white turnips
Chopped scallions (use sparingly)
Mushrooms, sliced in T's

Add to chicken broth after it has been strained and simmer gently for 5 minutes.

With Won Ton:

Won Ton skins are available at most Chinese grocery stores and supermarkets. These can be frozen and stored up to about 6 months. However, homemade ones are delicious and not too difficult to make.

Make a stiff dough, adding dry ingredients to the egg and water beaten together. Add more flour if dough is not stiff enough to roll. Allow to rest for 10 minutes and knead for a minute or two. Roll dough paper-thin on a well-floured surface. Cut dough in 3-inch squares.

2 cups flour
1 teaspoon salt
1 egg, well beaten
½ cup ice water

Filling:

Mix ingredients well. Place 1 teaspoon filling in center of each square of dough. Wet edges with a mixture of a tablespoon of cornstarch dissolved in ½ cup water. Fold to form a triangle and press edges together. Bring 8 cups salted water to a boil. Add Won Ton and simmer gently for 15 minutes. Remove Won Ton with slotted spoon and place gently in soup. Simmer together for 3 minutes.

½ pound shrimp, cleaned and
chopped in small pieces
½ pound ground pork or
chicken, ground twice
3 tablespoons light soy sauce
½ teaspoon salt
¼ teaspoon Accent (optional)
½ teaspoon sesame oil
(optional)
⅛ teaspoon pepper
¼ teaspoon minced ginger root
(optional)
2 tablespoons sherry
¼ teaspoon sugar
1 scallion, finely chopped
½ cup finely chopped or
ground Chinese cabbage

38

Chicken with Ham Soup

Follow recipe for making chicken soup, except use only ¼ tea-spoons salt. During the last half hour of cooking, add 2 slices of Chinese, Virginia or Smithfield ham. Take out meats when done cooking, strain soup and adjust seasonings. Cut chicken and ham into eating size pieces and place on a serving plate. Give each diner a small dish of soy sauce in which to dip meats. The meats and soup are eaten at the same time.

Cucumber Soup

¾ pound pork or flank steak,
      sliced thinly against
      the grain
2 tablespoons sherry
1½ tablespoons light soy sauce
1 tablespoon cornstarch
½ teaspoon sugar
12 cups chicken broth
¼ teaspoon salt
1 large or 2 small cucumbers,
      thinly sliced

Mix meat, sherry, soy sauce, cornstarch and sugar; set aside. Bring broth and salt to a boil. Add meat slices and boil gently 10 minutes if using pork and 3 minutes if using beef. Add cucumber slices and simmer gently for 3 more minutes. Taste and adjust seasonings. (Freezes well before adding cucumbers. Defrost; reheat; add cucumbers and proceed.)

Egg Drop Soup

¾ pound pork or veal, sliced
      thinly against the grain
2 tablespoons soy sauce
1 tablespoon sherry
2 teaspoons cornstarch
12 cups chicken broth
¼ teaspoon salt
3 tablespoons cornstarch
¾ cup water
3 eggs

Mix meat with soy sauce, sherry and cornstarch. Bring broth and salt to a boil. Add meat and boil gently for 10 minutes. Mix cornstarch and water and add, stirring constantly, to the broth. Beat eggs well and add to soup very slowly, stirring vigorously with a fork all the while. Taste and adjust seasonings. (Freezes well.)

Corn and Crabmeat Soup

2   (16 ounce) cans cream-style
      corn
2   (7 ounce) cans crabmeat,
      shredded in large chunks,
      add juices from cans
¼   cup light soy sauce
2   cups light cream
½-¾ teaspoon white pepper
      Salt to taste

Combine all ingredients, mixing well. Taste to adjust seasonings. Heat to hot, stirring constantly. Serve immediately. (May be prepared before heating and refrigerated until serving time; heat and serve.)

Wintermellon Soup

1   pound wintermellon (peel,
      cut in ¼ inch-thick slices
      and into 1½ inch squares)
¼   cup diced pork or beef
¼   cup chopped shrimp
2   tablespoons peanut oil
8   cups chicken broth
1   tablespoon light soy sauce
      Salt to taste

Heat oil and fry meat, tossing, for one minute. Add shrimp and toss for 1 more minute. Add wintermellon and rest of ingredients except salt and bring to a boil. Reduce heat to a simmer and cook gently for one half hour. Taste and add salt if needed.

Chinese Celery Cabbage Soup

¾   pound pork, diced or flank
      steak, sliced thinly against
      the grain and diced
1½ tablespoons soy sauce
1   teaspoon sugar
1   tablespoon cornstarch
12 cups chicken broth
¼   teaspoon salt
1   Chinese celery cabbage,
      sliced fine

Mix meat with soy sauce, sugar and cornstarch. Bring broth and salt to a boil. Add meat and boil 10 minutes if using pork and 3 minutes if using beef. Add cabbage and simmer gently for 5 more minutes. Taste and adjust seasonings. (May be frozen before adding cabbage. Defrost and proceed.)

Steamed Lobster

1   lobster for each 2 people
½   tablespoon sherry, per
     lobster
1   tablespoon soy sauce, per
     lobster
1   scallion, finely chopped,
     per lobster
1   slice ginger root, minced,
     per lobster or 1 clove
     garlic, crushed, per
     lobster

Have lobsters cut in half lengthwise. Rinse and clean. Place shell side down on a rack in a large pot or steamer. Mix rest of ingredients and spread over meat of each lobster. Pour enough water in bottom of pot to allow to steam for 15-20 minutes or until lobsters are done. Serve with fried rice.

Lobster Cantonese

3   chicken lobsters, cut in
     chunks about 1½ x 1½
     inches
3   tablespoons dried black
     beans, rinsed, drained
     and crushed
2-3 cloves garlic, crushed
1   thin slice ginger root,
     crushed or grated
½   pound lean pork, ground
     twice
1   teaspoon salt
½   teaspoon sugar
⅛   reaspoon pepper
3   tablespoons sherry
2   cups chicken broth
2½ tablespoons cornstarch
1   egg, well beaten
1   scallion top, sliced fine
¼   cup peanut or vegetable oil

Have lobsters split just before cooking time. Using a poultry shears, cut into chunks. Heat oil to piping hot. Mix crushed black beans, garlic and ginger together well. Fry 30 seconds and add pork, seasonings and sherry and cook 3 minutes, stirring. Add lobster and cook, stirring, 1 minute; add stock, stir, cover, and cook 5 minutes or until lobster is bright red, stirring occasionally. Dissolve cornstarch in a little water and add. Cook, stirring, until sauce thickens. Remove from heat. (If freezing, cool and do so at this point. To use, defrost slowly in refrigerator; reheat at low temperature and when hot, remove from heat.) Stir in beaten egg, mixing through well. Garnish with sliced scallions to serve.

Fried Shrimp Sweet and Sour

40 large shrimp, cleaned, de-
    veined, with tails on
1 cup bread crumbs, fine,
    unseasoned
2 eggs
1 teaspoon salt
4 tablespoons water
    Oil for deep frying

1 cup water
¾ cup cider vinegar
1 cup sugar
4 tablespoons sherry
1 tablespoon soy sauce
3 tablespoons catsup
3 tablespoons cornstarch
1 green pepper, cut in
    thin strips
2 carrots, cut in thin
    match strips
3 medium gherkin pickles, cut
    in thin strips
2 buffet size cans pineapple
    tidbits, drained

Salt shrimp heavily and allow to stand 20 minutes. Rinse well and dry on paper towels. Beat together eggs, salt and water. Heat deep fat to 375°. Dip shrimp into egg mixture and then roll in bread crumbs. Drop into hot oil and fry to golden—about 3 minutes. Drain on paper towels and keep warm in 200° oven until ready to serve or cool shrimp, refrigerate or freeze until ready to use. To heat or defrost, place in 350° oven until crisp. Serve in the following sauce.

Sweet and Sour Sauce:

Combine vinegar, water, sugar, sherry, soy sauce and catsup in a saucepan. Cook until sugar dissolves. Mix cornstarch with a little water to make a thin paste. Add to sauce and cook, stirring until clear. Add green pepper, carrots, gherkin pickles and pineapple tidbits and simmer gently until vegetables are slightly cooked but still brightly colored and crisp. This sauce can be made in the morning without the vegetables and left unrefrigerated. Heat gently, adding vegetables just before serving. Pour sauce over hot shrimp to serve.

Steamed Stuffed Rolls

8 unbaked Parkerhouse or
    similar rolls
1⅓ cups finely chopped
    Chinese cabbage
⅔ cup finely chopped canned
    or fresh cooked shrimp
1 clove garlic, crushed
¼ teaspoon sugar
¼ teaspoon salt
1 scallion, finely chopped
1 teaspoon sesame oil
2½ teaspoons soy sauce
1 teaspoon sherry
1 teaspoon Brown Bean Sauce

Mix all ingredients except rolls, blending well. Split rolls almost in two and place some of the filling in each roll; replace top. Line a steaming tier with cheesecloth; leaving ends of cloth long enough to grab for easy removal. Place rolls about 1 inch apart on the cloth; cover and steam about 20 minutes.

42

Sauteed Prawns and Black Bean Sauce

2 pounds large prawns
    (shrimp), peeled, deveined
    and cut into thirds
½ cup peanut or vegetable oil
4 tablespoons black beans,
    rinsed, drained and
    mashed
4 cloves garlic, crushed and
1 teaspoon grated ginger
    root
4 tablespoons soy sauce
¼ teaspoon salt
2 teaspoons sugar
1 teaspoon monosodium
    glutamate (optional)
4 tablespoons sherry
2 teaspoons cornstarch mixed
    with 2 tablespoons water
4 scallions, sliced

Salt prawns heavily and allow to stand 20 minutes. Rinse well and prepare, dry with paper towel. Heat oil to piping hot and add prawns. Fry, tossing until prawns are just turning pink. Remove from pan and keep warm in 200° oven. Combine black beans, garlic and ginger root and add to remaining hot oil; cook 30 seconds. Add rest of ingredients except scallions and cook until thickened and clear. Add prawns and cook, stirring, 30 seconds. Add scallions and serve.

Shrimp Omelet (Foo Young)

8-10 large shrimp, cleaned, de-
    veined and cut in half,
    lengthwise
½ cup thinly sliced celery
¼ cup bean sprouts, rinsed
    and drained
2-3 scallions, chopped fine
1 tablespoon soy sauce
1 teaspoon sugar
8 eggs, well beaten
1 teaspoon salt
1 tablespoon cornstarch

In a large skillet, heat oil of ⅛ inch depth to piping hot. Add shrimp and cook, stirring constantly, for 1 minute. Add celery, bean sprouts and scallions and cook for 1 more minute, stirring. Add soy sauce and sugar and mix well; cook 1 more minute. Remove mixture to a warm platter and place in 250° oven. Rinse and wipe skillet and heat oil of ⅛ inch depth on medium heat. Add well beaten eggs and salt; cook, stirring, for just 1 minute. Remove from heat and with a slotted spoon lift shrimp and vegetable mixture onto partially cooked eggs. Save juice from shrimp and vegetable mixture to make gravy. Return eggs to medium heat and cook 1 minute or until eggs begin to set around filling; turn omelet over and finish cooking, about 1 more minute. Put on heated platter in 250° oven while making gravy. Heat the saved juice; gently add to water to make 1 cup. Mix cornstarch with a little water to make a thin paste and add to juices. Cook, stirring, until clear and pour over omelet to serve. May be kept warm in 250° oven for a few minutes, without the gravy, before serving.

43

Shrimp in Shells

2 pounds shrimp with shells on
2 tablespoons peanut or
   vegetable oil
1 tablespoon sugar
2 tablespoons soy sauce
1 teaspoon salt
2 tablespoons sherry
1 scallion, finely sliced
1 teaspoon minced ginger root

Wash shrimp, drain and dry. Heat oil to piping hot. Add shrimp and fry 6-8 minutes, to pink. Stir in sugar, soy sauce and salt, stirring vigorously. Add sherry, chopped scallion and minced ginger and cook, stirring, for 30 seconds. Leftovers are good cold.

Fried Phoenix Tail Shrimp

2 pounds jumbo prawns
   (shrimp)
2 eggs, beaten
8 tablespoons flour
8 tablespoons water
1 teaspoon salt
   Oil for deep frying

Shell and devein shrimp, keeping on the "Phoenix tails," which will turn a beautiful red when fried. Salt shrimp heavily and allow to stand for 20 minutes. Rinse well and dry. Mix beaten eggs, flour, water and salt very well. Heat oil for deep frying to 360°. Take each shrimp by its tail, dip in batter, drip off, and fry to a rich golden brown, about 3 minutes. Drain on paper toweling and keep hot in 200° oven a few minutes before serving.

Fried Phoenix Tail Shrimp Sauce:

1 cup sugar
½ cup water
½ cup cider vinegar
1 tablespoon catsup
1 tablespoon soy sauce
4 tablespoons currants, dried
4 tablespoons crushed pineapple with juice
¼ teaspoon salt
2 teaspoons cornstarch
1 tablespoon water
1 teaspoon paprika

Plump currants in hot water, soaking a few minutes. Drain well on paper toweling. Mix first 8 ingredients in sauce pan. Simmer gently for 5 minutes. Mix cornstarch with water and add, stirring all the while. Cook until thickened and clear. Add paprika and cool. Store in refrigerator for future use. Allow sauce to reach room temperature before using.

Five Willow Fish (Enn Low Zet Yaf)

4-6 pound sea bass, red snap-
     per, doria or pike
    Egg white, if frying
    Water chestnut flour, if fry-
     ing, smooth in blender
    Salt and pepper
½ teaspoon minced ginger
    root, if steaming
2 scallions, chopped fine,
    if steaming
1 teaspoon black beans,
    rinsed and drained,
    if steaming

To Fry: Have fish scaled and cleaned and eyes removed at market, leaving skin, head and tail on. Wash and wipe very dry. Air-dry further for 30 minutes. Beat egg white and 2 tablespoons water until frothy. Salt and pepper fish and brush thinly with beaten egg white. Roll in water chestnut flour; shake off excess. Deep fry in 350° hot peanut or vegetable oil in French fish frier or steamer or fry in deep oil in roasting pan, preheating oil and oven to 450°, browning well on a large piece of aluminum foil covered with paper towels. This will facilitate easy removal to serving dish. Place in 250° oven to keep warm. Will keep up to ¾ hour. Serve with sauce and garnishes.

To Steam: Have fish scaled and cleaned and eyes removed at market, leaving skin, head and tail on. Wash and wipe fish and sprinkle with salt and pepper. Place on a large plate and sprinkle with minced ginger root, scallions and black beans. Slip onto fish steamer rack or place plate on large rack in a larger kettle. Fill with water to just barely reach bottom of place or 1 inch deep. Cover tightly and steam gently for about 30 minutes, until fish flakes easily but is still moist. Follow instructions for keeping warm under frying. Serve with or without sauce and garnishes.

Sauce:

¾ cup vinegar
1 cup water
1 cup sugar
4 tablespoons sherry
2 tablespoons soy sauce
3 tablespoons catsup
¼ teaspoon minced ginger
    root
4 tablespoons cornstarch
1 carrot, cut in thin sticks
1 green pepper, cut in strips
½ cup canned, shredded
    sweet cucumber (at
    Chinese grocery)
    Cocktail tomatoes and
    maraschino cherries

In saucepan, combine vinegar, water, sugar, sherry, soy sauce, catsup and minced ginger root. Simmer gently until sugar dissolves. Mix cornstarch with a little water to make a thin paste. Add to sauce and cook, stirring constantly, until clear. Make to this point until just before serving. Then add carrot and green pepper strips and ¼ cup of the shredded cucumber. Reheat by simmering gently for just a few minutes, stirring all the while, making sure not to cook too long so that the vegetables retain their natural color and are still crisp. Place cooked fish on a larger platter, surrounded with tomatoes; pour over sauce and garnish with rest of the shredded cucumber and maraschino cherries. (Use cherries for eyes if desired.)

Steamed Fish and Ginger Sauce

4-6 pound sea bass, red snapper,
     doria, or pike
1   whole scallion
1   tablespoon ginger
     root, minced

To Steam: Have fish scaled and cleaned and eyes removed, leaving skin, head and tail on. Wash and wipe fish and air dry for 30 minutes. Place a whole cleaned scallion inside fish. Place on a large plate and sprinkle with 1 tablespoon ginger root, minced. Add water to 1½ -2 inches deep; cover tightly; or place fish in a fish steamer and add water to bottom of steamer; place cover or pouch in fish poucher or roasting pan with water to cover. Steam 12 minutes per pound. Serve with following sauce.

Sesame and Ginger Sauce:

1   cup salad or peanut oil
½   cup ginger root cut in
     julienne
⅔   cup sliced whole scallions
1½ tablespoons sesame oil
½   cup soy sauce
2   teaspoons sugar
¼   teaspoon pepper

Mix all ingredients in small saucepan and have ready. When fish is fully steamed, heat sauce to hot. Remove fish to larger platter and pour sauce over all.

Abalone with Vegetables

6   tablespoons peanut or
     vegetable oil, 3 table-
     spoons at a time
1   pound can abalone, thinly
     sliced with edges fringed
½   teaspoon minced ginger root
1   package frozen snow peas,
     defrosted and dried, or
     ½ pound fresh snow peas
3   scallions, cut in 1 inch
     slices
½   cup diced bamboo shoots
1   cup sliced water chestnuts
2   teaspoons sesame oil
2   tablespoons light soy sauce
2   tablespoons sherry
1½ teaspoons sugar
2   cups chicken broth
2   tablespoons cornstarch
2   tablespoons water

Heat oil and fry abalone and ginger root, tossing, until abalone turns white. Remove and place in 200° oven. Rinse pan and heat oil to piping hot. Add vegetables and seasonings and cook, stirring, 1 minute. Add chicken broth and cornstarch mixed with water. Cook, stirring, until thickened and clear. Add abalone and heat 30 seconds.

Chicken with Mushroom and Wine

2 fowls or fryers, cut in 2-3 inch pieces, bone in
1½ teaspoons Chinese 5 spices
1 tablespoon sugar
2 teaspoons sesame oil
9 dried Chinese mushrooms
4 tablespoons sherry
2 teaspoons salt
6 tablespoons dark soy sauce
6 tablespoons light soy sauce
2 bunches scallions
4 cups warm water
4-6 cloves garlic, crushed

Thoroughly wash dried mushrooms and soak in warm water. Clean scallions and cut into 1 inch pieces. Skin chicken, do not attempt to skin wing pieces. Cover bottom of a large kettle with ¾ inch of peanut or vegetable oil; heat. Brown chicken pieces on all sides in piping hot oil, removing pieces as they are nicely browned. Pour off remaining oil after all have been fried; put chicken back in pot without washing the pot. Add mushrooms and rest of ingredients and mix well. Cover; cook gently until tender, stirring occasionally. Add warm water as liquid cooks away to keep gravy to about 2 cups. Flavor improves if made the day before. (Freezes well. The long cooking makes for what the Chinese call Red Cooking.)

Fried Chicken (Jaur Zee Guy)

4 chicken breasts, halved
8 tablespoons soy sauce
1½ tablespoons sesame oil
1½ tablespoons peanut or vegetable oil
1½ tablespoons sugar
2 tablespoons sherry
1½ teaspoons salt
¼ teaspoon pepper
1 clove garlic, crushed
  Cornstarch or water chestnut flour
1 clove garlic or sliced ginger root
  Accent (optional)
  Coarse salt
  Chinese 5 spices, cinnamon or Szechwan pepper

Marinate chicken in soy sauce, sesame oil, peanut or vegetable oil, sugar, sherry, salt, pepper and garlic for at least 30 minutes. Pat dry with paper towels and then dredge lightly in cornstarch or water chestnut flour. In largest size frying pan or wok, heat oil of about ⅛ inch deep to medium heat (350°). Put in piece of garlic or ginger root and cook to brown all over; remove. Fry chicken slowly to a rich golden brown on all sides, making sure chicken is cooked through. Add more oil, heated, if needed. Drain cooked chicken on paper toweling; place on a wooden board and cut with a meat cleaver or Chinese knife into about 2 inch pieces. Mix Accent with a little coarse salt and very little 5 spices, cinnamon or Szechwan pepper, whichever you prefer, and heat to barely warm. Place in small dishes near each diner so that they may dip pieces of chicken into mixture just before eating.

Chicken with Vegetables (Moo Goo Guy)

4 boned and skinned chicken
    breasts, cut in thin slices
1 tablespoon cornstarch
2 tablespoons soy sauce
1 tablespoon sherry
1 tablespoon cornstarch
2 tablespoons soy sauce
1 tablespoon sherry
1½ teaspoons sugar
¾ teaspoon salt
1 scallion, chopped
1½ teaspoons sesame oil
¾ teaspoon minced ginger root
    or 2 cloves garlic, crushed
¼ pound mushrooms, sliced
    in T's
⅔ cup sliced water chestnuts
⅔ cup sliced bamboo shoots
1½ cups snow pea pods
1½ cups chicken broth
1 tablespoon cornstarch
1 tablespoon oyster sauce
    (optional)
¼ teaspoon salt
⅓ cup toasted almonds

Marinate chicken slices with cornstarch, soy sauce, sherry, sugar, salt, scallion, sesame oil and ginger root or garlic for 20 minutes. In the largest size frying pan or wok, heat oil of about ⅛ inch depth to about 350°. Remove chicken slices from marinade with slotted spoon and keep warm in 250° oven. Heat oil of about ⅛ inch depth to piping hot and put in mushrooms, water chestnuts, bamboo shoots and snow pea pods. Fry, tossing constantly, for 3 minutes. Add chicken slices and chicken broth which has been mixed with cornstarch and salt. Cook, stirring, until thickened and clear. Add oyster sauce if using it. Taste to adjust seasonings. Add toasted almonds; cook, stirring for 1 more minute.

Tangerine Peel Marinated Roast Chicken

1 piece dried tangerine peel*,
    about the size of a third
    of a large tangerine
1 clove garlic, crushed
1½ cups chicken broth, heated
½ cup soy sauce
1 tablespoon sugar
1 teaspoon salt
⅛ teaspoon pepper
1 teaspoon sesame oil
1 large roasting chicken

Combine all ingredients listed except chicken; breaking the tangerine peel into small pieces. Place cleaned chicken and marinade in plastic bag. Marinate overnight or all day, turning several times. Place chicken on a roasting rack in pan; cover loosely with aluminum foil and place in 325° oven. Roast 4-5 pound bird for 2½-3 hours, bird over 5 pounds for 3-4 hours. Allow to rest 15 minutes before carving.

* Best purchased at a Chinese grocery.

48

Walnut Chicken

2   chicken breasts, cut in tiny
      ¼ inch cubes of meat
1   bunch celery, cut in thin
      slices on the slant
½   pound mushrooms, cut in T's
4-5 scallions, slivered and cut
      in 1 inch lengths
2   cups water or chicken broth
2   tablespoons soy sauce
2   tablespoons sherry
1   teaspoon sesame oil
2   teaspoons sugar
1-2 teaspoons oyster sauce
      (optional)
1½ teaspoons salt
3   tablespoons cornstarch
2   cups walnut meats, fried*

In the largest size frying pan or wok, heat oil of about ⅛ inch depth to hot. Add chicken and cook, stirring constantly, for 1 minute. Add vegetables and cook for 3 minutes, stirring all the time. Remove from heat and add water or broth and seasonings. Add cornstarch mixed smooth to a thin paste with a little water. Return to heat and cook until clear, stirring all the while. Add fried walnut meats and cook, stirring, for half a minute.

*To fry walnut meats, boil first in water to cover for 3 minutes. Plunge in cold water and slip off as much of the skin as possible. Dry on paper towels. Fry in a little hot oil, stirring constantly, to a rich golden brown. Drain on paper towels; set aside.

Pork and Pickled Mustard Cabbage (Harm Choy)

2   cups diced pork, Char Siu
      or fresh pork steak
2   cups shredded pickled
      mustard cabbage,
      Harm Choy
8   scallions, sliced
1   cup diced bamboo shoots
1½ cups diced celery
2   tablespoons soy sauce
1   teaspoon salt
1   tablespoon sugar
¼   teaspoon pepper
1   tablespoon sherry
2-3 teaspoons sesame oil
1-2 tablespoons oyster sauce
      (optional)
1½ cups chicken broth
3   tablespoons cornstarch

Fry pork in oil that is ⅛ inch deep in largest size frying pan until pork is done and slightly browned. Add Harm Choy, scallions, bamboo shoots and celery; cook, stirring frequently, for 3 minutes. Remove from heat and add rest of ingredients which have been blended well until cornstarch is smooth. Return to heat and cook, stirring, for about 3 minutes, until thick and clear. (See recipe for making your own Pickled Mustard Cabbage, listed with side dishes.)

49

Stuffed Cucumber or Mushrooms

Cucumbers, peeled and cut
    into 2-inch sections,
    enough to serve 8 *or* use
1½ pounds large fresh mush-
    rooms
¾ pound ground pork
    or chicken
1 egg, beaten
1 teaspoon sugar
1½ teaspoons salt
2 tablespoons sherry
2 cloves garlic, crushed
1½ teaspoons cornstarch
    Chinese or Virginia ham
    to garnish

1 tablespoon peanut or
    vegetable oil
1 tablespoon minced scallion
    Sliced mushroom stems,
    if using mushrooms
½ teaspoon onion flakes
1 tablespoon soy sauce
8 water chestnuts, sliced
1½ cups broth from simmered
    stuffed vegetables
1 tablespoon sesame oil
1 teaspoon sugar
1 tablespoon cornstarch

With teaspoon remove the seeds from one end of each cucumber section, to within ½ from other end. If using mushrooms wipe and remove stems. Mix the meat with the following 6 ingredients, mixing well. Stuff meat mixture either into cucumber sections or mushroom caps, rounding the tops. Place in a shallow pan and top with a small piece of ham. Pour water to 1 inch depth and add ½ teaspoon salt to the water. Cover and cook, gently simmering, for 30 minutes, adding water if it boils away. Serve with gravy. Keep stuffed vegetables warm in 250° oven, without broth and covered. Save broth for gravy.

Gravy:

Heat the tablespoon oil and saute the minced scallion and mushroom stems 2 minutes. Pour off oil and add next 6 ingredients, bringing to a gentle boil. Mix cornstarch with a little water to make a thin paste and add. Cook, stirring, until clear. Pour gravy over stuffed vegetables to serve. (May be frozen and reheated in oven to piping hot, freezing stuffed vegetables and gravy separately. Add an ice cube to gravy when warm to smooth when reheating.)

Chinese Dried Mushrooms with Lettuce

½ pound dried mushrooms
1 head lettuce
½ cup oil
4 tablespoons light soy sauce
3 tablespoons sherry
1½ teaspoons sugar
3 teaspoons sesame oil
½ cup oyster sauce
2 cups warm water
2 tablespoons cornstarch
2 tablespoons water

Soak ½ pound of the large Chinese dried mushrooms in warm water for 1 hour. Drain and remove stems.

Heat oil to 350°. Add mushrooms and fry 3 minutes, stirring. Add light soy sauce, sherry, sugar, sesame oil, oyster sauce and warm water. Cover and cook 4 hours, simmering gently. (If you are going to freeze, cool and do so at this point, defrost and reheat to proceed.) Dissolve cornstarch in 2 tablespoons water; add and cook stirring until sauce is clear. Rinse and drain head of lettuce, shred coarsely, place in pot with ½ cup water; cover and boil ½ minute, remove and drain in colander. Place drained lettuce on platter and top with mushrooms, top side up, pour over sauce.

Canton Roast Duck with Sauce (Garaung Arp)

1 (5-6 pound) duckling, whole
1 cup water
½ cup sherry
2 scallions, cut very fine
2 teaspoons Hoisin Sauce
½ cup soy sauce
¼ cup sherry
2 tablespoons sugar
1 cup Sweet and Pungent Sauce (recipe follows, use for marinade)
2 cloves garlic, crushed
 Hoisin sauce, to serve after cooking (optional)
 Chopped scallions (optional)

Slide sharp knife between inside of skin and meat of duck, being careful not to pierce skin; separate meat from skin all over body of duck. Sew up duck at both ends. Mix water, ½ cup sherry and scallions. Fill cavity with this mixture using a basting syringe forcing the tip between stitches making as small an opening as possible. Mix rest of ingredients well and marinate duck in them for 24 hours, turning occasionally. Heat oven to 350°, place duck on a rack in a roasting pan, make a tent over it lightly with aluminum foil; and roast 1 hour and 40 minutes. Meantime, place marinade in saucepan; heat over low heat, stirring for 5 minutes. Set duck aside to cool. (If freezing, do so at this point; when ready to use, defrost and continue cooking according to the following directions.)

Turn heat up to 450°; baste duck with marinade; roast 15-20 minutes until duck is done, basting occasionally. Serve duck with marinade for sauce on side or with a bowl of Hoisin sauce in which you have cut up 2 scallions very fine. Have the host carve in small pieces, cutting through bone with poultry shears. This is a particularly delicious and the skin of the duck will be crisp and delectable.

1½ tablespoons peanut or vegetable oil
1 tablespoon chopped onion
1 clove garlic, crushed
¼ cup dried apricots, chopped fine
¼ cup water
¼ cup cider vinegar
¼ cup plus 1 tablespoon sugar
1 tablespoon lemon juice
1 pound can sliced peaches with juice, diced
⅛ teaspoon salt
¼ teaspoon grated ginger root
⅛ teaspoon red pepper (optional)
¼ teaspoon almond extract
1 teaspoon Kirsch or gin

Sweet and Pungent Sauce: (This may be purchased but is easy to make and especially delicious.)

Fry chopped onion and garlic in oil to a light golden color; drain off oil. Add next 8 or 9 ingredients and simmer gently until sauce begins to thicken, about 45 minutes. Remove from heat and cool. Add flavoring and mix well. Optional: Put through blender; add soy sauce for color. Store in a tightly covered jar and refrigerate. Use wherever Sweet and Pugent Sauce is called for.

51

Chicken with Cashews or Peanuts

3 tablespoons peanut or
   vegetable oil
4 chicken breasts, boned and
   skinned and diced ½
   inch in size, marinate in
   marinade given below
2-3 cloves garlic, crushed
1 inch slice ginger root,
   finely minced
2 tablespoons sherry
1 teaspoon sugar
1 scallion, sliced
1 green pepper, cut in ½
   inch cubes
1 cup sliced bamboo shoots
1 cup water chestnuts, sliced
½ cup chicken broth
2 1 teaspoon Chinese Hot Chili
   condiment
1 cup roasted cashews or dry
   roasted peanuts
1 teaspoon cornstarch
1 teaspoon water

2 tablespoons cornstarch
2 tablespoons soy sauce
¼ teaspoon salt
2 teaspoons sesame oil
1 tablespoon oil

Heat oil to piping hot. Add chicken, garlic and ginger root and cook stirring for 1 minute. Add sherry and sugar and cook, stirring, 30 seconds. Add vegetables, tossing well, and cook 1 minute. Add broth, condiment, and roasted nuts and bring to a boil. Mix cornstarch and water to make a thin paste; add to broth and cook, stirring, until mixture is thickened and clear.

Marinade:

Mix well, add chicken, toss to coat and marinate for half hour. Drain off marinade and proceed as above.

Short Ribs of Beef with Chestnuts

1½ cups dried chestnuts, water
        to cover, soaked overnight,
        drained
3   pounds lean beef shortribs
½   teaspoon Chinese 5 spices
4   tablespoons sherry
1½ teaspoons salt
12 tablespoons soy sauce
2   bunches scallions
1   tablespoon sugar
8   dried mushrooms (Chinese)
4-6 cloves garlic, crushed
6   cups warm water

Soak dried mushrooms in warm water after thorough washing. Clean scallions and cut into inch size pieces. Heat enough peanut or vegetable oil to cover bottom of large size kettle ⅛ inch deep. When piping hot, add short ribs and brown well on both sides. Remove beef as pieces are browned; when all is done, pour off fat from pot and put beef back in. Add rest of ingredients and stir well. Cover and cook gently until tender, about 3½ hours, stirring occasionally. Add warm water as it cooks down to keep gravy to about 3 cups. Taste and adjust for salt. (Freezes well.)

Chinese Celery Cabbage (or Other Vegetables) and Beef

1   pound flank steak, sliced
        thinly against the grain or 2
        boned and skinned chicken
        breasts, cut in 1-inch cubes
4   teaspoons soy sauce
1   teaspoon baking soda
2½ teaspoons sesame oil
4   teaspoons cornstarch
1   teaspoon sugar
1½ teaspoons salt
¼   teaspoon pepper
2   scallions, cut in 1½ inch
        pieces
1   tablespoon Brown Bean
        Sauce (optional)
1   large Chinese celery
        cabbage, cut in 1½ inch
        slices
1   teaspoon sugar
½   cup hot water
2   slices ginger root or
        2 cloves garlic

Marinate meat in the following listed 8 or 9 ingredients. Rinse the cut cabbage and drain dry. Fry a small slice of ginger root or clove of garlic in hot oil, enough to cover the largest size frying pan or wok to about ⅛ inch deep. When brown, remove ginger or garlic and add prepared vegetables and 1 teaspoon sugar mixed in ½ cup hot water. Cover and cook about 3 minutes. Take out vegetables from pan with a slotted spoon and place in a dish in a warm oven at 250°. Pour off juice from pan and save. Wipe pan and again fry a piece of ginger root or garlic in enough hot oil to cover pan to ⅛ inch deep. Remove ginger or garlic when brown and add the marinated meat and cut up scallions. Fry, tossing, over the hottest heat until meat is just cooked, about 1 minute. Add juice from vegetables and stir thoroughly; cook until slightly thickened. Pour all over vegetable and serve.

Diced pork may be used instead of beef but be sure and cook, stirring, at least 8 minutes. Any other vegetables, such as broccoli, string beans, asparagus, green peppers, spinach and etc. may be used instead of the cabbage. If using broccoli, cut off the flower ends; cut stems in match-like sticks. Cook stems for 5 minutes and then add flower ends and cook 3 minutes more using 1 cup water and 2 teaspoons sugar to cook with the vegetable.

53

Cook this while guests are finishing their hors d'oeuvres. If you have everything ready it will take only about 7 minutes to prepare. Read through the recipe and understand the sequence of the steps to be taken in making this delectable dish.

In the morning or night before: Soak half a package of the Sha Ho Fun rice sticks overnight or all day in water to cover and 1 tablespoon peanut or vegetable oil; drain before starting to cook.

In the afternoon: Soak 2 pounds fresh bean sprouts, if you have them, for 1 hour and then drain until ready to use or wash and drain a 2 pound can of bean sprouts thoroughly.

1	pound flank steak, thinly sliced against the grain
2	teaspoons cornstarch
2	teaspoons light soy sauce
4	tablespoons sherry
½	teaspoon sugar
½	teaspoon sesame oil

Marinate for several hours:
Mix together and marinate.

2	tablespoons black beans, rinsed, drained and crushed
2	cloves garlic, crushed
1	teaspoon salt
2	wedges ginger root, size of a quarter, 1 piece minced
4	green peppers, sliced in 1 inch pieces
1	large Spanish type onion, cut in slices lengthwise
2	tablespoons dark soy sauce
½	teaspoon sugar
½	teaspoon salt
¼	teaspoon pepper
1½	cups chicken broth (mixed with above 4 ingredients)
4	teaspoons cornstarch
4	teaspoons water
8	tablespoons peanut or vegetable oil

To Cook:

Heat 4 tablespoons oil in wok or large frying pan; add drained noodles and bean sprouts and cook, stirring and tossing, 4 minutes. Set aside on a large platter in 250° oven. Rinse wok or pan and dry. Heat 2 tablespoons oil; add black beans, garlic, minced ginger and salt and stir a few seconds. Add green pepper and onion and stir 1 minute. Add soy sauce, sugar, salt and pepper to chicken broth and add all to peppers and onions. Mix well. Cover and cook 2 minutes. Strain off broth and save. Place green pepper and onion in bowl and keep warm in oven. Rinse and dry pan. Heat last 2 tablespoons oil to piping hot and add piece of ginger root; remove ginger when browned. Add beef and flatten against pan; cook; stirring 1 minute, until beef is about ¾ done. Add saved broth and stir in cornstarch which has been mixed with water. Cook, stirring until broth is translucent and clear. Add green peppers and onions, mix well and pour all over rice sticks and bean sprouts. (May be kept in 250° oven for up to half hour successfully.)

Chicken Wings or Short Ribs of Beef with Anise and Mushrooms

3 pounds chicken wings, split
8 lean beef short ribs
¼ teaspoon Chinese 5 spices,
   if you have it
1 tablespoon sugar
1 teaspoon sesame oil
8 dried Chinese mushrooms
2 tablespoons sherry
1-1½ teaspoons salt
6 tablespoons soy sauce
2 bunches of scallions
2-3 anise flowers
4-6 cloves garlic, crushed
4 cups warm water

Soak dried mushrooms in warm water after they have been thoroughly washed. Clean scallions and cut into inch size pieces. Heat enough peanut or vegetable oil to cover bottom of a large size kettle to ⅛ inch deep. When piping hot, add chicken wings or short ribs of beef and brown well on all sides. Remove chicken wings or beef as pieces are browned. After all wings or beef are browned, pour off excess oil in pot and put wings or beef back in pot. Add mushrooms and water they were soaked in, and rest of ingredients and mix well. Cover and cook gently until tender, about 3-4 hours, stirring occasionally. Add warm water as it cooks down to keep gravy to about 3 cups. Taste and adjust for salt. (This is one Chinese dish that really improves with flavor if made the day before.)

Ginger Fried Steak (Tut Pa Noug Pa)

4 slices tenderloin steak,
   1 inch thick, cut in half,
   or 1 flank steak, sirloin
   or boneless rib steak cut in
   serving size pieces
6 tablespoons soy sauce
1 teaspoon baking soda
1½ tablespoons sesame oil
1½ tablespoons peanut or
   vegetable oil
1 tablespoon sugar
1½ teaspoons salt
¼ teaspoon pepper
   Smoothed water chestnut
   flour or cornstarch
1½ tablespoons minced or
   grated ginger root
4 large onions, cut in slices
   vertically

Marinate meat in soy sauce, baking soda, sesame oil, peanut or vegetable oil, sugar, salt and pepper for 30 minutes. Pat dry with paper towels and then dredge lightly in water chestnut flour or cornstarch. In the largest skillet or wok heat oil about ⅛ inch deep to piping hot, put in steak, minced ginger root and onions. Fry, tossing onions frequently until onions are golden and steak is browned on both sides. Cook to desired doneness, but best if left pink inside. Serve on a hot platter.

Stuffed Doilies or Lettuce Envelopes (Moo Chou Pork or Beef)

1 pound very lean pork, or
    beef steak, finely diced
1½ tablespoons soy sauce
1½ tablespoons cornstarch
3 tablespoons peanut or
    vegetable oil
12 dried Chinese mushrooms,
    soaked ½ hour, drained
    and thinly sliced
1 cup finely sliced water
    chestnuts
½ cup diced bamboo shoots
1 teaspoon cornstarch
¾ cup chicken broth
¼ teaspoon salt
2 teaspoons sugar
3 tablespoons sherry
1 teaspoon sesame oil
1 cup finely sliced celery
4 scallions, finely sliced
1 tablespoon oyster sauce
2 teaspoons Black Bean
    Sauce with Chili

3 cups flour
1½ cups water, heated to
    simmering
3 tablespoons vegetable oil
    mixed with 1 teaspoon
    sesame oil

Stuffing:

Marinate prepared meat in soy sauce and cornstarch for 20 minutes. Heat 3 tablespoons oil to piping hot and add meat. Cook, stirring, until meat is cooked through, about 3 minutes. Add mushrooms, bamboo shoots and water chestnuts and cook, stirring, 2 minutes. Add combined cornstarch, chicken broth and next listed 4 ingredients. Cook, stirring, until broth is thickened and clear, about half a minute. Add celery, scallions, oyster sauce, and Black Bean Sauce with Chili, tossing together well. Heat through and serve in one of the following.

Doilies: (These may be purchased at Chinese grocery.)

Place flour in a medium size bowl. Holding water about 1 foot above the bowl, gradually add to flour; knead to smooth, to make gummy and translucent dough. Cover dough with plastic wrap and allow to rest 20 minutes. Divide dough into 24 pieces. Taking a piece of the dough in the palm of the hand, flatten to make a 2-inch cake. Wet 1 side of cake with some of the combined vegetable and sesame oil. Place another prepared cake on top of oiled one and roll out with a rolling pin to about 6 inches diameter. Do the same with rest of the pieces of dough and you will have 12 double doilies. Heat an iron griddle over low heat and bake each doily for about 3 minutes under cover. Turn doilies and bake other side about 3 minutes, covered. Pile done doilies on a plate and cover all with a dish cloth. Separate doilies to serve. Each diner takes a doily and places a row of the filling in the center of his doily, having the smooth wet inside face up. Fold in top end and roll the doily over the stuffing to facilitate easy eating. Delicious! (Doilies may be made ahead and kept in refrigerator. To reheat place on steaming tray or warm, covered with foil, in a preheated 300° oven for 10 minutes.) Makes 24 doilies.

Lettuce Envelopes:

1   large head iceburg lettuce

Separate leaves; wash and place in large bowl. Pour over boiling water and blanch 3 minutes; drain and dry. Serve on separate plate allowing each diner to take a leaf of lettuce; place a few tablespoons of filling in center; fold in sides and roll up for easy, delicious eating.

Meat and Vegetables with Fried Noodles (Chow Mein)

1   pound flank steak, chicken or pork, slivered against the grain
½   pound shrimp, sliced in 2 along the back (optional)
3   cups celery, cut in thin slants
½   pound mushrooms, cut in T's, or 1 pound fresh or canned bean sprouts, rinsed and drained
1   cup water chestnuts, sliced fine
6-8 scallions or 2 onions, sliced
1   teaspoon minced ginger root
2   tablespoons soy sauce
1½ teaspoons sugar
1   tablespoon sherry
1-2 cloves garlic, crushed (optional)
3   cups chicken broth
4   tablespoons cornstarch

Cut celery across top and slant into thin slices. Slice mushrooms into thin T's. Sliver scallions and cut into 2 inch pieces. Heat enough oil to cover the largest size skillet or wok to ⅛ inch deep, piping hot. Add prepared beef, chicken or pork and cook, stirring constantly, for 3 minutes or until meat is cooked. Add shrimp and cook, stirring, for 1 minute. Add vegetables and cook, tossing, for 3 minutes. Remove from heat and add seasonings and broth. Mix cornstarch with a little water to a thin paste and add. Return to heat and cook, stirring, until clear. Serve with fried Chinese noodles and rice. (Recipe for homemade noodles listed under side dishes.)

Fancy Fried Rice

6   cups cold cooked rice, tossed
      lightly to separate grains
1   pound shrimp, cut in ½
      inch chunks
¾   cup finely diced Char Su
      pork
1   Chinese sausage, or hot
      Italian sausage, sliced
1   cup chopped scallions
1   pound washed, drained
      bean sprouts
2   teaspoons salt
2   teaspoons sugar
3   tablespoons oyster sauce
      or light soy sauce
¾   cup cooked baby peas
2   eggs, beaten
6   tablespoons peanut or
      vegetable oil

Heat peanut or vegetable oil to hot and add shrimp and Char Su pork; cook, stirring, 1 minute. Remove to keep warm with slotted spoon and place in 200° oven. Add sausage and fry 1 minute, stirring. Add bean sprouts and scallions to skillet and cook, stirring. Add bean sprouts and scallions to skillet and cook, stirring, 2 minutes. Add rice, salt, sugar and oyster sauce. Add shrimp and pork and mix well, heat, stirring. Pour in beaten eggs and stir, tossing until eggs are set. Add peas and cook, mixing gently, to hot. (Freezes well. Reheat in 350° oven until fluffy and hot, covered, about 30-35 minutes after defrosting.)

Plain Fried Rice

3   tablespoons peanut or
      vegetable oil
2   eggs, well beaten
1   teaspoon salt
1   cup chopped onion
1   cup dried, cold, cooked
      chicken, shrimp, pork or
      veal
1   pound bean sprouts, rinsed
      and drained, or ½ pound
      mushrooms, finely
      chopped
6   cups boiled rice
4   tablespoons soy sauce
2   teaspoons sugar
      Salt and pepper to taste

Heat 3 tablespoons oil in the largest size skillet or wok. Pour in eggs which have been beaten together with salt. Tip pan so that eggs will thinly spread. Fry eggs until thoroughly cooked and delicately browned on both sides. Slide onto a plate and cut in long thin strips. Heat oil of ⅛ inch depth to piping hot and fry onions, stirring constantly, until lightly golden. Add meat or shrimp, bean sprouts or mushrooms. Salt and pepper well. Cook, stirring, until mushrooms are done, about 3 minutes. Add boiled rice and stir thoroughly but lightly with a fork until heated through. Mix soy sauce and sugar together and add to rice mixture, stirring through gently until rice is well coated with soy sauce mixture. More soy sauce and sugar may be needed as different rices absorb more liquid; add to taste. Add strips of egg and heat for another minute on a low heat, gently lifting to stir. Can be prepared ahead of time and gently reheated, stirring frequently. (Freezes well.)

58

Celery and Radish Salad

2   cups Julienne celery blanch-
    ed in 1 quart of boiling
    water for 3 minutes; drain
    and rinse in cold water
1½ cups thinly sliced red
    radishes
1   tablespoon sesame oil
1   tablespoon light soy sauce
1   teaspoon salt
1   teaspoon sugar

Toss together lightly. Refrigerate 10 minutes. Re-toss before serving.

Pickled Mustard Cabbage (Harm Choy)

2-3 fresh mustard cabbages
2   tablespoons coarse salt
1   cup white vinegar
3   tablespoons sugar
     Water
1   (5 ounce) jar prepared
     Diablo mustard (optional)

Get mustard cabbages at Chinese grocery.

Soak mustard cabbages in cold water and wash clean. Place in 2 quart container with rest of ingredients, adding enough water to cover cabbages, and stir in mustard if a hot Harm Choy is desired. Cover tightly and store in a cool place for about 1-2 weeks or until pickled. Keeps in refrigerator indefinitely. Serve as a pickle, slicing each leaf crosswise, thinly, as accompaniment to meal or use, if made without the mustard, to make Pork Harm Choy (see page 49).

Snow Pea Pods and Mushrooms

1   pound snow pea pods
½   cup chopped almonds
     Peanut or vegetable oil
½   cup sliced mushrooms,
     sliced in T's
1   teaspoon sugar
1   tablespoon oyster sauce
     or soy sauce

Remove strings from pea pods. Cook in boiling, salted water, about 1 cup, for 2 minutes; drain. Saute almonds and mushrooms in oil ⅛ inch deep for about 2 minutes. Add drained pea pods and cook, stirring constantly, for 2 minutes. Stir in sugar and oyster or soy sauce and heat briefly.

Rice and Noodles

Rice and noodles are of great importance to every meal the Chinese eat. Noodles may be purchased at a Chinese grocery and cooked according to directions. Rice is used as a soup, Congee, which is in fact a thin gruel made of rice and water. Rice accompanies all main dishes and is cooked properly by boiling or steaming.

Boiling:

1 cup rice
2 cups water

Wash rice and place with water in a saucepan; Chinese do not use salt when cooking rice. Bring to a boil; turn heat low and cover. Cook 20 minutes or until rice has absorbed all water and there are small holes on the surface. Shut off heat and keep covered for another 5-10 minutes before serving. Serves 4.

Steaming: (If you are lucky enough to have a rice steamer.)

1 cup rice
3 cups water

Wash rice and place with water in a pot. Bring to a boil and boil for 5 minutes. Put in strainer and drain off all water. Place rice in steamer and steam for 30 minutes. Shut off heat and allow to stand for 5 minutes before serving. Serves 4. (Will keep warm in covered steamer for half an hour.)

Stir Fried Vegetables

2 slices ginger root or
   1 clove garlic
1 teaspoon salt
1 tablespoon soy sauce
1 ½ teaspoons sugar
½ cup hot water
1 pound vegetables
   Peanut or vegetable oil
   Toasted, slivered almonds
    (optional)
1 ½ teaspoons vinegar, if
   using spinach

If cooking broccoli cut stems lengthwise to slim pieces and cut off flower tops to cook less time; French cut string beans; cut stems off spinach; prepare other vegetables in usual manner. Rinse well in a colander and drain. Use enough oil to cover the largest size frying pan or wok to about ⅛ inches deep. Fry fresh ginger root or garlic clove in hot oil until brown. Remove ginger or garlic and add vegetables, just the stem ends first if using broccoli. Add salt and soy sauce; add vinegar if cooking spinach; add sugar for all other vegetables; add hot water. Cover. Stir occasionally and cook for 3-4 minutes or until just cooked but still green and crisp. If cooking broccoli add flower tops and cook 2 more minutes. Add toasted almonds and stir well.

60

Steamed Chinese Cabbage (Chow Choy Sum)

2 pounds Chinese cabbage
2 inch wedge of ginger root
4 tablespoons peanut or
   vegetable oil
1 teaspoon salt
½ cup chicken stock
½ teaspoon sugar
½ teaspoon monosodium
   glutamate (optional)
⅛ teaspoon pepper
1 tablespoon soy sauce
¼ teaspoon sesame oil

Slice cabbage into ½ inch slices and wash and drain thoroughly. Heat oil to piping hot and add ginger and salt. Add Chinese cabbage and stir for 1 minute. Add stock, sugar, monosodium glutamate, soy sauce, sesame oil, and pepper; mix well. Cover and cook on highest heat for half a minute. Lift cabbage out of pan with a slotted spoon, allow to drain; place on warmed serving dish to serve.

Noodles

1 package Won Ton wrappers

Cut Won Ton wrappers in ½ inch strips. Deep fry in deep hot oil to a rich brown. Drain on paper towels. Keeps well in brown store bag up to a month. Good for nibbling or whenever fried noodles are used.

Jasmine, Oolong or Litchi Tea

1 teaspoon tea, per serving,
   in tea ball
1 cup boiling water
   per serving

Preheat the teapot with boiling water. Pour off and proceed.

Fried Pastries (Ju Won Ton)

2 cups flour
3 tablespoons sugar
⅛ teaspoon salt
2 eggs, beaten
1½ cups water
   Peanut or vegetable oil

Mix dry ingredients. Combine beaten eggs and water; add to dry ingredients and beat with wire whisk until smooth. Dip pretzel iron ¾ deep into batter and then deep fry in piping hot deep oil at 375° until golden, rich brown. Drop off iron and drain on paper towels. Store in brown paper bag. Optional: Dust with confectioners sugar.

Honeyed Apples

6 apples, peeled, cored and
  cut in wedges
3 egg whites
4 tablespoons cornstarch
2 tablespoons flour
1/3 cup peanut oil
2/3 cup honey
1 tablespoon sesame seeds
  Oil for deep frying

Make a batter from egg whites, cornstarch and flour; beat well. Coat wedges with batter and fry in deep oil heated to 375° until golden brown. Drain on paper toweling and keep warm in 250° oven. Heat the third cup peanut oil and stir in honey thoroughly; heat through and add sesame seeds. Add apples and coat well. Serve immediately. Apples and honey mixture may be served separately with each diner coating his or her apple in honey mixture.

Almond Cookies

3 cups flour
1 cup sugar
1/2 teaspoon salt
1 teaspoon baking powder
1 cup shortening or butter
1 egg, beaten
1 tablespoon almond extract
1/4 cup blanched almonds

Sift dry ingredients and cut in shortening until mixture is like corn meal. Add beaten egg and knead until egg is absorbed. Add almond extract and knead again. Roll out dough on lightly floured surface and cut into 1 inch circles about 1/2 inch thick. Place on ungreased cookie sheets and press an almond with a tip dipped in red food coloring on top of each cookie. Bake at 350° about 20 minutes or until lightly golden and done. Makes about 3-4 dozen cookies. (Freezes well.)

Almond Junket

2 packages unflavored gelatin
2/3 cup cold water
1 cup boiling water
1 cup milk
2/3 cup sugar
1/4 teaspoon salt
3 teaspoons almond extract

Soften gelatin in cold water; add rest of ingredients except flavoring. Simmer gently until sugar is dissolved and blended. Remove from heat; add almond extract; mix well and pour into lightly oiled 8 inch square baking pan. Chill and when firmly set; cut into small squares. (Freezes well after gelatin is set.)

Almond Junket and Mandarin Oranges:
Divide canned chilled Mandarin oranges and their juice into 8 dessert dishes; add several squares of almond junket to each dish.

Sesame Seed Cookies

2   cups flour
½   teaspoon baking soda
¼   teaspoon salt
1   cup shortening or butter
1   cup sugar
1   egg, beaten
1   teaspoon vanilla
¾   cup sesame seeds, toasted

To toast sesame seeds, heat in a shallow pan in 275° oven, or in a dry skillet over low heat; stirring constantly. Toast only until golden brown; be careful not to get too brown.

Sift flour, soda and salt. Cream shortening and sugar and add beaten egg and vanilla. Add sifted dry ingredients and mix well. Shape dough with hands into small balls. Roll in toasted sesame seeds and press flat on a greased cookie sheet with the bottom of a glass. Bake at 400° about 10-12 minutes or until golden. Makes 6-7 dozen. (Freezes well.)

63

German

Filled Lemons

8   lemons
3   cans boneless and skinless
      sardines, mashed with
      their oil
½   teaspoon grated onion
½   teaspoon salt
¼   teaspoon cinnamon
1½ teaspoons lemon juice

Wash lemons and cut off a tip end so that they will stand upright; cut off top for cover. Scoop out all lemon pulp and reserve for other uses. Put shells in a bowl of ice water to keep crisp. Mix all the rest of the ingredients well. Drain lemon shells dry; fill with sardine mixture and top with sliced off lemon covers. Refrigerate.

Chopped Wurst Canapes

1   cup ground hard wurst
1   small onion, ground
5   eggs, well beaten
     Salt and pepper

Mix all ingredients together well. Drop in hot greased frying pan by small spoonfuls and fry on both sides to golden. Drain on paper towels keep warm in 150° oven. Serve on pumpernickel rounds which have been spread with German Mustard.

German Mustard:

1   cup dry mustard
1   cup vinegar
2   eggs, beaten
1   cup sugar

The night before making, mix the cup of dry mustard and cup of vinegar in top of a double boiler; stir to smooth and allow to stand overnight. Next morning add rest of ingredients and cook over simmering water, 18 minutes, stirring occasionally. Place in a glass jar when done and keep refrigerated. Keeps indefinitely. Excellent on ham and other meats, also good spread over surface of a cake of cream cheese and served with crackers; each guest spreading some of the cheese and mustard on his or her cracker.

Baked Herring in Sour Cream Sauce

2   salted Herrings
     Pepper
6   tablespoons butter
1   cup chopped onions
½   cup bread crumbs
¼   teaspoon pepper
¾   cup sour cream
8   boned anchovies

Fillet and skin herrings. Soak overnight or all day in cold water. Drain on paper towels. Place in a well buttered serving-baking dish. Sprinkle with pepper. Fry chopped onions in butter until golden, add bread crumbs and mix well. Spread sour cream over fish fillets and sprinkle onion and bread mixture over sour cream. Garnish with anchovies. Cover lightly with aluminum foil and bake in 350° oven for 30 minutes, removing aluminum foil during last 10 minutes of baking. Place baking dish on a tray, surround with points of toast and ask guests to help themselves.

Poached Salmon with Cucumber Sauce

Whole salmon or salmon
  steaks
Cheesecloth
Dry white wine

Use a whole salmon, if you can get it, or salmon steaks cut thickly, about 4 inches. Wipe, brush with salad oil and season with salt, pepper and dill weed. Place a rack in a large pot to make a steamer if you do not have one. Cover salmon with a piece of cheesecloth large enough to encase the entire fish and leave ends long enough to grasp when removing fish after it is poached. Place cheesecloth wrapped fish in steamer gently. If using fresh salmon or fresh salmon steaks, poach in half white dry wine and half water with 1 tablespoon salt to 2 quarts of liquid. If using thawed frozen salmon, add the ingredients at left.

1   large carrot
1   cup sliced onion
12   mashed peppercorns
3   cloves
3   medium bay leaves
3   stalks celery, cut in thirds
4   large sprigs parsley
½   teaspoon dried thyme or
     1 sprig of fresh thyme

Simmer all gently for 30-40 minutes, until fish flakes easily. Remove by grasping cheesecloth ends and place on a cold, dry surface. Unwrap and carefully remove skin. Take a small paring knife and gently pare away the thin layer of brown flesh, revealing lovely salmon colored flesh underneath. Wrap tightly in plastic wrap and aluminum foil and place in refrigerator until serving time. Make a wine aspic with 1 envelope unflavored gelatin sprinkled over ½ cup cold water in top of double boiler. Place over hot water and stir until dissolved. Add 1¼ cups dry white wine, mix well, remove from heat and refrigerate until egg-white consistency. Place fish on serving platter and brush with the slightly thickened gelatin mixture. Arrange pimiento halves on surface, top with sliced hard boiled eggs and sliced ripe olives. Pour aspic over all and allow extra aspic to run onto serving platter. Refrigerate until aspic is set. Crumble aspic in platter surrounding salmon and garnish with watercress, parsley and/or cherry tomatoes. Serve with Cucumber Sauce.

Cucumber Sauce:

2   cups sour cream
2   cucumbers, peeled, seeded
     and coarsely grated
½   cup chopped ripe (black)
     olives
3   tablespoons capers, chopped
     (optional)
½   teaspoon grated onion
¼   teaspoon garlic powder
     Salt and white pepper
     to taste

Mix all together well. Taste and adjust seasonings to individual preference. Serve in separate bowls next to salmon.

Chopped Herring Salad

1 (12-16 ounce) jar of herring
    fillets in sour cream
1 small onion
1 sour apple, peeled and
    cored
3 hard boiled eggs
1 slice bread (soaked in cider
    vinegar and sugar)
2 tablespoons cider vinegar
    mixed with 2 teaspoons
    sugar
1 teaspoon salad oil
    Dash cinnamon
    Dash pepper

Grind or put through food processor herring, onion, apple and two of the hard boiled eggs. Squeeze bread which has been soaked in vinegar and sugar, reserving liquids, if any. Put bread through grinder or food processor and mix all together well. Add reserved vinegar and sugar mixture, left from soaking slice of bread. (Some breads absorb more liquid than others, depending on their texture.) Add oil, dash of cinnamon and pepper, seasoning to taste. Pat with a fork into a serving dish. Garnish fish with the other hard boiled egg, sliced, and finely chopped scallions. Refrigerate. Serve with party rye.

Calf's Aspic (Sulze Von Kalb)

6-8 large beef knuckle bones,
      not marrow bones
2   pounds meaty veal bones
3   onions, quartered
6-8 cloves garlic, cut thin
1   tablespoon salt
1   teaspoon whole pepper seeds
¼   teaspoon coarse black
      pepper
2   bay leaves
      Juice of 2 lemons
1   cup dry white wine
½   teaspoon sugar
2   egg whites, slightly beaten
      with 2 tablespoons water
1   teaspoon vinegar
4   hard boiled eggs

Place knuckle bones and meaty veal bones in a large kettle and cover well with water. Add onion, garlic, seasoning, lemon juice and wine. Boil gently for 4½ hours, until liquid is reduced in half. Strain broth; measure 4 cups. (Should there not be enough liquid to make 4 cups, reheat liquid and add hot water to make 4 cups. Dissolve 1 package gelatin with ¼ cup cold water and add to hot mixture.) Refrigerate. Place bones and meat in bowl and refrigerate until cool enough to remove meat and glutinous flesh. Coarsely chop meat and glutinous flesh, making about 2 cups. Skim all fat from cooled liquid and melt slowly if jellied. Add sugar and slightly beaten egg whites; boil vigorously for about 10 minutes, stirring constantly. Strain through cheesecloth; add vinegar; taste and add more salt, pepper or crushed garlic, as this broth must be highly seasoned. Set broth in refrigerator until it begins to gel. Stir in bits of chopped meat. Wet a large mold; place slices of hard boiled egg on the bottom to make a design. Chop rest of hard boiled eggs coarsely and add to aspic. Pour into mold and refrigerate until solid. Turn out and cut in slices to serve. Serve with cocktail size pumpernickle bread.

Pink Pickled Eggs

1   large can tiny whole beets
8   hard boiled eggs
¾   cup sugar
1   cup beet liquid
1   cup vinegar
1½ tablespoons salt
¼   teaspoon white pepper
2   bay leaves
10 cloves

Place beets and eggs in a large bowl or jar. Bring rest of ingredients to a boil and simmer 5 minutes. Pour over beets and eggs. Cover and refrigerate for at least 12 hours.

Thick Lentil Soup (Dicke Linsensuppe)

1   pound lentils
2   large soup bones or 1 pound
      smoked beef cheek
1   carrot, whole
1   large stalk celery
1   medium onion, whole
12 cups water
1½ teaspoons salt
¼   teaspoon pepper
½   teaspoon peppercorns
1   bay leaf
2   tablespoons butter
2   tablespoons flour

Wash lentils thoroughly and place in large soup kettle. Add meat, carrot, celery, onion, water, salt, pepper, peppercorns and bay leaf. Cover; bring to a boil; skim; turn down heat and simmer gently for 3-4 hours, until lentils are very soft. Remove meat, vegetables, peppercorns and bay leaf; skim off fat. Heat butter in a small skillet; add flour and make a roux. Gradually add 2 cups of the soup and cook, stirring for a few minutes. Pour all back into soup kettle and cook, stirring constantly, for about 3 minutes. Taste and adjust seasonings. Cut meat into small pieces and return to soup. Put cooked carrot through a food mill or food processor and add to soup for color. (Freezes well.)

Beer Soup

1½ pound German dark rye or
      pumpernickle bread
4   cups water
2   quarts beer
1   cup sugar
4   egg yolks
4   tablespoons sour cream
    Salt and pepper to taste
    Cinnamon to taste
    Dabs of sour cream

Cut bread in small cubes and place in a bowl. Pour water over bread and let stand overnight. Remove bread to a soup kettle and simmer, stirring, until completely disintegrated. Put bread mixture in blender, a little at a time, and blend to smooth; set aside. Mix beer and sugar together in a soup kettle and simmer until sugar dissolves. Beat egg yolks well with the sour cream and gradually add a little of the hot beer mixture, blending well; add all at once to rest of beer mixture. Cook, stirring, for 1 minute. Add bread mixture; mix well; season with salt, pepper and cinnamon to taste. Simmer gently for 10-15 minutes, stirring occasionally. Serve hot with a dab of sour cream in each dish.

70

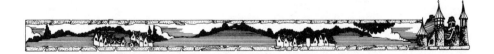

Potato Soup (Kartoffelsuppe)

4 tablespoons butter
4 tablespoons flour
12 cups beef or chicken broth
8 large potatoes, diced
1 large onion, diced
1 cup diced celery
⅓ cup chopped parsley
¼ cup dried precooked beans
½ cup cauliflower
1 cup peas
1 bay leaf
6 peppercorns
Salt and pepper to taste
Diced bread

Melt butter in a large soup kettle and add flour, stirring constantly, to make roux. When lightly brown, slowly add some of the broth, stirring, then gradually add rest of the broth. Add the vegetables and spices. Simmer gently for about 40 minutes. Press all through a food mill blender or food processor; return to soup kettle and season highly. Fry bread cubes in a little butter until golden and serve with soup. (Freezes well.)

Broiled Herring

10-12 salted herrings

Fillet and skin herrings. Soak overnight or all day. Drain on paper towels; dry. Place on oiled serving broiler dish; brush herring with melted butter. Broil under moderate heat for about 10-15 minutes, until herring is cooked and lightly brown. Serve with lemon wedges or with scallions minced into sour cream. Surround with toast points and ask guests to help themselves.

Meat Loaf and Cabbage

3 pounds ground beef
1 medium onion, grated
¾ cup fine dried bread crumbs
3 eggs, beaten
¾ cup milk
4 teaspoons caraway seeds
2½ teaspoons salt
¼ teaspoon pepper
1 small head cabbage, shredded

Mix meat, grated onion, bread crumbs, beaten eggs, milk and 3 teaspoons caraway seed. Add salt and pepper and mix well, preferably with hands. Form into a loaf and place in center of a large greased baking pan. Toss the other teaspoon of caraway seeds through shredded cabbage. Surround meat loaf with cabbage and caraway seed mixture; salt cabbage lightly. Bake covered for 1 hour in 375° oven. Remove cover and baste cabbage frequently with meat juices and bake uncovered for 30 minutes more. Excellent served with potato pancakes. (Freezes well.)

Breaded Veal Steak (Wiener Schnitzel)

3 pounds round steak of veal,
   cut very thin in serving
   pieces
5 tablespoons vegetable
   shortening
   Flour
2 eggs, beaten
3 tablespoons water
1 ½ cups fine bread crumbs
1 ½ teaspoons salt
¼ teaspoon pepper
¼ teaspoon ginger
2 onions, sliced (optional)
¾ cup sour cream (optional)
½ cup meat stock (optional)
   Juice of 1 lemon (optional)

Pound veal steaks very thin; dredge lightly in flour. Dip into beaten eggs to which you have added the water. Coat all over with bread crumbs to which you have added salt, pepper and ginger. Melt vegetable shortening in a skillet until hot. Fry breaded steak until brown on both sides. Reduce heat to low and finish cooking until done, about 10 minutes. For variation prepare as directed but add sliced onion when browning veal. When meat is browned and onion golden, lower temperature and add sour cream and ½ cup of meat stock and juice of 1 lemon. Cover and simmer ½ hour.

Stuffed Rolled Round Steak (Rouladon)

8 slices top round steak,
   cut very thin
   Hot mustard or German
   mustard
2-3 carrots, chopped
3 medium onions, diced
1 large green pepper, diced
1-2 large dill pickles, diced
8 strips bacon, diced
   Salt and pepper
   Shortening
1 (8 ounce) can tomato sauce
3 cans water
1 bay leaf
2 peppercorns

Tenderize steak and pound thin. Spread with hot or German mustard on one side of each steak. Mix chopped carrots, diced onion, diced green pepper, diced pickle and diced bacon. Spread all over the mustard side of steaks. Sprinkle with salt and pepper. Roll up as for jelly rolls and tie with string or close with toothpicks. Bring to piping hot enough shortening to cover bottom of a large skillet to ⅛ inch deep. Brown rolls and add rest of the ingredients; simmer slowly for 45 minutes. Remove Rouladon and cut off string or remove toothpicks. Slice and serve with the sauce. (Freezes well.)

Roast Beef in Wine

Rolled rib roast for 8
Dry red wine
Water
4 tablespoons flour
1 cup sour cream

Marinate a rolled rib roast or a standing rib roast in dry red wine for at least 8 hours, turning meat frequently. Roast in 325° oven with wine marinate, basting frequently. Roast 35 minutes per pound for well done, 30 minutes per pound for medium and 20 minutes per pound for rare standing rib roast. Add 10 minutes for a rolled rib roast. Use a meat thermometer for accuracy. When done, remove meat, skim off fat, and add water to make 2 cups of liquid in the pan. Mix 4 tablespoons flour with water to make a thin paste and add to liquid. Cook, stirring until thickened, over medium heat. Blend in 1 cup sour cream and simmer briefly. Serve gravy separately. Very rich and elegant.

Braunschweiger Olives

1 pound Braunschweiger
cheese
40 small pimiento olives
Chopped parsley

Mash cheese well with fork. Scoop a teaspoonful into palm of your hand and pat and flatten. Place an olive in center and roll mashed cheese over it into a covering ball. Roll in chopped parsley and serve on picks.

Pot Roast (Sauerbraten)

5-6 pound sirloin roast, larded
with suet thickly
1½ teaspoons salt
¼ teaspoon pepper
2 cups water
2 cups vinegar or dry
white wine
2 large onions, sliced
5-6 bay leaves
2 teaspoons peppercorns
12 cloves
½ cup sugar
Vegetable oil
12 gingersnaps
½ cup flour
1 cup sour cream

Rub meat well with salt and pepper and place in a large bowl. Heat water and vinegar or wine to lukewarm. Add sliced onion and next 4 ingredients. Heat until mixture is hot and pour over meat. Allow to marinate in this for at leat 48 hours; turning several times; keeping refrigerated. Remove liquid; strain and save. Heat ⅛ inch oil in a large kettle to piping hot. Add meat and brown well on all sides. Add marinade and gingersnaps. Cover tightly and simmer slowly for 3-4 hours, or until meat is tender. (Freezes well at this point. Defrost; heat and proceed.) Remove meat to a platter. Mix sour cream and flour together with a little water to make a smooth thin paste. Gradually add some of the hot liquid to sour cream mixture until well thinned. Add to remaining liquid in pan and cook, stirring, until gravy thickens. Strain if necessary; serve with sliced meat.

73

Rabbit Stew (Hasenpfeffer)

3	rabbits, quartered
2¼	cups vinegar
2¼	cups water
3	onions, sliced
3	teaspoons salt
1	teaspoon peppercorns
½	teaspoon red pepper
7	whole cloves
7	bay leaves
1½	teaspoons sage
10	tablespoons butter
2¼	cups sour cream

Clean rabbits and place in a large crock. Cover with vinegar and water, mixed together. Add onions and seasonings. Marinate, placing crock in refrigerator for 2 days and turning meat several times. Drain meat and wipe dry. Brown on all sides in melted hot butter. Add 3 cups of marinade and simmer gently, covered, until tender. (Freezes well. Reheat and proceed.) Add sour cream to sauce, blending well, and simmer gently for a few minutes. Serve with sauce.

Roast Venison

	Venison roast for 8
2	teaspoons salt
¼	teaspoon pepper
¼	cup parsley, chopped
2	cucumbers, diced
1½	cups dried apricots
2	cups hot water
2	medium apples, diced
1½	tablespoons vinegar
3	tablespoons butter or margarine

Rub roast well with salt and pepper. Place in roaster with rest of ingredients. Roast at 350°, covered, for 1 hour. Remove cover, add water if needed and roast uncovered until browned and tender, basting frequently with juices. Allow 3½-4 hours roasting time in all.

Brisket of Beef with Sauerkraut

6-7	pound brisket of beef
	Salt and pepper
2	quarts sauerkraut
2	tablespoons vinegar
4	tablespoons brown sugar
	Grated large potato
2	teaspoons caraway seed

Wipe meat and salt and pepper well. Place in bottom of a large pot and pour sauerkraut with juice over it; cover. Simmer gently or bake in 350° oven until beef is tender, about 3½ hours. Add vinegar, brown sugar, grated raw potato and caraway seeds; stir lightly with a fork. Cover and cook 10 more minutes. To serve, slice brisket and surround with sauerkraut; pour sauce over all. (Freezes well.)

Partridges with Chestnut Gravy

Partridges
Flour
Salt and pepper
½ cup small cubes fat pork
Butter
2 cups heavy cream
1 cup chestnut puree
Paprika

Cut up birds as for fried chicken or just use breasts, as you prefer. Mix flour, salt and pepper together in a plastic bag and drop in partridge pieces, shake to cover all with flour. Try out pork and add an equal amount of butter. Fry partridge pieces to a delicate brown. Remove partridge pieces and add cream, chestnut puree and paprika enough to give a nice pink coloring to sauce. Season to taste and add browned partridge pieces and reheat. (May be prepared several days ahead and then reheated.)

Filled Pork or Veal Steak (Gefulte Schwein, Kalb Filet)

8 very thin veal or pork steaks, pounded thin
½ pound beef hamburg
2 slices bread, soaked in milk and squeezed out
1 egg
2 onions, grated
1 large can broiled, chopped mushrooms
3 large tomatoes or 1½ cups stewed tomatoes
3 cups hot water
1 cup sour cream
1½ tablespoons flour
Salt and pepper

Pound steaks as flat as possible and sew two together, leaving one end open to make a pocket. Make a stuffing by combining hamburg, moistened bread, eggs, one of the onions and half of the mushrooms. Season with salt and pepper. Fill steaks and sew open ends together. Heat ⅛ inch shortening to piping hot and brown steaks on both sides. Salt and pepper. Add other grated onion, tomatoes and mushrooms and cook 20 minutes over low heat, stirring frequently. Place in 350° oven for about 30 minutes, basting occasionally. Add sour cream, salt and pepper to gravy to taste. Thicken with flour mixed with a little water to make a thin paste, simmering gently and stirring constantly. Slice in halves and serve with gravy. (Freezes well.)

Sauerkraut

6½ pounds cabbage
1 tablespoon sugar
5 tablespoons coarse salt
1 tablespoon caraway seed
3 cups water

Remove hard core of cabbage and outer leaves. Shred fine and pack in layers of 4-5 inches deep in a crock or plastic keg. Sprinkle each layer with rest of dry ingredients, mixed, repeating the process until cabbage is used as well as rest of the dry ingredients. Pour water over cabbage and press cabbage down until brine about covers it. Place a plate with a heavy washed rock on top of it over cabbage so that it will weigh the whole thing down. Tie or lay a cloth over top of crock or keg. Keep at room temperature for 5-7 days, mixing with a large wooden spoon once every day. Taste and when sour enough put into glass jars and refrigerate. Keeps a long time.

Sauerkraut with Apples (Sauerkraut Mit Appfeln)

4	tablespoons bacon drippings or vegetable oil
1	onion, diced
8	cups sauerkraut
3	apples, diced
1	teaspoon salt
¼	teaspoon caraway seed
2	raw potatoes, grated
	Boiling water or broth
	Brown sugar or honey

Heat bacon drippings or vegetable oil; add onion and fry until golden brown. Add sauerkraut and cook, stirring occasionally, for 5 minutes. Add apples, salt, caraway seeds and grated potatoes. Mix thoroughly and cover with boiling water or broth. Cook, uncovered, for 30 minutes. Cover and continue cooking for another 30 minutes. (Freeze, if doing so, at this point. Defrost and proceed.) Sweeten to taste with brown sugar or honey; mix well. Reheat for a few minutes before serving.

Potato Dumplings (Kartoffel Kloesse)

8	large boiled, peeled potatoes
3	eggs, beaten
1½	cups dried fine bread crumbs
¼	teaspoon nutmeg
2-3	teaspoons salt
1¼	cups milk
4	cups flour
1¼	teaspoons baking powder

Force potatoes through a food mill or put in food processor until finely mashed. Add eggs, bread crumbs, nutmeg and salt. Beat well with a fork and gradually add milk. Sift flour and baking powder together and stir into potato mixture. Beat until light; shape into small golf ball dumplings with wet hands. Drop dumplings into boiling salted water. When dumplings rise to surface; allow them to simmer for about 15 minutes. Remove from water with a slotted spoon and drain. Arrange on a large platter and cover with the following sauce.

Sauce:

1	cup butter
1	grated medium onion
1	cup dried fine bread crumbs

Melt butter in small frying pan; add rest of ingredients; stir and cook for 1 minute. (May be made up ahead, cooled, and frozen. Bring to room temperature and boil and proceed.) Serve with crumb sauce poured over all.

Potatoes in Sour Cream Dill Sauce

16 small potatoes, in jackets
3   tablespoons butter
     Salt and pepper
¾ cup sour cream
1   teaspoon dill weed or
     minced fresh dill

Boil potatoes in their jackets until barely tender. Peel while hot. Heat butter in skillet and when hot, brown potatoes well all over. Drain on paper towels. Heat sour cream and dill weed; season with salt and pepper and add potatoes. Simmer gently for a few minutes, turning potatoes gently, until heated through.

Stuffed Potatoes (Wiener Kartoffel Kloesse)

8   potatoes, peeled
1   cup flour
2   eggs
     Salt to taste
     Grated nutmeg
     Goose fat or butter
1   tablespoon dried instant
     onion
½ cup dried fine bread crumbs
½ teaspoon salt

Boil potatoes until soft; drain thoroughly. Mash while hot adding flour a little at a time, or put through food mill or food processor, mixing flour in frequently as potatoes are mashed. When thoroughly mashed and all flour is in, add eggs, one at a time, mixing well. Salt to taste and add a little grated nutmeg for flavor. Flour surface thickly and roll out potato dough about ½ inch thick. Heat goose fat or butter and fry onion to lightly golden; add dried bread crumbs and season highly; remove from heat. Spread mixture over potato dough and roll as for jelly roll. Cut in 2 inch widths. Drop into boiling salted water and boil uncovered for about 15 minutes; remove with slotted spoon. May be fried in goose fat or butter until golden or boiling. If boiled, serve with seasoned melted goose fat or butter poured over all. May be made ahead and reheated.

Cucumber Salad (Gurkensalat)

3   large cucumbers,
     thinly sliced
¼ teaspoon salt
1½ tablespoons sugar or to taste
⅛ teaspoon cayenne pepper
2¼ tablespoons cider vinegar
1½ cups sour cream

Add salt, sugar, cayenne pepper, vinegar to sour cream and stir until smooth; taste and add sugar if desired. Pour over thinly sliced cucumbers and place in refrigerator for ½ hour before serving.

Potato Pancakes (Kartoffelpuffer)

8 raw potatoes
2 eggs, beaten
²/₃ cup flour
½ teaspoon baking powder
1 teaspoon salt
   Dash of pepper
½ cup milk
3 tablespoons melted butter

Cover potatoes, after peeling, with cold water and allow to stand for several hours. Grate or put through blender or food processor. Remove as much of the potato starch as possible, rinsing in a strainer, draining well and pressing out all liquid. Put grated potatoes in a bowl and add rest of ingredients, mixing thoroughly. Fry by tablespoon portions in hot vegetable oil until pancakes are brown and crisp on both sides. Drain on paper toweling. Serve with applesauce. (May be fried, drained on paper towels, cooled, and frozen on cookie sheets. Place frozen in 350° oven until hot.)

Red Cabbage And Apple (Rotkohl)

1 medium head red cabbage, shredded
3 tablespoons butter
2 cups water
2 medium apples, diced
2 tablespoons vinegar
3 tablespoons brown sugar or
   ¼ cups honey
   Salt

Heat butter in deep pan and add shredded cabbage. Cook, stirring, for 4-5 minutes. Add water and apple; cover; cook over low heat, stirring occasionally, for 1 hour. Add vinegar, brown sugar or honey and salt to taste. Reheat for a few minutes to dissolve sugar and blend. Serve with meat. (May be frozen. Bring to room temperature to reheat over low heat, stirring occasionally.)

Chestnut Torte

6 eggs, separated
⅓ cup sugar
1 (8 ounce) can chestnut puree with vanilla
²/₃ cup flour
3 teaspoons baking powder
⅛ teaspoon salt
1 pint heavy cream, whipped, sweetened and flavored
10 ounce jar raspberry jam or jelly
   Candied violets

Beat egg yolks with sugar until lemon colored. Reserve 3 tablespoons of the chestnut puree and add rest to egg mixture, blending well. Sift flour, baking powder and salt and blend into egg mixture. Beat egg whites very stiff and carefully fold into egg yolk mixture, blending very well. Bake in two 10-inch buttered and floured round cake pans in 350° oven for 20-25 minutes or until cake springs back at light touch of your finger. Cool. When cold carefully split each layer in two, making four layers. Put together by spreading raspberry jam or jelly over bottom layer, then prepared whipped cream, continuing between all layers. Put together with sweetened whipped cream into which you have stirred the reserved chestnut puree. Decorate with candied violets after covering top layer thickly with whipped cream. Refrigerate. (Freezes well before assembling. Defrost and assemble.)

Meringue Shells (Schaum Torte)

8   egg whites (1 cup)
¼   teaspoon cream of tartar
2¼   cups sugar
⅛   teaspoon salt
1   tablespoon white vinegar
      or lemon juice

Beat egg whites until fluffy; add cream of tartar; beat few minutes more. Gradually add sugar and salt and beat until stiff. Add vinegar or lemon juice and continue to beat until very stiff and glossy. With decorator bag, using large metal end, form into desired shape on greased heavy brown paper placed on a cookie sheet or pile into three 9-inch pie plates, shaping up sides in a swirl. Bake in 250° oven for about 50-60 minutes or until very lightly off white. Remove and cool. Refrigerate for several hours before using. Makes about 2 dozen individual nests. (Freezes well.) Serve topped with fresh fruit or favorite chiffon pie filling and decorate with sweetened and flavored whipped cream. Also very good filled with Mocha Filling in four 8-inch circles or meringue made 1 inch high by 1½ inches wide, using one 8-inch meringue layer as a base.

Mocha Filling:

2   (7½ ounce) milk chocolate
      bars with almonds
½   cup strong coffee
2   packages whipped topping
      or 1⅓ cups cream, whipped with 6 tablespoons
      sugar and 1 teaspoon
      vanilla

Melt chocolate bars with coffee in top of double boiler. Cool. Beat topping according to package directions or beat cream with sugar and vanilla to very stiff. Fold cooled chocolate mixture through whipped mixture, blending thoroughly. Refrigerate until it begins to really thicken. Place meringue layer on serving plate; spoon little chocolate mixture along outer edge and top with another meringue circle, adding all meringue circles in this way. Allow to set and then pour filling into torte. Refrigerate. At serving time, decorate with dollops of more whipped topping or cream and sprinkles of chocolate.

Bremen Apple Torte

7   large apples, quartered,
      cored and peeled
6   tablespoons sugar
4   tablespoons butter
1   cup sour cream
4   eggs, beaten
1   tablespoon vanilla
½   teaspoon cinnamon
2   tablespoons butter
1½   cups Zwieback crumbs
      (6 ounce box)

Place apples, sugar and 4 tablespoons butter in a pan and cover. Simmer over medium heat, stirring occasionally, for about 30 minutes, until almost mushy. Remove from heat and break apples into small pieces. Add sour cream, eggs, vanilla, cinnamon, butter and half cup of Zwieback crumbs; mix well. Return to heat and cook, stirring, until thick and just starting to boil. Cover bottom of a 9-inch springform pan with ¾ cup Zwieback crumbs; pour in filling; sprinkle rest of Zwieback crumbs over top and dot well with butter. Bake in 350° over for 1 hour. Cool and refrigerate. Serve topped with sweetened and flavored whipped cream. (Freezes well.)

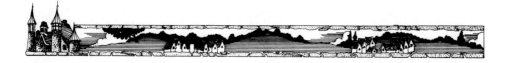

Linzer Torte

Custard Filling:

⅓ cup sugar
2 egg yolks, beaten
¼ cup flour
1 tablespoon arrowroot or cornstarch
¼ teaspoon salt
1½ cups milk
1 teaspoon vanilla
1 tablespoon cognac

In top of double boiler, add sugar to beaten egg yolks; beat until thick and lemon colored. Add flour, arrowroot or cornstarch and salt and blend. Add milk, a little at a time; blend well with wire whisk. Cook over simmering water, stirring with whisk, until thick and smooth. Add vanilla and cognac and blend. Cool in refrigerator, covered with waxed paper.

Raspberry Filling:

1 package thawed frozen raspberries
2 tablespoons sugar
2 tablespoons cornstarch
1 tablespoon lemon juice

Combine all ingredients in a saucepan. Simmer gently, stirring constantly, until mixture is thick and clear, about 5 minutes. Cool in refrigerator covered with waxed paper.

Pastry:

1½ cups flour
1½ tablespoons sugar
½ teaspoon baking powder
½ teaspoon salt
½ teaspoon cinnamon
3 tablespoons firmly packed brown sugar
¼ pound butter
1 egg, beaten
1-2 tablespoons cold water
½ cup sliced unblanched almonds, for pastry
Unblanched sliced almonds, for trim
¾ cup whipped cream, slightly sweetened

Mix flour, sugar, baking powder, salt, cinnamon and brown sugar. Cut in butter as for pie. Add beaten egg and almonds; work into pastry ball, adding water as needed to hold together. Take ½ cup of dough and chill. Press remaining dough into bottom and sides, covering edges of a 9-inch pie plate. Fill with cooled custard filling, then top with raspberry filling. Take dough from refrigerator and place on well-floured surface. Add 1 tablespoon flour to dough and knead in well. Roll out dough to about ⅛ inch thick, cut in ½ inch strips. Make lattice over filling; use remaining strips to place around edge of torte, pressing to seal. Lightly damping top of edge of dough, decorate with thin slices of almonds. Bake in 375° oven for 30-35 minutes, until lightly brown. Cool. Refrigerate until serving time. Garnish with a border of whipped cream just inside the torte edge to serve. (Freezes very well without whipped cream garnish. Bring to room temperature and garnish to serve.)

Strawberry Bavarian Cream Mold

1 quart fresh strawberries, or
    1 large package frozen
    whole strawberries and 1
    large box frozen sliced
    strawberries
1½ cups sugar or if frozen
    berries, ¾ cup sugar
1 tablespoon gelatin
¼ cup cold water
¾ cup hot milk
2 egg yolks
⅛ teaspoon salt
1 cup heavy cream, whipped
½ cup light cream
1 teaspoon vanilla

Hull and wash berries. Save about 16-18 for decoration. Mash rest and add 1 cup sugar. If frozen berries are used, set aside in refrigerator 16-18 whole berries for decorating, and slice the rest; set aside. Soften gelatin in cold water. Add ¼ cup sugar to hot milk. Beat egg yolks and add rest of sugar and salt; beat again. Dilute egg mixture gradually with a little of the hot milk; add rest of hot milk. Cook over medium heat, stirring, until mixture coats spoon. Remove from heat; add gelatin, blending well; strain and place in refrigerator to cool. Beat cream stiff and save half for garnish. As soon as gelatin mixture thickens slightly, add half of whipped cream, light cream and vanilla. Fold in sliced or mashed berries, very gently, and pour into a mold. Refrigerate until firm. Unmold and garnish with whipped cream and whole berries. (Will keep frozen up to 1 month.)

Frozen Chestnut Fruit Pudding

1 cup chestnut puree
5 egg yolks
1 cup sugar
2 cups light cream
⅛ teaspoon salt
¼ pound candied cherries,
    cut in half
¼ cup currants
½ cup candied pinapple,
    cut up fine
½ cup maraschino cordial
¼ cup citron, cut fine
2 tablespoons powdered sugar
2 cups whipped cream
½ teaspoon almond extract

Beat egg yolks with sugar until light; add chestnut puree, light cream and salt. Pour into top of double boiler and cook over simmering water, stirring frequently, until mixture begins to thicken. Set in refrigerator to cool. Put fruit and cordial in a bowl and set aside. When chestnut cream is cool put in freezer trays and freeze for 10 minutes. Take out and stir through cream which has been whipped stiff with powdered sugar and almond extract; stir through fruits and cordial. Return to trays and freeze until mush. Take out and place in cold bowl and stir well. Return to trays and freeze. Makes 2 quarts.

81

Greek

Philo Dough

Please read through completely.

This is the extra special something that makes Greek cooking such a treat. This paper thin dough, used in layers, makes for a pastry that is crisp and flaky and unforgettable. The dough is used both in cooking and baking. Philo may be purchased at many Greek grocery stores or in Armenian stores where it is known as Paklava Dough; it is also called Strudel Dough in many large supermarkets. The dough keeps beautifully for 2 months in the freezer, but must be carefully packaged and should not be kept beyond 2 months. Making the dough sheets is quite time consuming, but I offer the following recipe for those who are not fortunate enough to be able to purchase it. It is well worth the effort.

5 cups flour
1 teaspoon salt
1 egg, beaten
¼ cup olive oil
1½ cups lukewarm water
Cornstarch

Sift flour and salt into a large bowl. Make a well in center and add rest of ingredients, except cornstarch. Mix well and knead dough until smooth, about 5 minutes. Cover and allow to rest for 1 hour or overnight. Break off a piece of dough about the size of an egg; give it the shape of a patty; sprinkle well with cornstarch and roll out on a surface heavily covered with cornstarch. Take 4-5 pieces, after having rolled them as thin as possible; stack on top of one another with cornstarch in between. Take a long thin rolling pin; cover with cornstarch and roll, pushing forward and out in all directions. Turn over and roll in the same manner making sure that there is plenty of cornstarch in between, so they will not stick to one another. Roll to paper thin, separate, and roll to almost transparent, about 30 inches across. Cover each sheet of dough with a piece of waxed paper after rolling and place under a damp towel while rolling rest of dough. Stack and fold; wrap in waxed paper and then in aluminum foil. Place in tightly covered box to store. *When Philo dough is to be brushed with butter, do so lightly. If a thicker layer of the dough is desired, simply add a few more sheets of the dough.* (Freezes well.)

Cheese and Custard Filled Triangles (Tirothrigona)

Buy Philo dough if possible; see recipe and explanation for buying or making dough in preceding recipe.

Filling:

2	tablespoons sweet butter
2	tablespoons flour
¾	cup milk
⅛	teaspoon salt
¹⁄₁₆	teaspoon white pepper
⅛	teaspoon nutmeg
1¼	cups finely crumbled Feta cheese
1	egg, beaten
1	pound sweet butter

Melt butter and blend in flour. Remove from heat and gradually blend in milk. Return to medium heat, stirring constantly; cook until thickened and boiling. Remove from heat and add rest of ingredients, blending well. Cool. Have ready 1 pound sweet butter. Melt a quarter pound at a time as needed.

To Make Triangles: Place a pile of 25 sheets of Philo dough on a dry dish towel. Cover with waxed paper and then with wrung out dish towel. Lift waxed paper and dish towel and draw out 2 inches of the pile of dough beyond the dish towel. Cut off exposed strip with a scissors and lift off top piece of dough; place rest under waxed paper until needed. Brush strip of dough with melted butter on top side. About an inch down from top of strip, place a teaspoon of the cheese mixture. Fold the right hand corner of dough over to the left, down far enough to cover cheese mixture. Then take left hand corner and fold to right; continue folding dough over and over in described manner, as folding a flag, using whole strip, ending with a filled triangle. Place triangles on baking sheet and brush tops with melted butter. (Freeze at this point if planning to do so. Defrost to use and proceed.) Bake in 350° oven until golden, about 20-22 minutes. Drain on paper toweling a few seconds. Serve hot. (See page 101 for Spanakopita filling.)

Fried Potato Covered Meat Balls (Keftethakia)

Use meat filling as for Meat-Filled Triangles (see page 87). Shape into tiny meat balls.

Potato Covering:

4	cups mashed potatoes
1	egg, beaten
	Salt and pepper to taste
	Flour
1	egg, beaten

Mash potatoes well; add beaten egg and season highly to taste. Make circle of mashed potato in the palm of your hand, about ¼ inch thick. Place a small meat ball in the center and cover with circle of mashed potato. Roll in flour and then in beaten egg. Fry in deep hot fat at 350° until golden brown. Drain on paper toweling and serve hot on toothpicks. (May be lightly fried and frozen. To reheat, finish frying in deep hot fat.)

Boerch with Feta Cheese Triopitas

¾ cup butter, melted
6 eggs, beaten well
3½ cups yogurt
½ teaspoon baking powder
2 tablespoons finely chopped parsley
25 sheets Philo dough
⅓ pound Feta cheese, crumbled

Allow butter to cool to room termperature. Mix beaten eggs with yogurt, baking powder, parsley and 6 tablespoons of the melted butter. Brush 9 x 13 inch baking dish with melted butter. Place a sheet of dough on bottom of dish; brush with butter and add 6 more sheets of dough; brushing each with butter. Spoon ⅓ of filling over dough, spreading evenly, and sprinkle with half the Feta cheese. Top with 6 more sheets of dough, cutting these to fit inside the dish and brushing with butter. Spoon another third of the filling over dough; sprinkly with remaining cheese. Cover cheese with 6 more of the buttered sheets of dough. Spoon remaining filling over and spread evenly. Fold in edges of the bottom sheets of dough. Top with 6 more sheets of dough; buttering between each sheet. With a knife, cut top layers of dough into 24 small diamonds. Bake at 375° for 30-35 minutes, until puffed and golden brown with custard set. Allow to cool for 10 minutes and then cut through diamonds completely. Serve hot. (Does not freeze.) Will keep in refrigerator several days. Lightly cover with foil and reheat in 350° oven for 20-30 minutes.

Meat-Filled Triangles (Kreapopita)

1 package Philo dough

Buy or make Philo dough. Have ready ½ pounds sweet butter. Melt quarter pound butter at a time as needed.

Saute onions in butter until lightly golden. Remove from heat and add rest of ingredients, mixing well, preferably with hands.

Meat Filling:

2 tablespoons butter
1 cup diced onion
¾ pound lean beef, ground twice
¼ pound lean pork, ground twice
⅔ cup fine dried bread crumbs
1 egg, beaten
3 tablespoons tomato sauce
2 cloves garlic, crushed
¼ teaspoon oregano
¾ teaspoon crushed dried mint
1¼ teaspoons salt
¼ teaspoon pepper

To Fill: Cover unused Philo dough tightly with a piece of waxed paper and a slightly dampened dish towel. Take a sheet of dough and place on a dry dish towel, cutting off just about 2 inch strips at a time cutting through all layers. Put all but 1 strip under waxed paper, and cover the rest of the sheets of dough with waxed paper and another dampened dish towel. Brush cut off strip of dough with melted butter. About 1 inch down from top of strip place 1 teaspoon of meat mixture. Fold right hand corner of dough over to the left, down far enough to cover filling, then take left hand corner and fold to right. Continue folding dough over and over in described manner, using whole strip, ending with a filled triangle. Place triangles on a buttered baking sheet and brush tops with melted butter. (If freezing, do so at this point. Defrost to use and proceed.) Bake in 375° oven until golden, about 20 minutes. Drain on paper toweling and serve hot.

Stuffed Grape Leaves

4 cups diced onions
1 cup long grained rice
1 cup olive oil
1 teaspoon crushed dried mint
2 teaspoons fresh dill or
  dill weed
2 tablespoons lemon juice
¼ cup currants (optional)
¼ cup pine nuts (optional)
50 grape leaves, fresh
  or canned

Squeeze chopped onions well with hands until they lose their crispness and become soft. (This is best done by placing chopped onions in a plastic bag, closing securely and squeezing through the bag.) Add to rice and rest of ingredients, except grape leaves; mix well. If grape leaves are fresh, soak them in boiling water about 5 minutes, drain, squeeze dry and cut off stems. If canned leaves are used, taste the brine and if very salty, rinse leaves in warm water; drain and squeeze dry. To fill, place a leaf on a small plate, dull side up, with stem end toward you, being sure to cut off stem. Place a teaspoon of the rice mixture near the stem end and fold in sides, and start rolling away from you. Arrange a few grape leaves on the bottom of a large kettle and place the rolled filled leaves in layers on top. Add 2 cups water and lay a plate on top of leaves so that it will hold them tightly in place. Cover and cook over low heat for about 1½ hours, or bake in 350° oven for the same length of time. Test to make sure rice is soft. After they are cooked, allow them to remain covered until cool. Sprinkle with 2 tablespoons olive oil and squeeze over all the juice of 1 lemon. Serve cold. (Does not freeze. Keeps a month refrigerated.)

Variation: Fry onions in olive oil until golden. Add rice and 2 cups hot water. Cover and simmer until all water is barely absorbed. Remove from heat and add rest of ingredients, cutting down the mint to half a teaspoon and dill to ¼ teaspoon. Also add:

¼ teaspoon cinnamon   ½ teaspoon allspice
1 teaspoon paprika   ¼ teaspoon pepper

Cool and proceed as directed above.

Lobster Salad on Toast Points (Astakos)

2 cups cooked lobster meat,
  diced
½ teaspoon salt
⅛ teaspoon white pepper
⅛ teaspoon thyme
¼ cup chopped celery
2 tablespoons olive oil
2 tablespoons lemon juice
  Toast fingers
  Green peppers
  Pimientos

Mix all ingredients, except toast, green peppers, and pimientos together lightly. Refrigerate for 1 hour before using. Toss lightly with a fork. Serve on toast fingers. Garnish with chopped green peppers and pimientos.

Red Fish Roe Dip (Tarama)

4 ounces or 5 tablespoons Greek Tarama (red fish roe)
4-7 tablespoons lemon juice, to taste
4 slices white bread, without crust, soaked in water and squeezed dry, or
¾ cup mashed potatoes
⅛ teaspoon pepper
1 cup olive oil
Julienne of seeded cucumber
Celery and fennel
Melba rounds

Put Tarama in a strainer and rinse well under cold water. Drain well on paper toweling. Put 4 tablespoons of the lemon juice in blender and add Tarama. Begin blending at high speed, add crumbled, squeezed out bread or mashed potato and then drop by drop gradually begin adding olive oil, keeping blender at high speed all the while until the first half of oil is used and Tarama consistency is like mayonnaise. Lower speed to medium and add rest of oil in a slow drizzle, blending all the while. Add pepper; blend a few seconds; taste and add more lemon juice, blending, if desired. Serve surrounded with julienne of seeded cucumber, celery and fennel, plus Melba rounds. Keeps for weeks, covered, in refrigerator.

Vegetable Soup

3 pounds beef for soup
16 cups water
½ cup barley
½ cup diced celery
½ cup diced carrots
1 large onion, diced
½ cup diced parsnip
¼ cup diced turnip
½ cup diced potatoes
½ cup peas
2 tablespoons chopped parsley
3 tablespoons diced green pepper
1½ cups cut up fresh tomatoes or canned tomatoes
¼ cup shredded cabbage
2½ teaspoons salt
½ teaspoon white pepper
½ teaspoon oregano

Place meat, water and barley in a large kettle; cover; simmer gently for about 3 hours. Add remaining ingredients and simmer gently until all vegetables are soft, about 1 hour. Taste and adjust seasonings. Better second day. (Freezes well.)

Clam and Rice Soup

16 littleneck clams
2 tablespoons corn meal
½ cup olive oil
3 onions, chopped
3 tomatoes, peeled and
  cut fine
½ cup chopped parsley
6 cups chicken broth
6 cups water
3 teaspoons salt
1½ teaspoons white pepper
1½ teaspoons oregano
1½ teaspoons crushed dried
  mint
4 cups cooked rice

Soak clams in water to cover with 2 tablespoons corn meal for 1 hour, then wash and brush clams under cold water; drain on paper towels. Saute onions in olive oil to golden. Add tomatoes; cover and simmer 3 minutes, until mushy. Add rest of ingredients except rice and clams and simmer gently, covered, for 20 minutes. (If freezing, do so at this point. Reheat and proceed to finish.) Add rice and clams; mix well. Simmer 5 minutes, or until clams open.

Fisherman's Soup

2 pound piece any large fish
12 cups water
½ cup olive oil
2 onions, diced fine
3 tomatoes, quartered
1½ teaspoons salt
½ teaspoon white pepper
¼ teaspoon oregano

Simmer fish with rest of ingredients gently for about 30 minutes, until fish is done. Remove fish and break into 1-inch size pieces, discarding bones and skin. Strain broth; adjust seasonings and add fish. Reheat gently for 10 minutes. Serve piping hot. (Freezes well.)

Chicken Rice Lemon Soup

10 cups chicken broth
1 cup rice
4 eggs, separated
⅓ cup lemon juice
  Salt and white pepper

Bring broth to a boil and add rice; simmer gently for 20 minutes. Beat egg whites to stiff and fold in beaten egg yolks and lemon juice, blending thoroughly. Add some hot broth, a little at a time, folding to blend; add about 2 cups, stirring gently. Pour all back into soup pot, stirring vigorously. Bits of chicken may be added if desired. Taste for salt and pepper. (Freezes well before adding egg mixture.)

Crabmeat Stuffed Artichoke Bottoms (Aginara Kavoura)

12 homecooked or canned
      artichoke bottoms
1 (7½ ounce) can crabmeat,
      flaked
1 tablespoon chopped stuffed
      olives
1 tablespoon chopped ripe
      olives
½ teaspoon salt
⅛ teaspoon white pepper
1 tablespoon olive oil
2 tablespoons lemon juice

Cook artichokes in water to cover with a little salt and juice of half a lemon, covered with cheesecloth, for about ¾ hour. Cool; remove outer leaves and save to use for soup or garnish. Remove the furry, prickly cover on artichoke bottom. Trim stem off. Mix rest of ingredients together lightly and pile on top of artichoke bottoms. Serve cold.

Chick-Pea Soup (Revithia)

2 cans chick-peas, juice of
      1 can
10 cups chicken broth
½ cup olive oil
1 cup frozen diced onion or
      ½ cup fresh diced onion
1 carrot
2 stalks celery
    Salt
    Pepper
1 teaspoon finely crushed
      dried mint

Combine chick-peas and chicken broth and bring to a boil. In the meantime, heat olive oil and fry diced onion until golden, stirring all the while. Add fried onion, carrot and celery to broth and simmer gently for 1 hour. Put all in blender, through food mill, or food processor; taste and adjust seasonings with salt and pepper. Add crushed mint; stir well and heat another 5 minutes. (Freezes well.)

Lentil Soup (Fahki)

1 pound lentils
10 cups beef or chicken broth
½ cup olive oil
1 onion, whole
1 carrot, whole
2 stalks celery, whole
1 tablespoon tomato paste
2 cloves garlic
1½ teaspoons salt
¼ teaspoon white pepper

Wash and pick over lentils; combine all ingredients. Simmer gently until lentils are soft. Put all through food mill, blender, or food processor. Return to pot and adjust seasonings. Reheat to serve. (Freezes well.)

Clams and Rice

3 pounds clams
2 tablespoons corn meal
2½ cups diced onions
1¼ cups olive oil
8 tomatoes, cut in eighths
4 teaspoons salt
½ teaspoon crushed dried mint
½ teaspoon oregano
1 teaspoon white pepper
3 cups rice
½ cup chopped parsley
6 cups water

Soak clams in water to cover with corn meal for 1 hour. Scrub clams with a stiff brush under cold water and wash until clean. Fry diced onions in olive oil until onions are lightly golden. Add tomatoes and cook, covered, stirring occasionally, until tomatoes are mushy. Add seasonings, rice, parsley and water and stir. Add clams, shells and all, and mix well. Cover and cook for 25-30 minutes, until rice is tender. Discard any unopened clams. Remove from stove and cool slightly before serving.

Lamb Baked in Foil (Psito Arni Sto Harti)

4 pounds tender lamb, cut in
  1½ inch cubes
3 tablespoons olive oil
1 cup chopped onion
2 large tomatoes or ½ cup
  canned tomatoes
1 teaspoon salt
¼ teaspoon pepper
½ teaspoon crushed dried mint
8 tablespoons lemon juice
1 pound Feta cheese

Cut aluminum foil into 8 squares about 9 x 9 inches. Saute meat and onion in olive oil until meat is browned on all sides. Remove meat and set aside. Add tomatoes, salt, pepper and crushed mint to onions and cook, stirring, for 3 minutes. Place pieces of meat in center of aluminum foil squares. Pour over it 1 tablespoon lemon juice and spoon over some of the sauce, save rest of sauce. Top with several good size pieces of cheese and wrap tightly in aluminum foil. Place bundles on a large baking sheet and bake 1 hour at 300°. Turn heat up to 375°, loosen foil, leaving open a few inches and bake another 30 minutes. Add saved sauce and bake 15 minutes more. Serve with rice pilaf.

Leg of Lamb (Psito Buti)

1 leg lamb
  Slivers of garlic
¼ cup butter
  Juice of 2 lemons
1 cup tomato sauce
1 teaspoon salt
¼ teaspoon pepper
½ teaspoon thyme
½ teaspoon rosemary
¼ cup olive oil

Wipe lamb leg. Sliver garlic. Make gashes about 3 inches apart all over the leg and insert a sliver of garlic with a dab of butter into each gash. Mix rest of ingredients together in a small bowl and brush all over lamb leg. Place, uncovered, in 325° oven for 1 hour. Add 1 cup hot water to drippings and finish roasting, basting frequently, until brown and tender. Allow about 30-35 minutes per pound for entire cooking time, depending on how well done you prefer. Place on hot platter and thicken gravy if desired.

Baked Smothered Trout

8 brook trout
   Salt and white pepper
6 tablespoons butter, melted
3/4 cup dried bread crumbs
3/4 cup finely chopped
   tomatoes
6 tablespoons chopped
   parsley
1/4 teaspoon thyme
1/4 teaspoon nutmeg
3/4 cup dry white wine

Clean and dry fish thoroughly; season well with salt and pepper. Grease bottom and sides of a large roasting pan with melted butter. Combine bread crumbs with tomato, parsley and seasonings and mix well. Spread half of mixture on bottom of pan, place fish on crumbs and add wine, then sprinkle top of fish with remaining crumbs. Bake in 350° oven for 25-30 minutes, until fish is done, basting frequently. Remove carefully from pan to hot serving platter.

Lamb, Beef Cubes or Chicken Livers on Skewers (Souflikia)

Leg or loin of lamb, cut in
   1 inch cubes, or beef
   tenderloin, cut in cubes,
   or chicken livers, cut in
   halves
Mushroom caps
Onions, cut in eighths,
   lengthwise
Bacon, cut in 1 inch squares
Green pepper, cut in 1 inch
   squares
Cocktail tomatoes
3/4 cup olive oil
   Juice of 3 lemons
1/2 teaspoon dried mint
1/2 teaspoon white pepper
1 1/2 teaspoons salt

String pieces of meat, vegetables and bacon alternately on skewers, placing tomatoes at the end of the skewers. Mix rest of ingredients in a large baking dish and lay skewers in this to marinate, turning frequently. Marinate for at least 2 hours and then grill over charcoal or under broiler, turning frequently, until crispy and brown outside and pink inside. (The meats may be prepared off the skewers in a plastic bag with the marinade and frozen. Defrost, string on skewers and refrigerate until time to broil.) Serve with pilaf.

Shrimp in Casserole (Garides Yiahni)

1²/₃ cups diced onions
²/₃ cup olive oil
6 tomatoes, cut in eighths
²/₃ cup dry white wine
²/₃ tablespoon celery salt
²/₃ cup chopped parsley
1²/₃ teaspoons salt
¼ teaspoon white pepper
¼ teaspoon oregano
¼ teaspoon crushed dried mint
4 cloves garlic, crushed
3 pounds shrimp, cleaned
   and deveined

Brown diced onions to golden in olive oil. Add tomatoes, cover, and cook about 5 minutes, until mushy, stirring occasionally. Add wine, celery salt, parsley, salt, pepper, oregano, mint and garlic, mixing well. Arrange shrimp in a casserole and pour sauce over all. Place in 350° oven and bake for 30 minutes. (Easily prepared ahead of time and even better for having marinated in sauce before baking.) Serve with pilaf.

Swordfish on Skewers

3 pounds swordfish skinned
   and boned, cut in 1½
   inch cubes
   Juice of 3 lemons
2 tablespoons olive oil
¼ cup finely chopped parsley
2 teaspoons salt
   Bay leaves

1½ cups olive oil
   Juice of 3 lemons
2 cloves garlic, crushed
¼ teaspoon oregano
1 tablespoon salt
1 tablespoon water
1 teaspoon dry mustard

Mix lemon juice, olive oil, parsley and salt in a bowl. Add swordfish cubes and toss lightly to cover. Allow fish to marinate for at least ½ hour. (May be prepared up to this point the day before.) Put skewers through fish with a bay leaf between each fish cube. Broil over charcoal or under broiler, basting frequently with marimade. Turn skewers frequently until fish is done. Serve with following sauce.

Sauce:

Beat all ingredients together very well. Pour on hot fish. Serve over rice. (May be prepared ahead of time and left on shelf; shake well to use.)

94

Baked Fish

3   pounds sea bass or any
       whole fish
6   lemons, juice of 5 and
       1 sliced
1   teaspoon salt
½   teaspoon white pepper
¾   cup strained canned
       tomatoes
2   carrots, sliced
½   cup diced celery
3   cloves garlic, crushed
½   cup chopped parsley
¾   teaspoon oregano
½   cup diced onion
3   scallions, chopped
1-2   bay leaves, crumbled
½   cup dry white wine
½   cup olive oil

Wash, wipe fish and cut along back almost to bone. Rub juice of 5 lemons all over fish and season with salt and pepper. Place fish in a large buttered baking-serving dish. Mix remaining ingredients, except sliced lemon, and pour over fish. Garnish fish with slices of lemon. Place in 375° oven and bake for 20 minutes, covered. Uncoved, turn heat down to 350° and bake for 30 minutes more or until fish is done, basting occasionally. Serve with sauce.

Chicken and Walnuts

3   frying chickens, cut
       for frying
2   teaspoons oregano
⅓   cup lemon juice
⅔   cup olive oil
2   teaspoons salt
½   teaspoon pepper
4   cloves garlic, crushed
2   tablespoons Worchestershire
       sauce
⅓   cup sweet butter
⅔   cup broken walnut meats
½   cup sliced mushrooms
4   tablespoons cognac
2   cups chicken broth
⅓   cup chopped parsley

Place oregano in a small pan and heat to just warm. Roll between palms of hands to make a powder. Mix oregano powder with following listed 6 ingredients. Pour all over chicken pieces, rubbing into chicken and coating well. Cover and place in refrigerator for several hours or overnight. Remove from refrigerator half hour before ready to cook. Place chicken on broiler 5 inches from heat and brown to rich brown on all sides. Reduce heat to 325° and bake until fork tender. Meanwhile, heat sweet butter and saute walnut meats to a rich brown; remove with a slotted spoon and set aside. Add more butter if necessary and saute mushroom slices for a few minutes. Add cognac; warm and flame. Add chicken broth and bring to a quick boil. Lower heat and simmer gently to reduce sauce to half. Add fried walnut meats and parsley and heat 2 minutes. Pour over prepared chicken and serve hot. (May be prepared ahead and frozen up to point of adding walnut meats and parsley. Freeze fried walnuts separately. Reheat chicken and sauce and proceed.)

95

Eggplant, Meat Casserole with Tomato Sauce (Moussaka)

8 tablespoons olive oil
2 fat large eggplants
2 onions, 1½ cups, diced
1 large clove garlic, crushed
1 pound lean lamb, 1 inch thick and diced in ½ inch pieces
1 pound lean beef, 1 inch thick and diced in ½ inch pieces
½ teaspoon pepper
1½ teaspoons salt
1 tablespoon dried parsley flakes
8 ounces tomato sauce
2 eggs, beaten
½ cup chunks Feta cheese (optional)

Quarter eggplants lengthwise; rinse and dry. Fry in 1 tablespoon of the oil over medium heat until lightly browned on both cut sides, making sure eggplant is just barely cooked through and adding oil as needed. With a sharp knife, cut out all of the cooked eggplant leaving ⅛ inch pulp in skin. Chop eggplant meat coarsely. Lightly grease a 1½ quart mold and place scooped out skins in mold to overlap vertically, forming an inner mold. Heat 4 tablespoons olive oil; add onion and garlic in skillet and fry until onion is lightly browned. Add meat and cook, stirring, until browned. Drain off all grease. Add scooped out chopped eggplant pulp, seasonings, parsley and tomato sauce; mix well and simmer 5 minutes. Remove from heat and add 2 beaten eggs; mix well. Add the chunks of Feta cheese if using them. Fill Moussaka and place mold in pan with 2-3 inches of hot water. Bake in 350° oven for 40 minutes. (Freezes well. To reheat, do so frozen in 350° oven for 1 hour and 30 minutes.) To serve, pour off juices into tomato sauce and cool Moussaka 5 minutes before turning out. Spoon tomato sauce over all.

Rich Tomato Sauce:

¼ cup olive oil
2 cloves garlic, crushed
1 large onion, finely chopped
1 medium green pepper chopped
1 carrot sliced
4 cups canned tomatoes in sauce
1 bay leaf
2 tablespoons chopped parsley
½ cup chopped celery tops
½ teaspoon dried thyme
¼ teaspoon dried sweet basil
½ teaspoon salt
¼ teaspoon pepper

Heat olive oil and add next 4 ingredients; fry gently until onion is golden. Add rest of ingredients and simmer gently for 30 minutes, until thick, stirring occasionally. Cool and put in blender or food processor, half of recipe at a time. Reheat and serve with about a cup and a half of the sauce spooned over Moussaka. Pass the rest of the sauce so that each guest may add some as he or she likes. (Freezes well.)

Chicken with Artichokes (Kota Me Aginares)

2   roasting chickens, cut in
      serving size pieces
¼   pound butter or
      margarine
2   cups diced onion
8   tomatoes, cut in eighths, or
      1 small can tomato paste
3   cups hot water
2   teaspoons salt
¼   teaspoon pepper
½   teaspoon crushed dried mint
2   cloves garlic, crushed
8   artichokes or canned
      artichoke hearts

Dry pieces of chicken and fry over medium heat in butter or margarine to a rich brown on all sides. Remove chicken and drain on paper towels. Fry diced onion in the same butter or margarine to golden. Add tomatoes or tomato paste, water, salt, pepper, crushed mint and crushed garlic. Cook together, stirring constantly, for 5 minutes. Add chicken and simmer gently until almost done, about 1 hour. In the meantime, wash artichokes in salted water and drain. Remove most of the leaves, including center leaves and cut out choke. Cook in salted water with juice of 1 lemon for 20 minutes; drain. If using canned artichokes, drain well. Place artichokes in sauce around the chicken and cook gently for 30-35 minutes, until chicken is tender and artichokes are done. Add hot water if sauce thickens too much. Serve with pilaf. (Freezes well.)

Stewed Chicken (Kapama)

2   fryers or broilers, cut in
      serving size pieces
½   pound butter or
      margarine
4   tablespoons lemon juice
3   teaspoons cinnamon
2   teaspoons salt
1½ teaspoons sugar
¼   teaspoon white pepper
1⅓ cups tomato paste
3   cups hot water
⅔   cup dry white wine

Fry chicken in butter to golden brown on all sides. Add lemon juice, cinnamon, salt, sugar, pepper, tomato paste and water. Simmer on low heat for 20 minutes. Add wine and simmer gently, basting occasionally, for 25 minutes or until done. (Freezes well.)

Rabbit Stew (Stifatho Lagos)

3   rabbits, cut in serving-
      size pieces
      Juice of 3 lemons
12 small white onions,
      peeled whole
1   cup olive oil
3   cloves garlic, crushed
6   tablespoons tomato paste
6   bay leaves
3   peppercorns, slightly
      crushed
3   teaspoons salt
1½ cups hot water
¾ cup dry white wine

Rub pieces of rabbit well with lemon juice. Heat oil in largest size frying pan and brown rabbit pieces and whole onions to golden. Add crushed garlic and stir well. Add rest of ingredients and simmer gently, basting occasionally, until meat is tender and sauce is thick. Add water and a little more wine if sauce thickens too much. Serve with rice. (Freezes well.)

Stuffed Roast Turkey (Yallow Parayemistos)

12-15 pound turkey
1   tablespoon salt
1   teaspoon white pepper
      Juice of 4 lemons
2   teaspoons crushed dried mint
¼ cup olive oil

Wash and clean turkey and wipe dry. Mix rest of ingredients and brush all on to all surfaces of the turkey after it is stuffed.

Stuffing:

½ pound butter or
      margarine
1½ cups diced onions
      Turkey liver, chopped fine
1   pound hamburg, ground
      twice
½ cup pine nuts (optional)
2½ cups rice
3   tablespoons tomato paste
1½ cups hot water
1   tablespoon cinnamon
2   teaspoons salt
½ teaspoon white pepper
¼ pound butter
      Juice of 2 lemons

Saute onions in butter or margarine until golden. Add chopped turkey liver and hamburg and fry until brown, stirring constantly. Add rest of ingredients and mix well. Cook over low heat for 10 minutes, stirring occasionally. Cool and stuff turkey. Roast in 500° oven for 1 hour, basting occasionally with hot water. Lower heat to 350° and roast for 2½ hours, or until turkey is almost done. Melt ¼ pound butter or margarine and mix with juice of 2 lemons and baste frequently for another half hour or until leg joint moves back and forth freely and turkey is done. Allow turkey to rest 20-30 minutes before slicing. Serve with juices, first removing the fats.

Stuffed Squabs

8 squabs
1½ pounds chicken livers
3 tablespoons butter
¾ pound Feta cheese, crumbled
¼ teaspoon white pepper
Juice of 5 lemons
1 teaspoon crushed dried mint
4 tablespoons butter
1 cup hot water

Clean squabs and wipe dry. Cut chicken livers into halves and fry gently in butter until just done. Cool and chop livers into small pieces. Place in a bowl and add cheese and pepper; toss lightly together with a fork. Stuff birds and sew or truss so that stuffing cannot escape. Place on a rack in a roasting pan and brush well with lemon juice mixed with mint. Dot each squab well with butter and pour hot water over each. Roast in 350° oven until squabs are done, about 1 hour, adding more water if necessary.

Duck in Wine Sauce

2 ducks, cut in serving-size pieces
¼ cup butter or margarine
⅔ cup chopped onion
1½ cups white dry wine
2 cups tomato puree
2 cups water
½ teaspoon cinnamon
1 teaspoon salt
1 tablespoon cornstarch

Wash and wipe duck pieces. Heat butter or margarine and brown duck on all sides. Remove from pan and add chopped onion to butter or margarine and fry until golden. Return duck to pan with onion; add wine and simmer gently for 15 minutes. Add tomato puree, water, cinnamon and salt and stir well. Cover and simmer until duck is done. Mix cornstarch with water to make a thin smooth paste; add to sauce and cook, stirring constantly, until thickened and clear. Serve with rice pilaf. (Freezes well.)

Roast Leg of Venison

Leg of venison
1 cup olive oil
Juice of 4 lemons
1 teaspoon oregano
3 cloves garlic, crushed
2 teaspoons salt
¼ teaspoon white pepper
1 cup red dry wine
½ cup water

Wash and wipe meat. Mix olive oil, lemon juice, oregano, garlic, salt and pepper and marinate meat in this for several hours. Place in 400° oven, with marinade, for 15 minutes. Dilute wine with water and pour over roast. Cover and reduce heat to 350°. Continue roasting, basting frequently, until meat is tender, about 3½ hours. If wine and water cook away, add more so that you may continue basting and keep the meat moist.

Rice and Noodles (Hatzim Pilaf)

6 tablespoons butter
½ cup rosamarina or orzo
   noodles
1½ cups long grain rice
1½ teaspoons salt
¼ teaspoon coarse ground
   black pepper
4½ cups hot broth

Melt butter in kettle that has a tight fitting cover. Add rosemarina or orzo. Cook over low heat, stirring constantly, until noodles are lightly browned. Add rice and seasonings and cook, stirring, until all rice is well coated with butter and turning slightly white. Add hot broth and stir well. Cover and cook over low heat until all moisture is absorbed and rice has little pit holes all over the top. Add a lump of butter the size of a walnut. Cover and allow to steep for 10 minutes. Lightly lift rice with a fork thoroughly just before serving. May be made ahead and placed, tightly covered, in 150° oven for a few minutes.

Stuffed Tomatoes

8 large tomatoes
1 cup converted long
   grain rice
2 cups tomato pulp and juice
1 medium onion, finely
   chopped
2-3 cloves garlic, crushed
⅛ cup chopped fresh dill or
   2 teaspoons dill weed
1½ teaspoons salt
¼ teaspoon white pepper
¼ cup finely chopped parsley
3 tablespoons tomato paste
¼ cup water
¼ cup olive oil
3 teaspoons sugar

Cut tops off tomatoes and set aside. Remove pulp and juice from tomatoes and set tomato shells aside in cold water. Mix rest of ingredients well. Drain tomato shells and stuff lightly with rice mixture. Place tops back on tomatoes and put in large baking dish. Add ¼ inch of water to pan. Cover with aluminum foil and bake in 350° oven for 45 minutes. Uncover, test to make sure rice is soft and bake 15 minutes. (May be made up to baking the last 15 minutes and refrigerated. Bring to room temperature and reheat, baking at 325° for 30 minutes.

Potato Plaki

8   medium potatoes
1¼ cups tomato sauce with
      tomato bits
3   tablespoons chopped
      parsley
½   cup diced carrots
¼   cup chopped celery
6   medium cloves garlic,
      crushed
1½ teaspoons salt
½   teaspoon white pepper
2½ cups water
½   cup olive oil
1   tablespoon Worchestershire
      sauce (optional)

Peel and slice potatoes about ¼ inch thick and place in largest size skillet or au gratin pan. Mix all vegetables and seasonings well and pour over potatoes. Add water and cover. Cook over low heat for 45 minutes. Add olive oil, baste and add Worchestershire sauce, if using it. Baste and continue cooking for 15 minutes. Serve hot or cold. (Dried beans may be soaked, parboiled and substituted for potatoes to make Bean Plaki. This may be made several days ahead. It freezes well. Defrost to reheat.)

Spinach Pie (Spanakopita)

3   packages frozen chopped
      spinach
8   large scallions, chopped,
      or 1 cup diced onion
2   tablespoons butter
1½ cups Feta cheese
2½ tablespoons lemon juice
½   teaspoon dill weed
      (optional)
5   eggs
      Salt to taste
¼   teaspoon pepper
⅔   cup melted butter
12 sheets Philo dough

Defrost frozen spinach and drain well, squeezing out moisture with hands. Fry scallions or onions in 2 tablespoons butter until lightly browned, stirring constantly. Add fried onions to spinach. Crumble cheese and add to spinach mixture. Add lemon juice and dill weed. Add eggs, one at a time, mixing well. Taste for salt and add if needed; add pepper; mix. Grease 2 (9-inch) pie plates or 1 (9 x 13) baking dish well with melted butter. Place 6 sheets of Philo dough in bottom of baking dish, brushing between carefully with melted butter. Pour in spinach mixture and cover with 6 more sheets of dough, brushing each sheet with melted butter. Bake in 350° oven for 30-45 minutes, until dough is richly golden and lightly browned. If using baking dish, cut into squares to serve. Otherwise, cut in wedges as pie. (Freezes well. To reheat, place frozen in 325° oven for about 45 minutes.) Serves 16. (May be shaped as in Cheese and Custard filled Triangles, page 86, and served as an Hors d'oeuvre.)

Macaroni with Flaky Pastry (Pasititsio Me Philo)

1 pound ground lamb
4 tablespoons butter or
   margarine
2 teaspoons tomato paste
⅛ cup water
¾ teaspoon salt
¼ teaspoon white pepper
½ teaspoon cinnamon
½ pound macaroni
   Salted water and 1 tablespoon olive oil
4 eggs, well beaten
2 cups milk, warmed
4 tablespoons butter, melted
¼ pound grated Parmesan or
   Kefaletiri cheese
   Melted butter
12 sheets Philo dough

Brown meat in butter or margarine, stirring. Add tomato paste which has been mixed with water. Add seasonings and simmer. stirring occasionally, until most of moisture has been absorbed. Meanwhile, cook macaroni in salted water with olive oil to almost tender; drain macaroni. Gradually stir warmed milk into beaten eggs and cook over low heat, stirring, for 2 minutes. Butter a 9 x 13 x 3 inch baking dish and place 6 sheets of Philo dough in casserole, brushing well with melted butter between each sheet. Mix cheese and other 4 tablespoons butter together with drained macaroni. Place half the macaroni mixture over buttered sheets of dough, then pour over half of the milk-egg mixture. Spread over all the meat mixture and cover with remaining macaroni and cheese. Pour over remaining milk and egg sauce. Shake dish so that the sauce will penetrate. Cover with rest of the Philo sheets, brushing each well with melted butter. Bake in 375° oven for 1 to 1½ hours or until pastry sheets are richly golden. Cool 10-15 minutes. Cut in diamond shapes or squares to serve. Serve hot with meat instead of rice or potatoes. (Does not freeze.)

Artichokes and Onions

2 (8½ ounce) cans artichoke
   hearts
8 very small onions or
   2 medium onions,
   quartered
1 cup chopped scallions
   Juice of 2 lemons
½ cup olive oil
1 tablespoon sugar
1½ teaspoons salt
⅛ teaspoon white pepper
¼ teaspoon crushed dried
   mint or dill weed
1 cup water

Place artichokes and onions side by side in serving dish that will go into the oven or on top of stove. Sprinkle with chopped scallions. Sprinkle with lemon juice and ½ cup olive oil. Season, sprinkling all over, add water. Cover with a plate and then pot cover. Bake in 350° oven or simmer on top of stove until onions are just tender; add more water if necessary without removing plate. Remove from heat. Allow to cool with plate still on. Remove plate and serve at room temperature. (May be made several days ahead.)

Tossed Salad with Feta Cheese

3 tomatoes, quartered
1 cucumber, scored and sliced
1 bunch scallions, sliced
3 stalks celery, sliced
1 medium green pepper, sliced thin
1 carrot, slivered
4 radishes, sliced thin
1½ teaspoons salt
¼ teaspoon pepper
8 ripe olives
8 whole green olives
1 or 2 heads lettuce, torn
1 head endive, cut in strips
½ cup olive oil
½ cup wine vinegar or lemon juice
½ teaspoon oregano
2 cloves garlic, crushed (optional)
16 small chunks Feta cheese

Toss first 7 ingredients together lightly; salt and pepper. Add olives, torn lettuce and endive. Cover with plastic and refrigerate until just before serving. Shake olive oil, vinegar or lemon juice, oregano and garlic, if you are using it, well in a tightly covered jar. Keep at room temperature until ready to dress salad. Pour over all and toss lightly. Taste for salt. Top with Feta cheese. Serve immediately.

Chicory Salad (Rathika Salata)

Clove of garlic
Head of lettuce, quartered, washed and dried
1 head chicory, washed and dried thoroughly, discarding outer pieces
2 tablespoons sliced scallions
½ teaspoon salt
¼ teaspoon fresh ground black pepper
4 tablespoons olive oil
3 tablespoons tarragon vinegar

Rub salad bowl with clove of garlic. Break head of lettuce into bite size pieces into bowl. Break chicory into large pieces into bowl; sprinkle scallions over all. Cover with plastic and refrigerate until ready to serve. Mix rest of ingredients in a jar with a tight cover and keep at room temperature. Shake together well and pour over greens. Toss lightly, just before serving.

Greek Sponge Yeast Bread

1 cake yeast dissolved in ½
     cup lukewarm water
¼ cup shortening
2 tablespoons sugar
2 teaspoons salt
2 cups lukewarm milk
3 cups flour for sponge
4 cups flour for dough

Add shortening, sugar, salt and milk to dissolved yeast. Place 3 cups flour in a large mixing bowl and add yeast mixture, blending thoroughly. Cover and let stand in warm place 1 hour. Mixture will be light and bubbly. Stir in 4 cups flour to make a stiff dough, kneading in last of flour. Grease a large bowl; place in dough turning to grease top. Cover with a piece of plastic wrap and a towel and allow to rise 45 minutes in a warm place. When dough keeps imprint of finger, punch down dough, turning and kneading in bowl. Cover and allow to rise again in a warm place for 45 minutes. Turn out on pastry cloth; cut dough in 3 pieces and knead each piece a few minutes. Spray bread pans with vegetable oil very well; place in prepared dough. Cover and allow to rise 30 minutes in a warm place. Bake in 375° oven for about 45 minutes, until done. (Freezes well. Defrost and wrap in aluminum foil and heat in 150° oven for 30 minutes to serve warm.)

Braided Rolls (Tsourekia)

1 package dry yeast
2 tablespoons sugar
¼ cup warm water
¼ cup melted butter
¾ cup milk
1 egg, beaten
2 teaspoons salt
3½-4 cups flour
1 egg, beaten with 2 table-
     spoons water
     Sesame seeds

In a large bowl, mix together yeast, sugar and warm water and allow to rest 10 minutes. Add melted butter, milk, beaten egg and salt and mix well. Gradually beat in flour, adding enough to make a firm soft dough. Knead on lightly floured surface until dough no longer sticks. Grease large bowl; put in dough and turn over to grease top. Cover with a piece of plastic wrap and a towel and allow to rise until double in size, several hours or overnight. Punch dough down and cut in 2 pieces. Roll each piece out to ¼ inch thick and cut into strips ¼ x 4 inches. Braid 3 strips together, pressing ends together firmly. Place on greased baking sheets and brush with egg beaten with water and sprinkle with sesame seeds. Cover and allow to rise for 45 minutes. Bake in 400° oven for 15-20 minutes. (Freezes well. Wrap frozen loosely in aluminum foil, leaving open, and place in 350° oven for 10-15 minutes to reheat. Serve warm.)

Stewed Okra

4   tablespoons butter
1   medium onion, diced
⅓   cup diced green pepper
2   tomatoes, quartered
¼   teaspoon oregano, crushed
2   packages okra, or 1½
     pounds fresh okra, washed
     and dried
¼   teaspoon oregano, crushed
1   teaspoon salt
¼   teaspoon pepper

Heat butter gently and add diced onion and green pepper. Fry, stirring occasionally, until onion is golden. Add quartered tomatoes and okra; season and toss lightly. Cover; lower heat to medium and cook until okra is tender, mixing several times. (May be prepared up to adding tomatoes, refrigerated and then finished few minutes before serving.) Do not overcook; okra should be still a lovely green. (Freezes well. Defrost and reheat to just hot.)

Pistachio Bird Nests

¼   pound sweet butter, melted
     without coloring
⅓   cup shelled pistachios,
     chopped finely (mix with
     the sugar)
2   tablespoons sugar
⅓   cup shelled pistachios,
     chopped coarsely
8   sheets Philo dough

Cover sheets of Philo with a sheet of waxed paper, a wrung out wet dish towel and another piece of waxed paper; this will keep the dough soft. Work with 1 piece of Philo at a time. Brush a sheet of Philo lightly with melted butter. Fold sheet in half crosswise; brush with butter lightly again. Place folded edge of dough nearest you and fold edge over about 1½ inches and butter it lightly. Spoon 1½ tablespoon of the finely chopped pistachio and sugar mixture on top of the buttered fold. Lift up outer edges nearest you and flip forward; roll forward to about 2½ inches from farthest edge. Fold in side edges and roll filled portion to form about 2 inch nest. Push bottom of pastry in to form base for each nest. Place the nests on buttered cookie sheet and brush all well with butter. Cover lightly with aluminum foil and bake in 350° oven for 15 minutes. Remove foil and bake 10 minutes, to lovely golden. Remove and fill nests with the coarsely chopped nuts. (Cool to store or freeze. To serve, reheat to just warm, lightly covered with foil.) Pour little syrup over the warm nests to serve and pass extra syrup.

Syrup:

1½   cups sugar
1   cup water
½   cup honey
½   teaspoon lemon juice
1   teaspoon rosewater

Simmer gently to make medium heavy syrup, about 25 minutes. Serve cold.

Flaky Pastry and Nut Diamonds with Syrup (Baklava)

50 sheets Philo dough
1   pound sweet butter

See page 85 for Philo dough. Use 1 pound of dough or about 50 sheets. Also have ready 1 pound sweet butter; melt ¼ pound at a time.

Syrup:

3   cups sugar
2   cups water
¼   teaspoon lemon juice or
     1 tablespoon rum flavoring
1   cup honey
2   tablespoons light Karo
       syrup
1   cinnamon stick
3-4 whole cloves

Simmer gently; do not stir; for 20 minutes. Syrup should be slightly thick when ready; cool.

Nut Mixture:

3   cups nutmeats (walnuts,
       pistachios, almonds,
       pecans, mixed or
       one kind), chopped
       not too fine
¼   cup sugar
1   tablespoon cinnamon

Grease 9 x 13 x 2 inch size baking pan lightly with melted butter. Place 6 layers of Philo dough in pan; brush top layer well with melted butter and sprinkle well with nut mixture. Add another 3 layers of dough; butter; sprinkle with nut mixture, etc.; proceeding to fill baking dish in like manner, ending with 3 layers of dough brushed with melted butter. Cut into 1½ inch strips; then cut diagonally to form diamonds. Bake in 350° oven for 15 minutes. Remove from oven and spoon 1½ tablespoons melted butter over each diamond; cover pan tightly with aluminum foil. Return to oven and bake for ½ hour. Remove foil and bake until lightly golden brown. Remove from oven and immediately pour cool syrup over all. It will bubble as it is poured on; do not pour any more syrup on than pastry seems to absorb. Reserve the remainder of syrup for future use. Cool Baklava in baking dish, first recutting along same lines and removing a small corner piece. Tilt pan on something so excess syrup will drain off to empty corner. Keep spooning off excess syrup until no more forms in open corner. Keeps well without refrigeration up to 1 month. Serves 16.

Nut Cake with Flaky Pastry (Kipenhayi)

Bottom Crust:

1 cup sweet butter
⅓ cup sugar
1 egg, lightly beaten
2 tablespoons brandy
    flavoring
1 teaspoon grated lemon rind
1 teaspoon orange bits
2⅓ cups flour
¼ teaspoon salt
1 teaspoon baking powder

Cream butter and sugar to light and fluffy. Beat in egg and brandy. Stir in rind and bits, flour, salt and baking powder; blend well. Press dough over bottom and ½ inch up sides of 14 x 10 x 2½ inch baking pan. Bake 15 minutes in 350° oven until lightly browned. Meanwhile, make following filling.

Filling:

7 eggs, separated
⅓ cup sugar
1 tablespoon flour
1½ teaspoons baking powder
1¼ cups toasted, blanched
    almonds, finely chopped
1 cup finely chopped
    walnut meats
1 teaspoon cinnamon
1 teaspoon almond extract
2 teaspoons brandy flavoring
½ pound sweet butter, melted
8-10 sheets Philo dough
3 cups syrup

Beat egg yolks and sugar until very thick and lemon colored. Mix together flour, baking powder, almonds, walnuts, cinnamon and flavorings; stir into egg mixture. Fold in ⅓ cup melted butter and then stiffly beaten egg whites, folding through gently but thoroughly. Pour onto baked pastry. Top with a sheet of Philo dough; brush with melted butter and repeat with remaining sheets of dough, pour over any remaining butter, spooning over evenly. Cut through Philo layers only to make serving diamonds. Bake in 350° oven for 45-50 minutes until lightly golden. While hot, spoon over cooled syrup and let stand 24 hours before serving. Will keep at room temperature for a week. Extra syrup may be added to keep cake moist. Serves 16.

Syrup:

3 cups sugar
1 cup honey
2 cups water
1 tablespoon rum flavoring
2 tablespoons light
    Karo syrup
1 cinnamon stick
3 cloves

Boil together all ingredients, stirring to dissolve sugar. Simmer gently for 20 minutes without stirring; cool. (If lemon flavor is preferred, omit rum, cinnamon stick and cloves and add 2 tablespoons lemon juice and ½ teaspoon lemon rind.)

Apricot or Pineapple Surprise Cake (Pasta Pari)

1 cup butter
½ cup sugar
¼ teaspoon almond extract
1 egg, beaten
2 cups flour
1½ teaspoons baking powder
12 ounce jar apricot or pineapple jam or preserves

Cream butter and sugar until light and fluffy. Add almond extract and egg, mixing well. Sift flour and baking powder together and gradually add to first mixture. Will make soft dough. Spread on well greased and floured 9 x 13 inch baking pan to about ½ inch thick. Spread evenly with apricot or pinapple jam or preserves. Top with the following topping.

6 eggs, separated
1½ cups confectioners sugar
1 teaspoon baking powder
⅛ cup cointreau or whiskey
½ teaspoon almond extract
1½ cups finely chopped, blanched and toasted almonds
Heavy cream, whipped

Topping:

Beat egg yolks, confectioners sugar, baking powder, cointreau or whiskey and almond extract together until light and fluffy. Add chopped almonds and mix well. Beat egg whites to very stiff and fold into egg yolk mixture. Pour over jam or preserves. Bake in 350° oven for 50-70 minutes or until golden brown and tests done. Serve topped with whipped cream, lightly sweetened and flavored with almond extract. (Cover after cooling; keeps for about a week.)

Almond or Walnut Cake

2 cups Zwieback or graham
cracker crumbs
2 cups finely chopped, blanched almonds or walnuts
½ teaspoon cinnamon
2 teaspoons baking powder
6 eggs, separated
1 cup sugar
2 teaspoons vanilla
½ teaspoon salt

Make syrup first so that it may be cooking and have time to cool while you are making cake.

Mix dry ingredients thoroughly. Beat egg yolks, gradually adding sugar, until light and lemon colored. Add vanilla and salt; mix well. Mixing very slowly, gradually add dry mixture to yolk mixture, blending thoroughly. Beat egg whites very stiff and fold first mixture into them, blending well. Pour into 9 x 13 inch baking dish which has been well greased and floured. Bake in 350° oven for 30-40 minutes or until cake tests done. Remove from oven and pour cooled syrup over cake.

3 cups water
2 cups sugar
2 tablespoons cointreau or
whiskey or 1 tablespoon
rum flavoring
Slice of lemon

Syrup:

Simmer 30 minutes. Cool and pour over hot cake. Should cake seem to be getting too wet, reserve rest of syrup for another time. However, cake will take almost all of syrup. Rest may be passed when serving. (Cake will keep for at least a week.)

Grape Juice Mold (Moustalervira)

2 cups unsweetened grape juice or 2 cups fresh grape juice
1 cup sugar
2 tablespoons gelatin
1/3 cup cold water
3 tablespoons lemon juice
3 egg whites, whipped stiff with 2 tablespoons sugar
1 cup heavy cream, whipped with 3 tablespoons sugar
2/3 cup walnut meats
1/2 pint sweetened and flavored whipped cream for topping
Lady fingers and candied violets
Walnut meat halves

Line 1 1/2 quart mold with lady fingers. Heat grape juice with sugar until sugar is dissolved. In meantime, soak gelatin in 1/3 cup cold water. Add gelatin mixture to grape juice mixture and stir until dissolved. Add lemon juice and refrigerate until mixture begins to thicken. Fold in stiffly beaten egg whites, stiffly beaten whipped cream and the 2/3 cup walnut meats. Pour mixture into mold. Refrigerate 4-5 hours. Unmold and garnish with sweetened and flavored whipped cream, candied violets and halves of walnut meats.

Almond Butter Cookies (Kurabiedies)

1 pound almonds, blanched
Sweet butter
1 pound confectioners sugar

Slit 36 almonds in half and set aside. Chop rest rather finely and place on cookie sheet. Dot with a little sweet butter and toast in medium oven, stirring occasionally until lightly golden. Have ready 1 pound confectioners sugar for garnishing.

Dough:

1 pound sweet butter, room temperature
2 egg yolks
1/4 teaspoon almond extract
18 tablespoons confectioners sugar
3 cups flour, plus 2-3 more cups flour
Toasted chopped almonds

Mix softened butter with electric mixer or food processor until well whipped. Add egg yolks, almond extract and confectioners sugar. Gradually add the 3 cups flour and beat well. Remove from mixer and kneading with hands add toasted almonds and 2-3 more cups flour, enough to make dough easily handled but not too stiff. Take pieces of dough about size of a walnut in your hand and roll between palms of hands to smooth. Place on baking sheet and press almond half on top of each cookie. Bake in 350° oven until lightly pinkish in color, about 1/2 hour; do not allow to brown. Remove from pans and cool on racks covered with waxed paper. When cool sift confectioners sugar over cookies, turning and coating each cookie heavily. Will keep up to a month refrigerated. Serves 20.

Polynesian

Fried Shrimp (Tempura)

Sauce: (Make first.)

1 cup sugar
½ cup cider vinegar
½ cup water
1 tablespoon catsup
1 tablespoon soy sauce
4 tablespoons chopped currants
4 tablespoons crushed pineapple with juice
¼ teaspoon salt
2 teaspoons cornstarch
1 tablespoon water
1 tablespoon paprika

Plump currants in hot water, soaking few minutes. Drain well on paper toweling and chop. Mix sugar, vinegar, water, catsup, soy sauce, currants, crushed pineapple, and salt in saucepan. Simmer gently for about 5 minutes. Mix cornstarch with water and add, stirring all the while. Cook until thickened and clear. Add paprika and cool. Store in refrigerator for future use, but be sure to allow sauce to reach room temperature before using.

Fried Shrimp:

40 jumbo shrimp
Flour
2 egg yolks
1⅞ cups water
⅛ teaspoon baking soda
¼ teaspoon salt
1⅔ cups flour

Clean shrimps, leaving tails on. Remove black vein, then slit open along back to within ⅛ inch from tail. Dip shrimp in flour; shake off excess; set aside. Beat egg yolks and water together and then stir in rest of ingredients, blending well. Deep fry in oil heated to 375°, holding shrimp by tail, dipping into batter and allowing excess batter to drain off for a few seconds before dropping into hot fat. Fry to a rich golden color, about 3 minutes. Drain on paper toweling. May be kept warm in oven for a few minutes before serving. The following vegetables are also delicious fried in tempura batter: fresh mushrooms, cut in half; julienne of sweet potato and zucchini squash, broccoli, cauliflower and snow pea pods. Summer squash, zucchini and tiger lily flowers also make a different and delicious tempura. (Freezes well. To reheat, place frozen on cookie sheet in 350° oven for 15 minutes or until hot.

Spiced Abalone

1 tall can abalone, cut in thin slices
2 tablespoons lemon juice
3 tablespoons soy sauce
¾ teaspoon salt
½ teaspoon dry mustard
¾ teaspoon grated ginger root
2 tablespoons brown sugar
¼ teaspoon Tabasco sauce
2 tablespoons sherry

Wash and drain abalone and slice in bite size pieces. Combine rest of ingredients and pour over abalone slices. Marinate overnight. Drain and serve with toothpicks handy for each guest to help himself.

113

Curried Shrimp in Pineapple Sauce

Pineapple Chutney: (Make first.)

1½ cups pineapple tidbits, or chunks cut in thirds, drained
1 cup pineapple juice from tidbits or chunks, add water if needed to make 1 cup
½ cup raisins
½ can frozen pineapple juice concentrate
½ cup white vinegar
½ cup sugar
¼ teaspoon salt

Simmer all ingredients gently for 45 minutes, stirring occasionally. Makes enough for 3 batches of curried shrimp. (Freezes to keep.)

Curried Shrimp:

4 tablespoons butter
1 tablespoon minced scallion
1½ teaspoons curry powder
²/₃-³/₄ cup pineapple chutney
2 pounds cleaned and deveined shrimp
Squeeze of lemon juice

Saute shrimp and scallion in melted butter for 1 minute. Add curry powder and chutney and cook, stirring until shrimp are done, about 5 minutes. Squeeze lemon juice over all for desired tartness. Serve with sauce with toothpicks stuck in each shrimp.

Beef and Mushrooms on Skewers (Makai Nue)

1 flank steak, cut in half lengthwise and sliced thinly against the grain
1 cup light Karo syrup
5 tablespoons soy sauce
2-3 cloves garlic, crushed
2 tablespoons sherry
2 tablespoons honey
1 scallion, finely chopped
2 tablespoons sugar
¼ teaspoon grated ginger root
³/₄ cup water
1 large can mushroom caps
Sesame seeds

Prepare meat. Combine next 9 ingredients, mixing well. Marinate meat in mixture for 30 minutes. Remove from marinade. Draw slice of meat on a toothpick, sort of sewing it on; add a mushroom cap and then another slice of meat. Roll all in sesame seeds. Bake on cookie sheet in 375° oven until meat is just done and sesame seeds lightly toasted, about 15-20 minutes. (Freeze before baking. Defrost to bake.)

Avocado Dip

2 ripe avocados, mashed
2 teaspoons lemon juice
1 teaspoon curry powder
½ teaspoon salt
  Few drops hot pepper
    sauce
1 clove garlic, crushed
1 teaspoon sugar
2 tablespoons toasted, blanch-
    ed, slivered almonds
4 slices bacon, fried crisp,
    crumbled (optional)
⅓-½ cup mayonnaise

Ripe avocados are soft to touch and rather darker skinned; by soft do not mean mushy but rather ones that will dent when gently pressed by a finger.

Mix all ingredients together in mixer or food processor. Makes about 2 cups. To keep in refrigerator, bury pit in center of dip and lightly cover dip with mayonnaise; cover with lid. May be frozen in the same manner. Defrost; remove pit, and mix in mayonnaise to serve. (We prefer this without the bacon.) Serve surrounded with potato chips.

Sweet and Sour Sparerib Bites

3-4 pounds spareribs, have
    butcher cut in 1 inch
    widths across the ribs
1½ teaspoons salt
½ cup cornstarch
  Oil for frying
2 cloves garlic, crushed
1 small onion, grated
1 large can pineapple
    chunks
½ cup pineapple juice
¼ cup Chinese bead molasses
2 tablespoons sherry
¾ cup sugar
½ cup vinegar
½ cup soy sauce
¼ cup pineapple preserves
¼ teaspoon minced
    ginger root
¼ teaspoon salt

Wipe meat and cut between bones to make 1 inch sparerib bits. Drop into enough water to cover, to which you have added the 1½ teaspoons salt. Boil until meat shrinks back and bone tips show. Skim and drain. Cool ribs. Put cornstarch in a paper bag and drop in cooled ribs; shake to coat well with cornstarch. Heat ⅛ inch oil in frying pan until hot. Add floured ribs. Fry, stirring constantly, until ribs are browned on all sides. Drain off excess fat. Add rest of ingredients and cook, stirring occasionally, for about 20 minutes. Serve hot with sauce.

Avocado Eggs

8	hard boiled eggs
1	ripe avocado
¼	teaspoon garlic powder
½	teaspoon salt
¼	teaspoon pepper
¼	teaspoon Chinese mustard
2	tablespoons mayonnaise

Peel and cut hard boiled eggs in half lengthwise. Remove yolks and put through sieve. Mash avocado to smooth paste and add rest of ingredients. Add sieved egg yolks and mix well. Put in pastry bag and fill egg whites. Serve on tray with pineapple tidbits topped with stuffed olives and little pickled onions, strung together on a toothpick.

Chicken Niblits

1	broiler or 2 whole chicken breasts, cut with cleaver, through bone, into walnut size pieces
3	teaspoons sugar
4	tablespoons sherry
½	teaspoon salt
6	tablespoons soy sauce
1	large clove garlic, crushed
1	teaspoon minced ginger root
	Flour

Place chicken pieces in a bowl. Sprinkle with sugar; add sherry, salt, soy sauce, garlic and ginger root, mixing well. Marinate for 1 hour. Drain chicken pieces on paper toweling. Place ½ cup flour in a plastic bag; drop in chicken pieces and shake to coat well. Heat vegetable oil, ⅛ inch deep, to 360° in frying pan and fry to rich brown on all sides. Drain on paper toweling and serve hot. (Freezes well. Place on cookie sheets, frozen, in 350° oven until hot, about 25 minutes.)

Chicken Livers, Water Chestnuts Wrapped in Bacon (Rumakie)

6	slices bacon, cut in half both ways so that 1 slice makes 4 pieces
12	chicken livers, halved
12	water chestnuts, cut in half

Hold half of a chicken liver with half of a water chestnut and wrap them together with a piece of bacon, going firmly around both of them, using a toothpick to secure the whole thing. Do this to all and then marinate for 6-8 hours in the following:

1⅓	cups soy sauce	6	tablespoons honey
9	tablespoons brown sugar	1	teaspoon sesame oil
		1-2	cloves garlic, crushed
2	tablespoons vinegar	2	tablespoons sherry

Remove from marinade and drain. Place on broiler pan and broil about 7 inches away from heat or bake in 475° oven. Turn often until livers are done and bacon is crisp.

Spiced Pineapple Spears

1   large can pineapple spears
       or chunks
¾   cup vinegar
1½ cups sugar
⅛   teaspoon ginger powder
⅛   teaspoon salt
8   whole cloves
1   stick cinnamon

Drain syrup from pineapple into pan. To ¾ cup of the syrup add rest of ingredients. Boil gently for 20 minutes. Add pineapple and simmer gently for 5 minutes. Refrigerate at least 1 day before using. Serve on toothpicks.

Clam Soup

16 large clams in shells
12 cups chicken broth
1   teaspoon salt
1   teaspoon soy sauce
1   tablespoon sherry, sake
       wine or gin
8   slices lemon

Wash clams well, using brush under running water. Heat broth and drop in clams. When shells open, add rest of ingredients, except lemon slices. Taste and adjust seasonings. Serve broth with 2 clams, shell and all, per serving. Float a slice of lemon in each soup bowl. (Freezes well before adding clams; defrost; reheat; add clams and proceed as above.)

Bean Sprout Soup

¼   pound flank steak, cut in
       thin strips across the
       grain
6   scallions, chopped fine
2   tablespoons butter
2   cloves garlic, crushed
2   pounds fresh bean sprouts,
       washed and drained
12 cups chicken broth
3   tablespoons soy sauce
1   tablespoon chopped
       pimiento

Saute meat strips, chopped scallions and garlic in butter until meat is lightly browned. Add drained bean sprouts and cook, stirring, for about 2 minutes over a low heat. Add broth, soy sauce and pimiento and simmer gently for 20-30 minutes. Taste and adjust seasonings. (Freezes well.)

Shrimp Soup

½ cup chopped onions
4 tablespoons butter
½ pound mushrooms, sliced
2 cups chopped uncooked, peeled and deveined shrimp
1 tablespoon minced pimiento
1 tablespoon soy sauce
9 cups chicken broth
3 cups light cream
3 teaspoons cornstarch
Salt and pepper to taste

Saute diced onion in butter until golden. Add mushrooms; cover and cook, stirring occasionally, until mushrooms are tender. Add shrimp, pimiento, soy sauce, broth and light cream. Mix well and simmer gently over low heat for about 10 minutes. Make a thin paste with cornstarch and water; add and cook, stirring, for about 2 more minutes. Taste and adjust seasonings. Serve with a spoonful of rice mounded in the center of the bowl. (Freezes well.)

Mulligatawny Soup

1 (2½-3 pound) chicken
¼ cup butter, melted
¼ cup chopped onion
¼ cup chopped celery
¼ cup diced carrots
2 sour apples, peeled and sliced
1 tablespoon flour
1 teaspoon curry powder
4 quarts cold water
1 clove
½ green pepper, chopped fine
⅛ teaspoon mace
1 teaspoon chopped parsley
1 teaspoon sugar
⅛ teaspoon pepper
4 teaspoons salt
1 cup canned tomatoes
½ cup cream of wheat

(handwritten: tomato paste for color)
(handwritten: 1 tsp tomato paste for color)
(handwritten: 2 celery)
(handwritten: 2 carrots)

Cut chicken in portions and brown in melted butter. Add vegetables and fruit and cook, stirring gently, until lightly browned. Stir in flour and curry powder and when blended slowly add water, stirring until well mixed. Add rest of ingredients and simmer gently until chicken is tender. Remove chicken and skin and cut meat from bones and into small pieces. Strain soup and force vegetables and fruit through a food mill or put in food processor in four portions. Pour back into soup pot. Add chicken meat and heat. Serve very hot with boiled rice. (Freezes well.)

(handwritten notes: onion, garlic, scallions, sauted / add dried coconut / w/ tomato paste in / ¼ cup flour (to brown off) / stock flour taste / 1 ripe banana / (curry powder, cumin) / puree w/ garlic & / to spice up / serve w/ cilantro)

Sea Bass or Mahimahi Chowder

3 tablespoons butter
¾ cup chopped onion
2 pound sea bass, filleted or
    fillet mahimahi, if you
    can get it
4 large potatoes, diced
1 teaspoon salt
    Water to cover
1 large can sliced, broiled
    mushrooms
2 cups heavy cream
    Salt and pepper to taste

Saute onion in butter until golden. Cut fish into bite size pieces. Place fish, sauteed onion, diced potatoes and salt in a soup kettle and add water to cover. Simmer gently until potatoes are tender. Add can of mushrooms with their liquid. Add warmed cream and stir gently. Season highly with salt and pepper to taste and simmer over very low heat for 2 minutes. (Freezes well.)

Portuguese Egg Soup

4 tablespoons olive oil
2 cups chopped onions
2 cloves garlic, crushed
10 cups beef or chicken broth
½ teaspoon salt
2 teaspoons thyme
2 teaspoons celery salt
½ teaspoon pepper
8 eggs
8 thick slices French bread,
    cut in 1 inch cubes and
    dried in oven

Saute onions and garlic in olive oil. Add broth, salt, thyme, celery salt and pepper; simmer gently for about 5 minutes. Turn heat to very low and poach eggs in soup until firmly set. Put bread cubes in soup bowls; pour soup over and place a poached egg in each bowl. Freezes well before poaching eggs. Defrost; reheat; poach eggs and proceed as above.)

Roast Pork

4-5 pound pork shoulder,
    sliced ½ inch thick
2 teaspoons salt
3-5 cloves garlic, crushed
1 cup soy sauce
1 cup water
3 tablespoons honey
2 teaspoons sugar
2 tablespoons sherry

Mix well all ingredients listed after meat. Place meat in single layer in large dish; pour marinade over and allow to marinate for 30 minutes. Lift meat out of marinade and place on baking sheet. Roast in 500° oven until brown on both sides, turning often, or broil, turning frequently, until brown on both sides.

Shrimp Luau

3   pounds raw jumbo prawns, peeled and butterflied, leaving tails on
¼   cup lemon juice
⅛   teaspoon salt
⅛   teaspoon minced ginger root
1   teaspoon curry powder
2   eggs
1½   cups milk
½   cup pineapple juice
¼   teaspoon salt
½   teaspoon baking powder
2   cups flour
    Few drops yellow food coloring
1½   cups shredded coconut
    Fat to deep fry

Mix lemon juice, salt, ginger root and curry powder together and pour over shrimp. Allow to marinate for 4-6 hours in refrigerator. Make a batter in blender, doing half at a time, with the next 7 ingredients. Makes a rather thick batter. Dip shrimp in batter and allow excess batter to drip off. Roll each shrimp in coconut. Fry in deep fat at 375° until batter is golden and coconut is browned. Serve topped with sauce. (May be made and frozen; reheat in 350° oven for 15-20 minutes or until hot, placing in oven still frozen.)

Pineapple Curry Sauce:

¼   cup salad oil
2   tablespoons instant minced onion
1   very small clove garlic, crushed
2   cups chicken broth
2   tablespoons lemon juice
½   cup sugar
2⅓   cups crushed pineapple with juice
1-1½   teaspoons curry powder
⅛   teaspoon salt
2   tablespoons cornstarch
2   tablespoons water

Fry minced onion and garlic lightly in hot oil. Add next 6 ingredients and simmer gently for a few minutes. Mix cornstarch with 2 tablespoons water to a thin paste and add. Cook, stirring, until thickened and clear. Serve hot over prawns.

Sweet and Sour Fried Fish

2 eggs
³⁄₄ cup flour
3 tablespoons water
2 pounds sea bass fillets or
flounder fillets
3 cups water
¹⁄₂ cup vinegar
⁵⁄₈ cup sugar
2 teaspoons soy sauce
¹⁄₈ teaspoon pepper
2 tablespoons sherry
1 teaspoon Chinese bead
molasses
4 tablespoons cornstarch
4 tablespoons water
1 green pepper, cut in
1 inch strips
1 carrot, cut in match strips
¹⁄₂ cup pineapple tidbits or
chunks cut in thirds,
drained
³⁄₄ inch slice ginger root,
minced
1 teaspoon monosodium
glutamate (optional)
12 cocktail tomatoes, washed
and dried

Mix eggs, flour and water to a smooth batter. Coat fish; drip off, and fry in 350° oil to golden brown on each side. Drain on paper towels and place in 250° oven to keep warm. Meanwhile, mix water, vinegar, sugar, soy sauce, pepper, sherry and bead molasses and heat to dissolve sugar. Mix cornstarch with water to make thin paste. Add cornstarch mixture to sauce and cook, stirring until clear. Add vegetables, pineapple, and ginger root; continue cooking, stirring, 2 minutes. Pour over fish and garnish with cocktail tomatoes to serve.

Teriyaki Steaks

8 slices tenderloin or sirloin,
1 inch thick
1 cup light soy sauce
1 cup water
4 tablespoons brown sugar
3 tablespoons honey
4 tablespoons sherry
¹⁄₂ teaspoon grated ginger root
2 cloves garlic, crushed
2 tablespoons wine vinegar

Make a marinade from all ingredients listed after meat. Place meat in large shallow baking dish, 1 layer, and pour marinade over. Marinate for several hours or overnight, turning occasionally. Broil about 8 inches away from heat to preferred degree of doneness.

Teriyaki Steak and Chicken Breasts with Fruit Kebobs

1   large flank steak, cut in
      thirds lengthwise and
      then cut into 1½ inch
      squares
3   chicken breasts, boned and
      skinned, cut into 1½
      inch squares
1   cup soy sauce
2   tablespoons brown sugar
1   cup water
½   cup salad oil
1   teaspoon grated ginger root
½   cup pineapple juice,
      from chunks
2   teaspoons finely chopped
      scallions
2   cloves garlic, crushed
2   tablespoons wine vinegar
     Water chestnuts, whole
     Marschino cherries
1   pound can pineapple chunks
     Melted butter
     Curry powder
16 bamboo skewers, soaked
      in water several hours
      or overnight

Mix soy sauce, brown sugar, water, salad oil, ginger root, pineapple juice, scallions, garlic, and wine vinegar together well. Pour over steak and chicken pieces and marinate at least one hour, mixing occasionally. String eight skewers alternating the beef and chicken, going through the pieces lengthwise. String eight skewers alternating the pineapple chunks, water chestnuts, and maraschino cherries, skewing on by twisting gently, until each skewer is full. Brush the fruit skewers with melted butter and sprinkle well with curry powder. Broil meat skewers first, turning until very lightly brown on all sides, then add fruit skewers turning also and basting until hot. Serve placing skewer of meat and skewer of fruit side on top of Pulao. (May be placed on broiler racks early in the day ready for broiling at dinner time, saving some of marinade and curried butter to brush on just before broiling. (If you want extras, better do recipe 1½ times.)

Cherry - Apricot Spareribs

6-8 spareribs
¾   cup soy sauce
1   teaspoon minced ginger
      root, if you have it, or
      ½ teaspoon ginger powder
3   tablespoons sherry
2   tablespoons sugar
4-5 cloves garlic, crushed
2   cups apricot jam/
      preserves
½   cup cherry jam/
      preserves
½   teaspoon salt

Leave spareribs in serving size sheets. Wipe clean and sprinkle with salt. Boil in water to cover for 15 minutes; drain. Combine rest of ingredients, mixing well. Place spareribs in a large baking dish and brush well all over with preceding mixture. Marinate for 1 hour. Bake in 350° oven for 1 hour, turning and basting frequently. Serve with hot mustard and sparerib sauce (see Chinese Sweet and Pungent Sauce), if desired, or serve as is. (May be made ahead and allowed to marinate for several days, baking just before serving.)

122

Roast Stuffed Suckling Pig (or Capons)

1   suckling pig, about 12 pounds dressed, or 2 large capons, 8-10 pounds
2   teaspoons salt
3   tablespoons sugar
½   cup soy sauce
2   cloves garlic, crushed
1   teaspoon instant minced onion
1   teaspoon grated ginger root
4   tablespoons butter, melted
6   medium size sweet potatoes, parboiled, cut in 1 inch chunks
4   bananas, mashed
3   packages frozen pineapple chunks or 3½ cups fresh pineapple, cut in 1 inch chunks
8   tablespoons brown sugar
12 tablespoons pineapple juice
½   pound chunk of bacon
2   (12 ounce) bottles of beer
4   apples (1 whole, 3 quartered)
    Flour
3   tablespoons butter
    Maraschino cherries
    Taro leaves or large spinach leaves

Wash and dry pig or capons well. Mix the following 6 ingredients and rub pig or capons thoroughly inside and out; set aside. Mix melted butter, potatoes, bananas, pineapple chunks, brown sugar and pineapple juice; coating all well. Stuff pig or capons loosely with this mixture and fasten with skewers; lace skewers with heavy string. Truss hind legs and forelegs of piglet close under body, facing forward. Lay pig or capons on a rack in a large roasting pan. Place a wooden plug or block in the mouth of the pig and cover ears and tail with aluminum foil to prevent scorching. Form a tent loosely over pig or capons. Roast pig in 350° oven, capons in 325° oven, for 4-5 hours. Soak bacon in beer and keep at room temperature. Baste every 15 minutes by rubbing beer-bacon over surface of pig or capon. This will make for a crisp crackling skin, one of the delicacies of roast pig or capon. Test for doneness by inserting a metal skewer into thickest part of the pig. If a watery liquid comes out, the meat is still not done; if fat spurts out, the meat is done. Capons are done when the joints of the leg and thigh move freely. When piglet is done, uncover ears and tail and replace plug in its mouth with a red apple. Serve on a bed of taro or spinach leaves; garnish with quarters of apple which have been dredged in flour and fried in butter. Attach maraschino cherries with toothpicks to each apple quarter. (The pig or capons may be roasted on a rotisserie over medium heat, keeping the cover on and basting as above.) Serves 16-20.

Turtle Steaks

8   portions turtle steak
1   tablespoon salt
1   teaspoon pepper
1   tablespoon thyme
1   tablespoon ground tarragon
1   tablespoon crushed bay leaves
    Olive oil

Wipe steaks with a damp cloth. Mix seasonings together and rub well all over steaks. Place in a large shallow baking dish, in a single layer, and pour olive oil over all to cover. Allow to marinate for 30 minutes, turning frequently. Remove from marinade and broil about 8 inches from heat, at low broil, until brown on each side.

123

Pork Chops

8 pork chops, fat removed
¾ cup soy sauce
1 tablespoon ginger root, minced
1 clove garlic, crushed
2 tablespoons honey
2 teaspoons sugar
4 medium sweet potatoes, peeled
4 bananas, halved
4 pineapple spears or 8 chunks, halved
  Brown sugar
  Pineapple juice

Marinate pork chops in next 5 ingredients, turning frequently, for about 15 minutes. Drain on paper towels. Brown in melted butter, browning on both sides. Drain again on paper toweling. Place sweet potatoes in bottom of a large greased baking dish; place browned chops on top of potatoes. Cover and bake in 350° oven for 15 minutes. Add bananas and pineapple, placing around and on top of chops. Sprinkle with brown sugar and dot well with butter; pour over all 1 cup pineapple juice. Bake 30 minutes longer, basting occasionally. (Freezes well.)

Short Rib Stew

10 dried Chinese mushrooms
   Water
6 pounds beef shortribs, cut in 1½ inch pieces, cut off excess fat
⅔ cup soy sauce
5 scallions, save green tops, chop rest
6 cloves garlic, crushed
2 teaspoons sesame seed, toasted
2 tablespoons sherry
1 teaspoon sugar
½ teaspoon pepper
1 teaspoon salt
2 teaspoons sesame oil
2 tablespoons flour
2 eggs, beaten

Soak mushrooms in warm water to soften and set aside. Score meat almost to bone. Put meat, soy sauce, chopped scallions, garlic, sesame seeds, sherry, sugar, pepper, salt and oil in heavy pot. Add water to just cover and bring to a boil; turn heat low and simmer for about 30 minutes. Drain mushrooms; rinse and add. Continue cooking over low heat until meat is fork tender. Adjust seasonings. Blend flour with a little water to make a thin smooth paste. Add to meat broth and cook, stirring, until thickened. Fry beaten eggs very thin in hot oil until golden on both sides. Drain on paper toweling and then shred very thin. Chop scallion greens very fine. Serve stew in bowls over rice and decorate with shredded eggs and chopped scallion greens. (Freezes well before garnishing with fried egg and scallions.)

Mushrooms with Beef

½ pound top round, ground
6 tablespoons soy sauce
½ teaspoon salt
1 teaspoon chopped scallions
2 cloves garlic, crushed
¼ teaspoon pepper
1 tablespoon crushed sesame
   seed, toasted
2 cups mushrooms, sliced in
   thick T's, or mushroom
   caps
4 tablespoons flour
4 eggs, beaten
4 tablespoons vegetable oil
1 cup water

Add 4 tablespoons of the soy sauce, salt, chopped scallions, garlic, pepper and sesame seeds to ground beef and mix well. Put a layer of beef, about ¼ inch thick, between 2 slices of mushrooms or caps and press together. Prepare all mushrooms this way. Roll in flour and then in beaten eggs; fry until brown on both sides. Add leftover meat to browned mushrooms and meat. Add other 2 tablespoons soy sauce and the cup of water and cook until tender and water is all absorbed. Cook remaining egg in a very thin layer of heated oil until lightly browned on both sides. Shred fried egg finely. Arrange mushrooms with meat on platter and decorate with shredded egg. (Freezes well before garnishing.)

Lion's Head

2 pounds lean ground pork
6 tablespoons soy sauce
4 tablespoons sherry
1½ teaspoons sugar
½ teaspoon pepper
2 cloves garlic, crushed
3 egg whites
1 cup rice flour or ½ cup
   wheat flour

Combine ground pork, soy sauce, sherry, sugar, pepper and garlic. Add slightly beaten egg whites and then slowly stir in flour. Form into small balls and fry in deep hot fat, 350°, until brown. Drain on paper toweling and serve hot. May be made ahead and formed into balls. Fry just before serving.

Sausage with Rice

1 pound sausage, sliced ¼
   inch thick
3 cups chopped celery
3 tablespoons minced onion
6 cups cooked brown rice
2½ cups chicken broth
¼ cup green pepper, diced
16 stuffed olives, sliced
½ cup chopped macadamia
   nuts

Brown sausage meat in a dry pan. Add celery and onion and fry until onions are lightly browned, adding a little butter if there is not enough fat from sausage. Remove from heat and add rice, chicken broth and green pepper. Pour into casserole and top with sliced olives and chopped nuts. Bake in 350° oven for 35 minutes. (May be made and frozen before adding chicken broth or green pepper. Defrost and finish.)

Snow Peas with Mushrooms, Water Chestnuts and Almonds

1 pound Chinese snow peas or 3 packages frozen snow peas, use as directed on package
4 tablespoons bacon grease or peanut oil
¾ pound mushrooms, sliced in T's
12 water chestnuts, sliced thin
½ cup chopped toasted almonds

Rinse, string and dry fresh snow peas. Bring 1½ cups water to a boil. Drop in fresh or frozen snow peas and boil 3 minutes; drain. Saute mushrooms in bacon grease or peanut oil for 2 minutes. Add rest of ingredients; mix well and cook, stirring, 1 minute or until all is heated. May be made up to combining rest of ingredients with mushrooms and reheated until hot, stirring.

Pulao

½ cup butter
2 cups diced onion
2 cups rice
2 tablespoons currants
2 tablespoons slivered almonds
1 stick cinnamon
3 cardamom seeds
¼ bay leaf
1 teaspoon salt
¼ teaspoon pepper
4 cups chicken broth or water
¼ cup minced boiled ham (optional)
   Powdered saffron (optional)

Melt 4 tablespoons of the butter and fry onions until golden. Add remaining butter and melt; stir in rice. Cook, stirring, constantly until rice has absorbed all butter. Add currants, almonds, cinnamon, cardamom seed, piece of bay leaf, salt, pepper and broth or water. Cover; simmer until rice is tender; stir through ham if using it. Pour rice in baking dish, removing stick of cinnamon, cardamom seeds and bay leaf. Add another cup of liquid and bake in 350° oven for 15-25 minutes. Sprinkle with a little powdered saffron if available, to serve. (May be frozen when cold. Defrost to reheat in 350° oven for 25-40 minutes, covered.)

Spinach with Sesame

2 pounds spinach
6 tablespoons sesame seeds
6 tablespoons soy sauce
¼ teaspoon M.S.G. (optional)
3 teaspoons sugar

Wash spinach and remove stems. Cook over low heat using only water that clings to the leaves. Toast sesame seeds in oven or over low heat, stirring constantly, until lightly browned. Drain spinach and chop in fairly large pieces. Mix with rest of ingredients, tossing lightly. Serve in sauce dishes with the sauce. (May be frozen, thawed and quickly heated.)

Tossed Salad with Avocado Dressing

3   cucumbers, remove ends
and half of peel length-
wise, but leaving some on
for color, slice thin
2   tablespoons sliced scallions
4   tomatoes, cut in eighths
¼   cup thinly sliced celery
1   head iceberg lettuce, torn
in bite-size pieces

Prepare vegetables and place in a plastic bag in the vegetable drawer in refrigerator. Toss just before serving with the following dressing.

Avocado Dressing:

¾ -1   cup finely mashed
avocado, save the pit
2   tablespoons lemon juice
3   tablespoons French dressing
½   teaspoon salt
5   tablespoons cream

Place all ingredients in a bowl and blend well with a wire whisk. Place pit in center and cover with dressing. Store covered with plastic, wrapped tightly, in refrigerator until time to dress salad. Dressing will keep several days.

Sparkling Ginger Salad

2   packages lemon gelatin
1   cup boiling water
2½   cups ginger ale
¾   cup finely chopped celery
¾   cup slivered avocado
2   teaspoons finely diced
candied ginger

Dissolve gelatin in boiling water. When slightly cool, add ginger ale and mix well. Refrigerate until gelatin begins to set. Fold in rest of ingredients and pour into 9-inch, 2½ cup ring mold, greased, until set. Place in refrigerator to set. Does not freeze. May be made several days ahead. Unmold on a bed of shredded lettuce and pass with dressing.

Dressing:

¾ cup mayonnaise
6 tablespoons heavy cream

½ cup sugar
1 tablespoon vinegar

Mix all ingredients well.

Guava Salad

8 slices pineapple
½ cup pineapple juice
2 teaspoons lemon juice
¼ teaspoon minced ginger
  root or ⅛ teaspoon
  powdered ginger
¾ cup guava jelly

Heat pineapple with juice, lemon juice and ginger. Bring to a boil. Remove from heat and allow to cool. Drain and arrange on lettuce leaves. Garnish with cubes of guava jelly and serve with Sesame Seed Dressing.

Sesame Seed Dressing:

⅓ cup sesame seeds, toasted
⅓ cup dry mustard
1 teaspoon paprika
¾ teaspoon salt
⅓ teaspoon hot pepper sauce
½ teaspoon Worchestershire
  sauce
1 teaspoon minced onion
1½ cups salad oil
¾ cup cider vinegar

Toast sesame seeds to a light golden over medium heat, stirring. Mix all ingredients well in tightly covered jar. Shake well before serving.

Quick Yeast Rolls

2 packages dry yeast
½ cup warm water
1 tablespoon sugar
½ cup vegetable shortening
2¼ teaspoons salt
3 tablespoons sugar
2 cups boiling water
2 eggs, beaten
6⅔ cups flour

Soften yeast in lukewarm water with 1 tablespoon sugar and let rest 10 minutes. In a large bowl combine shortening, salt and 3 tablespoons sugar. Add boiling water and stir until shortening is melted and water is lukewarm. Add yeast mixture, beaten eggs and flour; beat well to mix thoroughly. Place in greased bowl turning over to grease top of dough. Cover with plastic wrap and clean dish towel and refrigerate for 2 hours. Shape into balls and place in muffin tins. Brush tops with melted butter; cover and return to refrigerator. Remove from refrigerator and allow to rise, uncovered, 1¼ hours or until double in size. Bake at 425° for approximately 15-20 minutes. Loosen each roll carefully but leave in pan. Cover pan tightly with clean dish towel to keep warm. Will keep warm up to 30 minutes. If you wish to keep them warm for a longer length of time, place covered in oven on warm.

128

Korean Pickle Chinese Cabbage (Kimchi)

2   pound Chinese cabbage
¼   cup salt
1   tablespoon crushed red
     pepper
1   teaspoon ground red pepper
2   cloves garlic, crushed
1   inch fresh ginger root
     minced or grated
2   scallions, chopped fine
1   tablespoon salt

Slice cabbage in 2 inch slices; wash and drain. Sprinkle ¼ cup salt all over and allow to stand until tender, approximately 3 hours. Rinse cabbage of salt and drain. Mix rest of ingredients, except salt and sprinkle over cabbage, tossing well. Pack lightly into 2 quart jars and fill, leaving about 1 inch of air space at top. Wash bowl in which Kimchi was mixed with ¼ cup water; dissolve salt and pour over Kimchi. Cover tightly and keep at room temperature for 2 days. Refrigerate and when cold it is ready to eat. Kimchi sours as it keeps and should be used within 2 weeks. This is very hot to eat, but if you really like hot, hot foods, use 1 tablespoon of the ground red pepper instead of the teaspoon.

Coconut Honey Bread

3   cups flour
1½ teaspoons baking powder
1½ teaspoons baking soda
1½ teaspoons salt
¾   cup honey
4½ tablespoons shredded
     coconut
2   eggs, beaten
1½ cups milk

Mix flour, baking powder, baking soda and salt. Add rest of ingredients and blend thoroughly. Bake in a greased bread pan in 350° oven for 50-60 minutes, until bread tests done. (Freezes well.)

Mango Pie

10 inch baked pie shell
1   tablespoon gelatin
¼   cup cold water
4   egg yolks, beaten
½   cup sugar
2   cups mashed canned mango
     or fresh mango, sweeten-
     ed with sugar to taste
4   tablespoons lemon juice
¼   teaspoon salt
4   egg whites
½   cup sugar
1   cup heavy cream, whipped,
     sweetened and flavored
     with vanilla

Soak gelatin in water and set aside. In top of double boiler place beaten egg yolks, sugar, mashed mango, lemon juice and salt and mix well. Place on top of simmering water and cook, stirring, until thick and of custard consistency. Remove from heat and stir in softened gelatin; blending well. Place in refrigerator to cool. Beat egg white until very stiff, gradually adding the half cup of sugar. When custard is cool, fold in meringue, blending thoroughly. Pour into baked pie shell; allow to set in refrigerator. If freezing, do so at this point and defrost to finish. Top with whipped, sweetened and flavoring cream to serve. Decorate with grated or slivered lemon peel.

Aloha Pie

1   (9-inch) baked pie shell

Pineapple Layer Filling:

¼   cup sugar
1   tablespoon cornstarch
⅛   teaspoon salt
1   cup crushed pineapple, not drained
1   tablespoon lemon juice

Mix sugar, cornstarch and salt. Add crushed pineapple; mix well and cook, stirring until clear. Add lemon juice and cool. Spread layer of cooled mixture over bottom of pie shell.

Pineapple Custard Filling:

½   cup sugar
1¼ teaspoons cornstarch
1¼ cups milk, scalded
4   egg yolks, beaten
1   can frozen pineapple juice concentrate, melted or 6 ounce can pineapple juice
1   tablespoon gelatin
¼   cup cold water
4   egg whites
½   cup sugar
½   pint sweetened whipped cream, flavored with ¼ teaspoon almond extract

Mix sugar and cornstarch in top of double boiler. Add scalded milk slowly to beaten egg yolks, and stir gradually into sugar mixture. Blend in pineapple concentrate and cook over simmering water, stirring, until custard is thick. Dissolve gelatin in cold water and stir into hot custard, blending well. Cool in refrigerator. Beat egg whites until fluffy; add sugar gradually and continue beating until whites are stiff and glossy. Fold cooled custard gently through egg whites, blending well. Pour over pineapple layer; chill. (May be frozen at this point. Defrost and proceed.) Serve with whipped cream and top with toasted slivered almonds.

Tropical Fruit Baskets

8   oranges
1   fresh pineapple, cut in 1 inch cubes
    White after-dinner mints, crushed
    Grated fresh coconut, canned or in plastic bag

Cut oranges in halves, scalloping edges. Cut out orange sections and clean membranes from fruit and shells. Put shells in ice water. Sweeten cubed pineapple with crushed white after-dinner mints according to taste; set aside to mellow. Toss together with orange sections and grated coconut, saving some coconut for decoration. Heap into orange shells and garnish with a little coconut which has been toasted in oven to golden brown. Serve chilled.

Coconut - Pineapple Cake

½   pound butter, softened
1   cup sugar
2   eggs, well beaten
2   cups flour
2   teaspoons baking powder
¼   teaspoon salt
¼   teaspoon baking soda
1   cup sour cream
½   cup ground toasted Hawaiian coconut; save out 1 tablespoon
½   cup drained crushed pineapple; save juice and 1 tablespoon pineapple

Cream butter and sugar together. Add well beaten eggs and mix well. Sift dry ingredients together and add alternately with sour cream to butter mixture. Divide batter in half; add ½ to the ground toasted coconut and other half to the crushed pineapple. Butter and flour 8 inch square baking pan. Pour in coconut layer and the pineapple layer; do not mix. Sprinkle top lightly with 1 tablespoon drained pineapple and 1 tablespoon of the coconut. Bake in 350° oven for 50 minutes or until cake tests done. Serve warm with warm sauce over warmed cake. (Cake freezes well. Place in warm oven 15 minutes before serving.)

Sauce:

1   cup pineapple juice
1   cup water
1   cup brown sugar
2   tablespoons flour
2   teaspoons rum flavoring
2   teaspoons butter

Heat pineapple juice, water and brown sugar until sugar is dissolved. Make a thin paste of flour with a little water. Add to heated mixture and cook, stirring, until thick and clear. Remove from heat and add flavoring and butter, blending well, strain if lumpy. (May be made several days ahead.)

Cream of Wheat Pudding (Haloa)

½   cup butter
1   cup cream of wheat
2   cups milk, warmed
½   cup sugar
¼   teaspoon crushed cardamom seeds
¼   cup slivered, toasted, blanched almonds
2   tablespoons chopped pistachio nuts
¼   teaspoon orange flavoring
   Whipped, sweetened, flavored cream or guava jelly for topping

Melt butter in saucepan and add cream of wheat, stirring constantly. Fry until lightly browned. Slowly add milk, over sink as it spatters, stirring all the while. Add rest of ingredients and cook until thick, stirring. Serve hot with whipped, sweetened, flavored cream or refrigerate and when cold, cut into squares and top with a dab of guava jelly.

131

Mandarin Orange Filled Cupcakes

16 favorite recipe orange cupcakes, small, with center
 cut out
1 package orange gelatin
1½ cups boiling water
6 drops orange extract
⅛ teaspoon salt
1 tablespoon grated orange
 rind
½ cup drained Mandarin
 orange sections, diced
 Cointreau or Grand Marnier
1 cup whipped cream
1 large banana, riced
¼ cup slivered candied ginger

Dissolve orange gelatin in boiling water. Add orange extract, salt and orange rind, mixing well. Chill and when jello thickens, add drained Mandarin oranges, distributing well. Refrigerate until mixture is slightly gelled. Brush hollowed out cupcakes with Cointreau or Grand Marnier and fill with gelatin mixture. Place in refrigerator until filling is set. Whip cream until stiff and add riced bananas. Place heaping tablespoon of banana whipped cream on each cupcake and decorate with bits of slivered candied ginger. (Freezes well.)

Coconut Ice Cream

2 coconuts, drain and remove
 meat from shell, not re-
 moving brown skin
3 pints (6 cups) milk
2 tablespoons flour
⅛ teaspoon salt
1½ cups sugar
6 eggs, separated
1½ cups cream, whipped
2 teaspoons vanilla

Place a third of the milk and a third of the coconut meat in a blender or food processor at a time until all coconut is grated. Pour into top of double boiler and cook, stirring constantly, for 5 minutes. Cool and strain through double cheesecloth or dish towel, making sure to get all milk out. Put coconut milk back into top of double boiler and add flour blended with a little water to make a smooth thin paste; mix well. Add salt and sugar and cook, stirring occasionally, for 12 minutes. Pour a little of this into beaten egg yolks and then return all to double boiler mixture, blending thoroughly. Cook for 3 minutes, stirring. Remove from heat; add flavoring and mix well. Pour into refrigerator trays or plastic bowl and freeze 2 hours. Turn into a large bowl and fold in egg whites beaten stiff and whipped cream, blending thoroughly. Refrigerate and finish freezing.

Coconut Pineapple Rum Cocktail

1 coconut per person
1 jigger rum per person
3 jiggers frozen pineapple
 juice, prepared as directed,
 or canned pineapple juice

Have the eyes punched out of the coconuts, and drain out coconut milk. Using small funnel pour in the jigger of rum and as much pineapple juice as the coconut will hold. Put in plugs of carrot so it will not spill out and shake well. Refrigerate until serving time. Remove plugs and slip a straw in one of the eyes to serve. After drinking the cocktail, allow each guest to take home his coconut and hand out the recipe for making Coconut Ice Cream.

Champagne Punch

3   quarts champagne, chilled
2   quarts sauterne, chilled
½   cup Cointreau
3   bottles club soda
     Strawberries, sliced pine-
      apple chunks, sliced
      peaches, or mangoes
      as desired

Mix before serving, adding the champagne at the table. Surround bowl with cracked ice. Do not dilute punch with ice. Float strawberries, sliced pineapple chunks, slices of peaches or mangoes to decorate. Serves 50.

Israeli-Jewish

Rendered Chicken Fat

Rendered chicken fat lends a special, delicious flavor to most Israeli-Jewish foods. It keeps well in the refrigerator and freezes beautifully. Save bits and pieces of fat and skin in the freezer, adding to it until there is large enough amount to render. Refreezing after cooking is no problem.

Method of rendering chicken fat: Clean fat from chicken or fowl; wash well and drain on paper towels. Cut into small pieces, approximately 1-1½ inch size. Clean pieces of skin; drain and cut in same size pieces. Place together in a deep pot over medium heat and try. When fats are almost melted, add 1 medium onion, coarsely diced. Cook, stirring occasionally, until rest of fat has been tried and onions and pieces of skin are richly browned. Strain and use fat in cooking. Use browned chicken skin and onion to incorporate wherever fried onion is called for, or save and mash with potatoes; delicious! The browned skin and onions are called "Gribeness" and are enjoyed as a snack.

Tongue with Sweet and Sour Sauce

1	large fresh beef tongue
½	tablespoon salt
	Water to cover

Scrub tongue with a brush under running water to clean thoroughly. Place in pot; add salt and water; cover and boil until tender. Add water if it boils away and turn tongue occasionally. When tender, hold under cold running water and peel away outer skin; cut off root of tongue. Slice. Reserve liquid.

Sauce:

1	tablespoon chicken fat or shortening
1	cup diced onion
2	tablespoons flour
2	cups liquid from tongue
1½	tablespoons lemon juice
1	tablespoon sugar
1	tablespoon vinegar
2	dozen raisins
1	dozen almonds, pounded
1	stick cinnamon
3	cloves
½	teaspoon cinnamon
4	tablespoons maple syrup
1	tablespoon molasses

Saute onion until golden in shortening. Stir in flour to make smooth paste. Add liquid and cook, stirring, until smooth, about 1 minute. Add rest of ingredients and simmer, stirring constantly, until smooth and thickened. Remove cinnamon stick and cloves. Pour over sliced tongue. Allow to set for several hours before using. Heat and serve hot. (Freezes well.)

Sweet and Sour Fish (Pickled)

2 pounds whitefish, pike or
      other firm, white meat fish
      1-1½ inch thick, cut in
      serving size pieces
1 cup white vinegar
1½ cups water
1 cup dark brown sugar
1 onion, sliced fine
¼ teaspoon ginger
¼ teaspoon cinnamon
¼ teaspoon pepper
1 teaspoon salt
1 or 2 whole cloves
½ cup muscat raisins

Place fish in vinegar and water to which you add salt, pepper and onions. Cook over low heat for 20 minutes. Dissolve brown sugar in a little of the hot fish liquid and add this to fish broth. Add spices and raisins and cook until tender but still firm. Remove fish with slotted spoon and cook liquid, simmering gently, for about 30 minutes, or until thick and syrupy. Pour over fish. Keep in refrigerator and serve cold. Better on second day and keeps for several weeks.

Filled Rich Pastries (Knishes)

Pastry:

3 cups flour
3 teaspoons baking powder
¾ teaspoon salt
9 tablespoons shortening
1 egg
7-8 tablespoons water

Mix dry ingredients; cut in shortening as for pie; beat water and egg together; add to dry mixture and gather into a ball. This makes about 5-6 dozen small knishes. They freeze well and can be reheated in 5-8 minutes when placed frozen on a cookie sheet in 350° oven.

To form and bake: On lightly floured surface, roll pastry thin, about ⅛ inch. Cut into strips about 4 inches wide. Take a handful of filling and form into sausage like shape, just large enough in circumference so that pastry may be wrapped around with a small overlap; lightly dampen the edge of overlap. (You will have to make several of these sausage like shapes to go the length of each strip of pastry.) Pinch overlap down tightly. Cut into 1-1½ inch pieces. Place on greased cookie sheet, cut side down. Melt more vegetable shortening and spoon about 1 teaspoonful over each filled pastry. Bake in 400° oven for 30-35 minutes, until pastry is a light golden brown. Serve hot. Reheats in 350° oven without impairing the flavor. (Freezes well.)

Fillings:

Meat:

4 cups cooked leftover meat,
  ground
¼ cup chicken fat or
  margarine
2 cups diced onions
⅛ teaspoon ginger
1¼ teaspoons salt
½ teaspoon pepper
½ teaspoon sugar

Fry diced onion until lightly golden in the fat. Add to meat, add seasonings and adjust for taste. Should be highly seasoned.

Potato:

4 cups warm mashed potatoes
½ cup chicken fat or
  margarine
2 cups diced onions
1½ teaspoons salt
½ teaspoon pepper
⅛ teaspoon ginger

Directions as for meat filling.

Buckwheat Groats-Kasha:

4 cups cooked medium
  groats, cooked as directed
  on package
½ cup chicken fat or
  margarine
2 cups diced onions
1¼ teaspoons salt
½ teaspoon pepper
⅛ teaspoon ginger

Directions as for meat filling.

Chopped Chicken Liver

1 pound chicken livers,
  washed and drained
⅓ cup rendered chicken fat or
  vegetable shortening
1½ cups diced onion
4 hard boiled eggs
¾ teaspoon salt
⅜ teaspoon pepper
1 tablespoon rendered
  chicken fat or chicken
  soup

Broil, bake or boil chicken livers until thoroughly cooked. Cool. Fry diced onion in chicken fat or vegetable shortening until richly golden. Put livers, hard boiled eggs and fried onion through meat grinder. For those who prefer a coarser texture; chop by hand fairly fine in wooden bowl or put in the food processor. *Do not mash.* Season with salt and pepper; add rendered chicken fat or chicken broth until of spreading consistency; mix well; taste and adjust seasonings.

Chopped Herring

2	large salted herring or 12-16 ounce jar of herring in wine sauce
1	medium onion
3	hard boiled eggs
1½	slices dried bread, no crust; 1 slice if using jar of herring
4½	tablespoons vinegar; if using herring wine sauce reduce vinegar in half
3	tablespoons plus 2 teaspoons sugar; if using herring in wine sauce reduce sugar in half
1½	large apples, peeled
¼	teaspoon pepper
2	tablespoons fine dried bread crumbs

Skin and bone herring and soak overnight. Drain and wipe dry or if using herring in wine sauce, use herring and onions from jar also. Mix sugar and vinegar together in a small bowl and crumble in the slice and a half of dried bread; stir and set aside. Put through meat grinder or food processor the herrings, onions, 2 of the hard boiled eggs, bread mixture from bowl and the apple. Grind very finely. Add rest of ingredients and mix well; taste to adjust seasonings. Pat into serving platter and decorate with slices of other hard boiled egg.

Meat Tarts (Pirogen)

1½	cups flour
¼	teaspoon baking powder
½	teaspoon salt
¾	cup shortening
¼	cup water
¼	cup chicken fat or vegetable shortening
1½	cups diced onion
1	pound cooked lungs (best), or leftover meat
1	cup leftover chicken
1	broiled chicken liver
½	teaspoon salt
¼	teaspoon pepper
1	egg, beaten

Tart Pastry:

Mix flour, baking powder and salt together. Cut in shortening as for pie crust. Add enough cold water to hold together. Roll out on floured surface to thin, about ⅛ inch. Cut into 4-5 inch squares. May be made in larger pieces and when baked, cut to serve.)

Filling:

Fry diced onion in chicken fat or vegetable shortening until golden. Chop lungs or meat, chicken and chicken liver very fine. Add fried onion, salt, pepper and beaten egg; mix well. Place a tablespoon of filling on each square of tart pastry. Wet two opposite sides of pastry with a little water. Fold pastry edges in half and press together to form boat-like cases. Place on greased cookie sheet; brush exposed pastry with egg beaten in a little water. Bake in 400° oven for 25-35 minutes, or until rich golden in color. Serve hot.

אל ישראל ישראל ישראל ישראל ישראל

Sweet and Sour Cabbage Rolls or Meat Balls

2 pounds hamburg
2 slices white bread, without crusts
2 eggs, beaten
1½ teaspoons salt
¼ teaspoon pepper
1 teaspoon Accent (optional)

Soak bread in water to soften; drain and squeeze dry. Beat eggs well and gradually add softened bread; beating after each addition. Gradually add meat, beating with a fork after each addition to keep light and fluffy. Season. Form into small balls if not using the cabbage.

Cabbage Rolls:

1 large head cabbage

Core cabbage and place in a large pot with 2 inches water; cover and steam 5 minutes; cool and spearate leaves. Cut large leaves in half, removing hard vein. Place 1-1½ tablespoons of hamburg mixture on each piece of cabbage leaf; fold edges of sides towards the center and roll. Put a few of the cut out veins and small leaves on bottom of a large kettle. Place rolls in kettle with edge side down, piling one on top of the other; separate with a few small cabbage leaves. If you have more meat than cabbage, form into small balls and place on top of cabbage rolls.

Sauce:

1 (16 ounce) can tomatoes, strained
1 (8 ounce) can tomato sauce
1 cup water
½ teaspoon sour salt
½ cup brown sugar
½ cup white sugar
1¼ teaspoons salt
½ cup maple syrup or honey
Pinch of ginger
½ cup raisins (optional)

Simmer all ingredients about 15 minutes and taste for sweet and sour; adjust. Pour over meat balls and/or cabbage rolls and cook, covered, gently for 1½ hours for meat balls and 2½ hours for cabbage rolls. Add more sauce if too much cooks away. Check to make sure there is plenty of sauce for each serving. (May be baked in 350° oven for same length of time, uncovering and basting last half hour.)

Egg Puffs (Kiechel)

These are in a class of their own. They are an egg flavored, puffy type cookie and are eaten with pickled herring or any pickled fish, or pucha, and sometimes are eaten as a cookie with tea or coffee.

3 eggs
½ cup vegetable or peanut oil
2 teaspoons sugar
⅞ cup flour

Preheat oven to 300°. Beat all ingredients in electric mixer, scraping sides, for 20 minutes. Drop on ungreased cookie sheet by teaspoonful, about 2 inches apart. Round out edges with the bowl of a spoon to give them round shapes. Place in center rack and bake for 20-25 minutes, until golden. (Tops may be brushed with slightly beaten egg whites and sprinkled with sugar before baking, if sweet Kiechel is desired.)

Tuna Fish Balls (Tuna Gefilte Fish)

Broth:

1 large onion, sliced
1 carrot, sliced
¼ teaspoon salt
Dash of white pepper
6 cups water

Combine all ingredients in medium size kettle with a tightly fitting cover and bring to a boil.

Fish Balls:

1 large (12½ ounce) can white meat tuna fish, drained and saving the oil
1 medium onion
1 carrot
3 eggs
½ cup plus 2 tablespoons cracker crumbs, matzo meal
1 teaspoon salt
⅛ teaspoon white pepper
⅛ teaspoon sugar

Grind the tuna fish, onion and carrot through meat grinder or in food processor until very fine. Add the oil from the fish and one egg at a time, beating thoroughly after each addition. Add the cracker crumbs and seasonings and stir well. Allow to stand in the refrigerator for 15 minutes. Make into balls about 1½ inch in diameter and drop into the boiling broth. Boil briskly for 20 minutes. Remove from fire and allow the fish to cool to lukewarm in the broth. Remove balls gently and place in refrigerator. Serve cold with horseradish or mustard.

Fish Balls (Gefilte Fish)

2-2½ ounds pike

Filet and bone 2-2½ pound pike reserving heads and backbones.

Broth:

Backbones and heads of
  fish scaled and cleaned
4 large onions, sliced
1 carrot, sliced in rounds
1 teaspoon salt
⅛ teaspoon white pepper
¾ teaspoon sugar
  Water to 5 inches deep
    in large pot

Remove gills and eyes from fish heads and rinse all bones thoroughly. Remove all possible meat to use in fish balls. Put bones and heads in bottom of a large size kettle that has a secure cover. Add rest of ingredients and bring to a boil. Simmer and cook, covered, while preparing fish balls.

Fish Balls:

Fillet of fish
¼ medium carrot
1 stalk celery
1 small onion
½ slice dried bread
2 tablespoons cracker crumbs,
    matzo meal
1 egg beaten well with
    ½ cup water
1 tablespoon celery salt
1 teaspoon salt
¼ teaspoon white pepper
¼ teaspoon sugar
1 tablespoon oil

Grind fish, carrot, celery, onion and dried bread through meat grinder twice or put in food processor until finely ground together, then into chopping bowl. Add cracker crumbs, by sprinkling over surface. Beat egg and water well and gradually add to fish mixture, chopping all the while with chopping knife and folding mixture over onto itself and chopping more. Add seasonings and oil. Chop again. Fold mixture onto itself and chop again, chopping all together for about 5 minutes. Remove cover from kettle and turn up heat under broth to bring to a vigorous boil. Dip hands in cold water and take up enough of the fish mixture to make a small fish ball about 1½ inches in diameter. Drop into boiling broth, one at a time. Lower heat to a gentle boil; cover and cook for 2 hours, very gently, making sure the broth doesn't boil away. When done cooking, allow to cool to lukewarm in broth. Remove fish balls gently and place on a platter in refrigerator to cool. Serve cold with horseradish or mustard. (Fish mixture may be baked in a meat loaf pan and served for a luncheon main course. Also may be used as fish course for formal dinner, using twice the recipe and making the fish balls about twice as large.)

Spiced Jellied Loaf (Pucha)

6-8 large knuckle bones, not
    marrow bones
2 pounds meaty veal bones
    Water enough to cover
    bones and meat
3 large onions, quartered
6-8 large cloves garlic, sliced
1 tablespoon salt
¼ teaspoon white pepper
4 hard boiled eggs

Place knuckle bones and meaty veal bones in a large pot and cover with 1 inch water. Add onion, garlic, salt and pepper; cover. Boil gently for 3-3½ hours, or until liquid is reduced in half and glutinous flesh falls off from bones. Remove from fire and remove bones and meat. Strain broth and set aside. Remove glutinous flesh and meat from bones. Set meat aside to use for Knishes, or freeze until ready to use. Grind cooked onion, garlic and all glutinous flesh, and put back in liquid. Add chopped eggs and stir through. Pour mixture in loaf pan and place in refrigerator. When gelled, cut into squares or different shapes and serve. Can be kept in refrigerator for several days or can be frozen.

Chicken Soup

1 large fowl, quartered,
    fat removed
2 teaspoons salt
¼ teaspoon pepper
    Water to cover
1 small onion
2 stalks celery
1 large carrot
¼ teaspoon thyme
½ teaspoon sugar

Clean and wash chicken. Place in pot with salt, pepper and water. Simmer gently over medium heat for 1 hour. Add vegetables and continue simmering gently until chicken is tender. Remove chicken and set aside for another use. Strain broth; add thyme and sugar; bring to a boil; taste and adjust seasonings. Serve with one of the following.

3 eggs (separate 1 egg)
3 tablespoons rendered
    chicken fat or melted
    butter or margarine
1½ teaspoons salt
¼ teaspoon white pepper
¼ cup chicken broth or water
1 cup matzo meal

Matzo Meal Dumplings (Knaidlachs):

Mix well the 2 eggs and the 1 egg yolk with chicken fat, melted butter or margarine, beating about 2 minutes. Add salt and pepper. Stir in chicken broth or water, blending thoroughly. Stirring constantly, slowly mix in matzo meal, blending thoroughly. Beat egg white until stiff and dry and fold through first mixture, gently blending well. Cover and place in refrigerator for 1 hour. Wet hands and form mixture into small balls, about 1½ inches in diameter, dropping 1 at a time into boiling soup. Cover pot tightly and simmer gently for about 40 minutes. (These can be made using melted butter or margarine and water and served with a milk soup. Drop matzo balls into boiling salted water; cover and simmer gently for 40 minutes. Add warm milk to liquid left after boiling the dumplings and season this broth well with salt and pepper.)

אלישראלישראלישראלישראלישראל

Meat-Filled Triangles (Kreplachs):

⅓ pound hamburg or ground cooked leftover meat
¼ teaspoon grated onion
¼ teaspoon salt
¼ teaspoon garlic powder
⅛ teaspoon pepper
⅛ teaspoon ginger
1 egg, beaten
1½ cups flour
1 teaspoon salt
3 eggs
   Or use Won Ton Skins instead of last three listed ingredients

Mix well first 7 ingredients and set aside. If not using Won Ton Skins make a stiff dough from next 3 ingredients, beating eggs well and gradually stirring in flour and salt. Add more flour if dough is not stiff enough. Knead dough for a few minutes and then allow to rest for a few more minutes. Roll dough paper thin on a well floured surface. Cut dough into 2 inch squares. Put a dab of the meat mixture in the center of each square. Brush edges with a mixture of 1 cup water and ½ tablespoon cornstarch. Fold corner to opposite corner, forming triangle, pinch dough together firmly. Drop into a large pot of boiling salted water and cook, covered, for ¾ hour. Remove with slotted spoon, allowing to drain well, and add to soup to serve. These also may be placed in a baking dish with a little rendered chicken fat, sprinkled with cinnamon and sugar and baked in 350° oven until brown on both sides, turning frequently, and then served in chicken soup. (If one happens to have some ginger honey left from making Honey Drops of "Taglichs" (see page 162) these Kreplachs make a delicious side dish to serve with meats by baking them, covered with ginger honey and dotted with a little rendered chicken fat, butter or margarine, about 1 hour in 350° oven, turning often.)

Israeli-Style Stuffed Peppers

8 large size green peppers
2 pounds hamburg
⅓ cup rice or medium buckwheat groats
1 cup tomato juice
½ teaspoon pepper
2 teaspoons salt
¼ cup chopped parsley

Cut tops off peppers; clean out seeds; rib pulp and wash and drain on paper towels. Mix rest of ingredients well. Stuff into peppers and cook in following sauce.

1 large onion, diced
4 cloves garlic, crushed
1 teaspoon dry mustard
2 tablespoons vinegar
2 tablespoons Worchestershire sauce
1 large can tomatoes
¼ teaspoon pepper
2 teaspoons salt
½ cup lemon juice

Sauce:

Combine all ingredients and pour over stuffed peppers. Cook for 1½ hours over low heat. Cover for first hour. Uncover and finish cooking, basting frequently. Serve with sauce. (Freezes well.)

Roast Stuffed Veal Brisket

1 veal brisket
Sweetbread stuffing
Ginger
Salt
Pepper
Cinnamon
Sugar

Have butcher cut a pocket in the veal brisket. Make a sweet bread stuffing, seasoning with a few fried diced onions, cinnamon and sugar, and adding a little ginger and a few seedless raisins. Add 2 extra tablespoons of rendered chicken fat or margarine. Stuff veal brisket. Sprinkle top of brisket with ginger, salt and pepper and a little cinnamon and sugar. Pour over 2 cups hot broth or tomato juice. Cover and roast in 350° oven for 1 hour, basting often. Finish roasting, uncovered, basting frequently. Roast to a rich golden brown and very tender or undercook by half an hour, cool and freeze. Defrost and finish roasting until tender, about 1 ½ hours.

Roast Fresh Beef Brisket

5-6 pound fresh beef brisket
4-5 large onions, sliced
Salt
Pepper
3 cloves garlic, crushed

Place meat in a roaster that has a tight cover. Salt and pepper well all over and cover with onions and garlic. Cover roaster tightly and roast in 325° oven, allowing 35 minutes to the pound. Uncover the last hour, pushing onions into juices, basting often. Serve well done, slicing against the grain. Replace sliced meat in pan juices. Do not thicken gravy but use juices and onions from roasting as is. Very delicious served with a sweet baked noodle pudding as a side dish. (Freezes well. Undercook by 1 hour. Defrost and place uncovered in 325° oven for 1½ hours, basting often.) Very good too with thick slices of potato, in juices, added during last hour.

Beef, Prune and Potato Casserole (Floimen Tzimess)

9 medium white or sweet
potatoes, peeled and
sliced ½ inch thick and
cut in thirds
2½ cups dried prunes
1 cup sugar
¼ teaspoon sour salt,
citric acid
1¾ teaspoons salt
2½ cups water
4 pound front cut beef brisket

Combine all ingredients, placing meat on top of other ingredients, in a large covered casserole or roasting pan that will go on top of stove. Simmer gently, covered, for 1 hour. Place in 350° oven, covered, and bake for 3 hours, basting occasionally. Taste and adjust seasonings. Serve with sauce, slicing meat thinly against the grain and surrounding with prunes and potato mixture. (Freezes well.)

Sweet Potato, Carrot and Brisket Casserole (Tzimess)

3 pounds carrots, peeled
  and sliced thinly
2 pounds sweet potatoes,
  peeled and cubed, 1½
  inches
¼ cup washed apricots, soaked overnight in water to
  cover
1½ teaspoons salt
¼ teaspoon pepper
1½ cups brown sugar
1½ cups liquid from soaking
  apricots and water
4 pound front cut beef brisket
  Salt and pepper (optional)

4 tablespoons rendered
  chicken fat or
  margarine
2 tablespoons minced onion
¼ cup flour
  Juice from casserole

Combine all ingredients, placing meat on top of other ingredients if using it, in large covered casserole or roasting pan. Simmer gently over low heat on top of stove, basting occasionally, for 1½ hours. Make Inbren and add juice from casserole to thicken. Pour over all and bake, covered, in 325° oven for 1¾ hours. Uncover and then bake, basting frequently, for 1¼ hours. To serve, slice meat across the grain in thin slices if using with meat. Excellent with Baked Potato Pudding (Potato Kugal) and Stuffed Chicken Necks (see side dishes.) Using half of the Potato Pudding recipe or making all of the Chicken Necks, push vegetables and meat to one side and place either one of the above in the sauce when casserole goes into oven. Dot the pudding with rendered chicken fat or margarine. Bake uncovered and baste all frequently. Pudding or chicken necks should be added when casserole goes into the oven. (Freezes well.)

Inbren:

Melt fat or margarine; add onion and cook until onion is transparent. Remove from heat and blend in flour. Gradually add some of the juices from the casserole and blend. Return to heat and cook 1 minute, stirring. Pour into remaining juices in casserole and blend thoroughly. Proceed to bake as instructed above.

Baked Potato Pudding (Potato Kugel)

9 large potatoes, peeled
1 very small onion
½ cup matzo meal or fine
  cracker crumbs
2 eggs, beaten
¼ teaspoon baking powder
1 teaspoon salt
⅛ teaspoon pepper
9 tablespoons vegetable
  shortening or rendered
  chicken fat, melted
  and hot

Grate potatoes and onion or put in blender or food processor. Pour into fine mesh strainer and rinse with cold water. Allow to drain and squeeze dry. Melt shortening or fat in 375° oven in a baking dish you will bake pudding in, approximately 8 x 8 x 2 inches. Pour 6 tablespoons of the melted shortening into grated potatoes and onion. Reserve rest of melted shortening in baking dish. Add rest of ingredients to potato mixture; stir well. Pour mixture into baking dish and spoon some of the saved melted fat over top. Bake in 375° oven until very richly brown all over, about 1 hour. Remove from baking dish and drain on paper towels a few minutes. Cut into squares and serve piping hot. (This same mixture is delicious if poured over the Sweet Potato and Carrot Casserole and baked with it for 1½ hours, basting frequently with casserole juices.) (Freezes well.)

Stuffed Cabbage

3 tablespoons rendered chicken fat or 3 tablespoons vegetable shortening
¼ cup diced onion
2 pounds hamburg
1½ teaspoons salt
¼ teaspoon pepper
2 eggs, beaten
½ cup water
½ cup uncooked rice
1 large head cabbage

1 pound can tomatoes, strained
1 (8 ounce) can tomato sauce
1 cup water
½ cup white sugar
½ cup brown sugar
4 tablespoons honey or use honey left from making Honey Drops (Taglichs)
4-5 tablespoons lemon juice or ½ teaspoon sour salt
⅛ teaspoon pumpkin pie spice or pinch of ginger and cinnamon
1¼ teaspoons salt
½ cup plumped raisins, drained

Heat fat and fry diced onion until golden. Add to hamburg with rest of ingredients, except cabbage; mix well. Set aside. Core cabbage; place in large kettle with 2 inches water and boil 5 minutes; cool; drain and separate leaves. Cut large leaves in half, removing hard vein. Place 2-3 tablespoons of the meat mixture on each cabbage leaf, 1 at a time. Fold edges toward center and then roll. Place rolls in a large pot, with edges down, piling one on top of another, separating with a few of the small cabbage leaves. Cook in the following sauce.

Sauce:

Combine all ingredients and simmer 10 minutes. Taste and adjust sweet and sour to your liking. Pour over cabbage rolls and cook gently on top of stove, covered, for 2½ hours. Uncover, and place in 350° oven for 1 hour, basting frequently. Add warm water if too much sauce cooks away, adding a little at a time, making sure there will be enough sauce to accompany each serving. (Freezes well.)

Sour Milk Pancakes

2 cups flour
3 teaspoons baking powder
1 teaspoon salt
2 eggs, beaten
1¼ cups sour milk
2 tablespoons melted butter

Sift dry ingredients into bowl. Add sour milk and melted butter to beaten eggs; add gradually to dry ingredients while stirring constantly; beat until smooth. Fry in tablespoon portions in hot melted butter. When golden brown, turn and brown other side. Serve hot with powdered sugar or a mixture of cinnamon and sugar. (Keep warm in 200° oven while completing frying.)

Boiled or Roasted Beef Tongue

1   large fresh beef tongue
1½ tablespoons salt
⅛   teaspoon pepper
½   teaspoon sage
½   teaspoon paprika
½   teaspoon celery salt
½   teaspoon thyme
1   teaspoon brown sugar
1   clove garlic, crushed
1   carrot, sliced, if roasting
1   small onion, chopped,
      if roasting
    Water ⅓ way up on tongue

Wash tongue thoroughly with good stiff brush under running water. If boiling, place in a deep pot and add rest of ingredients. Cover and gently boil on top of stove until almost tender, approximately 3 hours, turning often and adding water to keep liquid ⅓ of the way up on tongue. Peel off outer skin after plunging first in cold water when tongue is almost tender. Cut off root section and set aside for other uses (making Knishes or Pirogen). Return tongue to pot; cover and finish cooking until tender. Slice and serve with juices.

For roasting, reduce salt to ¾ tablespoon; mix all seasonings in small bowl; rub seasonings well into washed tongue. Allow to stay in refrigerator several hours or overnight. Place in roasting pan with water up to 1½ inch depth; add carrot and onion. Cover and roast in 375° oven, adding water as it cooks away to keep liquid at this depth. Follow rest of instructions as for boiled tongue, however, roasting tongue, after peeling, for the last hour uncovered, turning and basting often. Slice and serve with pan juices. (Freezes well.)

Lima Bean, Barley and Potato with Beef Short Ribs Casserole (Cholent)

     Several joint bones, veal
       or beef
4-5 pound lean short ribs of
       beef cut in 3-inch pieces
6   medium potatoes, cut in
       1½ inch dice
1   cup dried baby lima beans,
       soaked in water to cover
       overnight, drained
½   cup barley
2   medium onions, diced and
       sauteed in 3 tablespoons
       rendered chicken fat or
       margarine
2   teaspoons salt
½   teaspoon pepper
1   teaspoon paprika
     Water to cover

Combine all ingredients in a large Pyrex casserole or kettle. Bake, partially covered, in 300° oven for entire day. Stir ingredients occasionally and add water if cooking down too fast. You should have just a little gravy to serve with when done. Can be baked in 200° oven overnight. Add water to cover again just before going to bed. Turn oven up to 250° on arising and bake until noon. Reheat to serve. (Freezes well.)

South Seas Sabra Chicken

South Sea Mixture:

2   pounds sweet potatoes,
      cut into ½ inch dice and
      parboiled to barely tender
1   (15½ ounce) can or 1½
      cups drained pineapple,
      saving juice
½   cup mashed bananas
4   tablespoons brown sugar
4   tablespoons Sabra Liqueur
6   tablespoons pineapple juice
¾   teaspoon salt
½   cup chicken broth or
      bouillon

Mix well and pour into large casserole or baking dish that has been lightly coated with butter or margarine. Set aside.

2-2¼ pounds chicken breasts
1½ pounds chicken legs or backs
1   cup flour
2   teaspoons salt
1   teaspoon paprika
¼   teaspoon pepper
½   teaspoon celery salt
½   teaspoon dried sweet basil
1   tablespoon finely chopped
      parsley
¼   cup butter or margarine
¾   cup Sabra Liqueur

Wash and wipe chicken parts and set aside. Place flour and the following 6 ingredients in a plastic bag and shake. Add chicken parts, a few at a time, and shake to coat well. Remove from bag and shake off excess flour. Heat butter or margarine until it foams and add chicken pieces. Fry over medium high heat until browned on both sides. Remove and place on top of South Sea Mixture. Add Sabra liqueur to frying pan in which chicken was prepared and light liqueur with a long match or lit candle. Allow flame to die out. Stir, scraping brown bits from the pan into sauce. Pour over chicken parts and South Sea Mixture. Bake, covered, in 350° oven for 30 minutes. Uncover and baste and bake another 15 minutes. (May be made ahead and frozen.)

Potato Pancakes (1) (Potato Latkes)

6   medium potatoes, peeled
2   eggs, beaten
¼   cup flour
½   teaspoon baking powder
1   teaspoon grated onion
1   teaspoon salt
      Dash of white pepper
½   cup milk
3   tablespoons melted butter

Grate potatoes and onion or put in blender or food processor. Pour into fine mesh strainer and rinse with cold water. Allow to drain and squeeze dry. Add rest of ingredients; mix well. Fry by tablespoon portions in hot vegetable shortening until browned well on both sides. Drain on paper toweling. Keep warm in 200° oven while completing frying. Serve with applesauce or cinnamon and sugar, mixed together. (To freeze, place pancakes on cookie sheets and freeze, uncovered. When frozen, place in plastic bags. To serve, reheat frozen on cookie sheets until hot in 350° oven.)

Potato Pancakes (2)

6   medium potatoes, peeled
1   teaspoon grated onion
1½ teaspoons salt
2   eggs, beaten
½   cup matzo meal or fine
     cracker crumbs

Grate potatoes and onion or put in blender or food processor. Pour into fine mesh strainer and rinse with cold water, allow to drain and squeeze dry. Add rest of ingredients and mix well. Fry by tablespoon portions in hot vegetable shortening until browned well on both sides. Drain on paper toweling. Keep warm in 200° oven while completing frying. Serve with applesauce or a cinnamon and sugar mixture. (To freeze, see instructions under No. 1.)

Pot Roast (Gedepfte Fleisch)

5-6 pound chuck, 2 inches
     thick
     Flour
3   tablespoons rendered
     chicken fat or
     vegetable shortening
3   onions, sliced
3   cloves garlic, thinly sliced
1½ teaspoons salt
¼   teaspoon pepper
2   carrots, sliced (optional)
1   stalk celery, sliced (optional)
1   bay leaf
6   peppercorns
8   medium potatoes, sliced
     ½ inch thick
1   cup boiling water
¾   cup V-8 juice or tomato juice

Coat meat well with flour. Heat fat and brown meat on all sides. Remove meat and lightly brown sliced onion; add sliced garlic and saute 1 more minute. Return meat to pan with onion and garlic. Add salt, pepper, carrot, celery, bay leaf, peppercorns, water and juice; cover and simmer 1 hour. Remove meat and add potatoes; salt and pepper potatoes. Replace meat; cover and cook slowly for another hour. Add more hot water or juice as juices cook away, keeping gravy no more than about 1 inch deep so as not to stew meat. Slice meat into serving pieces, accompany with vegetables and spoon gravy over all. (Freezes well.)

Cottage Cheese Pancakes (Keeze Latkes)

1   cup cottage cheese
1   cup sour cream
4   eggs, beaten
1   cup flour
2   tablespoons sugar
½   teaspoon salt

Combine cottage cheese and sour cream. Add beaten eggs and mix well. Add flour gradually, beating after each addition. Add sugar and salt and mix thoroughly. Fry by tablespoons in hot melted butter. Brown on both sides. (Keep warm in 200° oven while completing frying.)

Corned Beef and Cabbage (Pickling Own Beef)

Corned Beef:

10	pound brisket of beef
4	quarts water
¼	cup warm water
½	teaspoon saltpeter
2	cups coarse salt
¼	cup brown sugar
6	cloves garlic, thinly sliced
1	tablespoon paprika
1	tablespoon mixed pickling spices

Dissolve saltpeter in ¼ cup warm water. Add salt to water and mix with all ingredients except meat. Place in a 3 gallon crock; add meat. Cover with a plate and weight down with a large, clean stone. Leave in a cool place in the brine for 12 days, turning meat every other day. (You may buy your corned beef but for a delicious treat do try making your own sometime. If buying the beef already corned, add 3 cloves of garlic, thinly sliced and a teaspoon of mixed pickling spices when cooking.)

1	large head cabbage, cut in eighths
8	carrots
8	potatoes

Place corned beef in a large pot and fill with water to just cover. (See above if beef was bought already corned.) Simmer gently, covered, for about 3 hours, or until almost tender. About 30 minutes before corned beef is done, add vegetables and finish cooking. Serve on a large platter, meat sliced against the grain in center and vegetables arranged around. (Freeze without adding vegetables. Defrost, bring to a boil and add vegetables. Proceed as above.)

Cottage Cheese Casserole (Taygertz)

4½	cups uncooked wide egg noodles
¼	pound butter
1	cup sour cream
1	cup cottage cheese
2	eggs, beaten
1½	teaspoons salt

Boil noodles until just under tender; drain. Combine all ingredients. Bake in 10 x 6 x 2 inch baking dish. Bake in 350° oven until medium dark golden brown, about 1 hour and 15 minutes. Cut in squares to serve. (Freezes well.)

Hot Potato Salad

10	medium potatoes, peeled and boiled
6	large eggs, hard boiled
¼	pound butter
1	large onion, diced fine
	Salt and pepper

Drain potatoes and place in a large bowl. Add hard boiled eggs, diced onion and butter. Mash all together coarsely with potato masher. If not moist enough, add a bit more butter. Season highly with salt and pepper. Serve hot. Keep until serving time covered in 200° oven. (Does not freeze.)

אלישראלישראלישראלישראלישראלישראל

Stuffed Chicken Necks (Heldzel)

The whole skin from around the chicken neck is used. Cut the skin off from just above the wishbone and then pull it off the neck bones. Clean thoroughly, removing all pinfeathers, then wash and dry. Sew up larger opening and stuff through top.

Stuffing: (For 8 skins of chicken necks.)

1 cup flour
1⅓ cups matzo meal or fine cracker crumbs
⅔ cup oatmeal or cream of wheat
2 medium onions, grated
2½ teaspoons salt
½ teaspoon pepper
⅔ cup chicken fat or suet or vegetable shortening
Chicken broth

Mix dry ingredients, grated onion, salt and pepper well with a fork. Add chicken fat or shortening and work in lightly with fingers until of a pebbly consistency. Stuff neck skin loosely. Sew top together. Boil with chicken broth for 1 hour, then place in pan of Sweet Potato and Carrot Casserole (see page 147) and bake in oven. Basting stuffed necks with casserole juices, turn occasionally and brown nicely. Can be served without roasting after boiling by increasing time by ½ hour. Also may be roasted with chicken or meat. Slice to serve. Usually necks are small and 1 whole one is served per person. (Freezes well.)

Baked Noodles and Apricot Pudding

1 large and 1 small package of cream cheese, room temperature
½ cup sugar
¾ pound melted butter or margarine
8 eggs
1½ cups milk
1 pound medium width noodles, boiled until just underdone, drain
¾ cup dried, washed, apricots cut into small pieces

Beat cheese, sugar and cooled melted butter or margarine together. Beat eggs and add milk as for custard. Add all to boiled noodles, adding apricots as well. Sprinkle with topping.

Topping:

1 cup crushed corn flakes
¼ teaspoon cinnamon
1 tablespoon butter, room temperature

Mix together well and toss lightly with a fork.
Pour Noodle Mixture into a large 13 x 9 x 2 inch serving dish. Sprinkle all over with prepared topping. Bake in a 325° oven 1 hour and 15 minutes. Cut into square serving size pieces after allowing to rest 10 minutes. May be kept warm in a 250° oven. Serves 12.

Chick-Pea Salad

2 cans chick-peas, rinsed
  and drained
1 large onion, diced
½ cup salad oil
½ cup wine vinegar
½ teaspoon salt
¼ teaspoon coarsely ground
  black pepper
  Chopped parsley

Combine chick-peas and diced onion in serving bowl. Place oil, vinegar, salt and pepper in a jar with a cover; shake well. Pour over chick-pea mixture, tossing to coat well. Taste and add salt if desired. Garnish with chopped parsley. (Does not freeze. Can be prepared the day before.)

Stuffed Derma (Kishka)

Derma skins stuffing
(see page 153)

Use the Stuffed Chicken neck recipe for stuffing, but double or triple, depending on how much derma you have. Order the derma (Kishla) skin from a Kosher butcher shop. The butcher will get it for you cleaned and cut in lengths. Wash thoroughly; turn inside out and scrub with a brush under water. Turn back and sew one end. Now push sewed end in, stuffing loosely, and gradually pushing inside out, stuffing as you go along. When loosely stuffed, sew the other end. Boil in salted water 1 hour, then put in pan with a little rendered chicken fat; cover and place in 350° oven to brown, about 1 hour, turning frequently and basting. Can be browned with roast of meat or fowl or either potato casserole (see pages 146-147). Slice to serve. (Freezes well.)

Sweet Cottage Cheese and Noodle Casserole (Luckshen Kugal)

1 pound wide egg noodles
  (11 cups)
½ pound melted butter or
  margarine
1 pound cottage cheese
4 eggs, beaten
½ pint (1 cup) sour cream
1 teaspoon cinnamon mixed
  with 1 cup sugar
½ cup golden raisins
2 teaspoons salt
2 teaspoons vanilla

Boil noodles until barely tender; drain. Combine all ingredients, saving a little cinnamon and sugar mixture to sprinkle over top. Bake in dish approximately 12x9x2 inches. Bake in 350° oven until nicely browned. Can be made omitting sour cream and cottage cheese and substituting butter or margarine with half cup of rendered chicken fat. Serve with roasted meats or as luncheon dish. Cut in squares to serve. Will serve 12.

Green Pepper and Tomato Salad

6-8 large green peppers
3 large tomatoes
²/₃ cup salad or olive oil
¹/₃ cup wine vinegar
¹/₂ teaspoon salt
¹/₈ teaspoon pepper
   Chopped fresh parsley or
      parsley flakes

Place peppers directly on burner over low heat or flame. Cook until blackened, turning until peppers are cooked all over in this manner. Place peppers in a paper bag and gently squash bag together to just split peppers open a little. Place in refrigerator to cool. Remove from bag; cut off stem part; remove seeds and, while running cold water over them, peel off skin. Rinse and drain on paper towels. Cut into pieces about 1½ inches square and place on platter. Slice tomatoes and place on platter topping with peppers. Combine oil, vinegar, salt and pepper and pour over all. Sprinkle with parsley and keep in refrigerator. Remove and bring to room temperature before serving.

Cheese Blintzes

Skins (Crepes):

6 eggs, beaten
1 cup milk or water
¹/₂ cup flour
¹/₂ cup cornstarch
1 teaspoon salt
3 tablespoons melted butter
¹/₄ teaspoon vanilla (optional)

Do half a recipe at a time in blender, beating eggs and milk first and then adding rest of ingredients. Pour into a pitcher; cover and allow to rest half an hour before using. Grease a 6-inch frying or crepe pan with a little butter; heat until hot. Pour in enough batter to cover bottom of pan, about ¼ cup; tilt pan to coat all over and pour excess back into pitcher. Cook over medium high heat until edges begin to lift. Turn out, uncooked side down, on waxed paper. Repeat using all of batter, piling one skin on top of another.

Filling:

2¹/₄ pounds Farmers cheese or
      dry cottage cheese
4¹/₂ tablespoons sugar
1 teaspoon cinnamon
   Dash of white pepper
¹/₂ teaspoon salt
4 tablespoons sour cream
1 egg, beaten

Mix cheese and rest of ingredients together well. Place 2 or 3 tablespoons of filling in center of the upper third of a skin, on cooked side. Fold top down and sides of skin in, then roll down. Finish filling all skins. Fry in butter in a large frying pan until golden brown on both sides. Serve with sour cream and/or maple syrup. Makes 36 blintzes. (Freeze after frying. Cool; cover tightly with aluminum foil and then a plastic bag. Reheat on cookie sheets in 350° oven, covered lightly with aluminum foil and frozen, for about 25-30 minutes, until hot.)

Cottage Cheese Salad

1 pound cottage cheese
2 tomatoes, cut in small
   pieces
¼ medium green pepper,
   diced
4 scallions, finely sliced
½ cup diced cucumber
3-4 red radishes, finely sliced
1 cup sour cream
   Salt and pepper

Combine all ingredients and mix lightly. Add salt and pepper to taste. Serve on lettuce leaves. (May be prepared in A.M.)

Kosher-Style Dill Pickles (1)

   Pickling-size cucumbers
3 cloves garlic, cut in
   small pieces
1 heaping tablespoon
   coarse salt
1 heaping tablespoon mixed
   pickling spice
1 large piece fresh or
   dried dill

Wash pickling-size cucumbers. Place in quart jar with rest of ingredients.

Fill jar with cold water. Place jar rubber on and dry so it will seal or if using screw type cover, dry top of jar to insure tight seal. Turn jar upside down to see if it leaks, testing for several hours. Store in cool place. Ready to eat in about 3 weeks. Keeps indefinitely. (Half sours in 3-4 days.)

Kosher-Style Dill Pickles (2)

   Pickling-size cucumbers
2 tablespoons pickling spice
5-6 cloves garlic, cut in
   small chunks
1 tablespoon cider vinegar
¼ teaspoon powdered alum
1 spray fresh or dried dill
1 cup coarse salt
1 gallon hot water

Fill 2 quart jars with washed pickling-size cucumbers.

Place next 5 ingredients in jars with cucumbers; place dill in the top part of jar. Mix coarse salt with hot water; stir well; fill each jar to top. Put on jar rubber and dry so it will seal or if using screw type cover, dry top of jar to insure tight seal. Turn jars upside down for several hours to see if they leak. Store in cool place. Ready to eat in about 3 weeks. (Half sours in 2 weeks.) Keeps indefinitely.

Egg Bread (Challah)

½ cup lukewarm water
2 packages dry yeast
1 teaspoon sugar
5 cups all-purpose flour
1½ teaspoons salt
⅛ cup sugar
4 tablespoons salad oil
3 eggs, beaten
¾ cup lukewarm water
1 egg mixed with 2 table-
   spoons water
2 tablespoons poppy or
   sesame seeds

Stir ½ cup lukewarm water, dry yeast and teaspoon sugar together in a large bowl. Wait 2-3 minutes for yeast to dissolve. Add 2 cups of flour, salt, sugar, oil, eggs and ¾ cup of water. Beat all together very well. Add 2-2½ cups flour and beat dough until it comes away from side of bowl. Sometimes more flour or less is needed depending on how well the flour absorbs the water. Turn dough on to a lightly floured surface; knead for 10 minutes, adding more flour if necessary, so dough is plyable and not sticky. Place dough in an oiled warm bowl, turning it to grease dough all over. Cover bowl with plastic wrap and a towel and place in a warm area, at least 80°.

Allow to rise 1 hour until double in size. Punch down dough with your fist. Turn out on a floured surface. Cut dough in three parts. Cut two parts into six pieces. Shape each piece into a 12-14 inch long roll. Braid three pieces together to make 2 breads. Place each one on a greased cookie sheet. Divide the last piece of dough into 6 pieces and shape into 4-5 inch long rolls. Braid 3 pieces together to make small bread on top of each large bread. Secure with toothpicks. Place in a warm area for 45 minutes, until almost double in size. Preheat oven to 300°. Brush top of dough with egg and water mixture. Sprinkle with poppy or sesame seeds.

Bake at 300° ten minutes and then reset oven to 350° and bake 40 minutes. Immediately remove to a rack and let cool. Remove toothpicks. (Tests done when knuckles of hand tapped against bottom of bread sounds hollow.)

For Rolls:

After first rising cut dough into pieces about 3 inches square. Roll into 1 inch rope; tie into knot and tuck end under. Set on greased baking sheet and allow to rise to double in size. Brush with egg mixture and sprinkle with seeds. Bake as directed, but baking after resetting temperature only until rolls are rich golden brown. (Tests for doneness as for bread.) (May be made much smaller if desired. Freezes well and should be reheated in a microwave oven or placed in open brown bag at 300°.)

Pumpernickel

2   packages dry yeast
1½ cups warm water
2¾ cups rye flour
1   tablespoon salt
    Caraway seeds
1   tablespoon shortening
⅓   cup molasses
3¼-3¾ cups all-purpose flour
    Cornmeal

The night before, sprinkle the yeast into warm water in a large bowl. Stir until yeast is dissolved. Add the rye flour and beat to smooth. Cover with plastic wrap and place in a warm area to rise overnight. Next morning mix in salt, caraway seeds, shortening, molasses and half the flour; mix in more flour, a little at a time, until dough is stiff and cleans sides of bowl. Turn dough on floured surface and knead five minutes, to smooth. Place in a greased bowl, turning to grease top, and cover. Allow to rise 1 hour or until hole remains from fingerprint. Punch down and divide in half. Round each to a smooth ball. Place at opposite corners on lightly greased, cornmeal sprinkled cookie sheet. Cover with wax paper and let rise until dent of finger remains in dough, 35-45 minutes. Brush tops with cold water. Place a pan of warm water on lower rack in oven. Preheat oven to 375° and bake 35-45 minutes to well browned. (Tests done when knuckle of hand tapped against bottom of bread sounds hollow.)

Fruit or Poppy Seed Filled Pastry (Strudel)

Strudel dough may be purchased in large supermarkets in urban areas. This is a paper thin, stretched dough, similar to the Greek Philo dough, which indeed may be used as a substitute. The recipe for making the stretched Philo dough is listed in the Greek section. However, strudel is also delicious made with a tender sour cream dough as in the recipe that follows. The fillings are listed first as one of them must be prepared the night before. There is a choice of 3 fillings. (If using purchased strudel dough, use 6-8 sheets brushing with melted butter every 2 sheets and brushing top as well.)

Cherry Filling:

1   (12 ounce) jar cherry
    preserves
1   (16 ounce) jar maraschino
    cherries, chopped
1   orange, ground
1   lemon, ground
1   cup raisins, soaked in
    warm sweet wine for a few
    minutes and drained
¾   cup fine dried bread
    crumbs
½   cup chopped nuts

Mix first 6 ingredients of filling, including juice from maraschino cherries and leave overnight. Next morning, add chopped nuts. Place a strip of filling about 2 inches thick through center of prepared dough, which has been rolled ⅛ inch thick, in rectangles approximately 6 x 16 inches. Seal with a little water to dampen lower edge. Lift dough both ways to cover filling, placing dampened edge on top and pressing together. Place rolls on a greased cookie sheet. Whip egg whites slightly and brush over strudels. Slash every 1½ inches. Bake in 400° oven for 15 minutes; turn heat to 375° and bake 25-30 minutes, until lightly browned. Cool and slice across into about 1½ inch pieces. (Keeps well but may be frozen.)

אל·ישראל·ישראל·ישראל·ישראל·ישראל·ישראל

3 pounds grated greening
apples
1 cup sugar
1½ teaspoons cinnamon
3 tablespoons chopped nuts
(optional)
3 tablespoons golden raisins
(optional)
6 tablespoons fine dried
bread crumbs

¾ cup poppy seeds
1½ cups sugar
½ cup raisins
A little hot coffee to
make sticky paste
1 teaspoon lemon rind

3 cups flour
½ pound butter or
margarine
¾ cup sour cream
1 egg, separated

Apple Filling:

Mix all ingredients and allow to rest 30 minutes. Cut dough into 3 parts. Roll each part into rectangle about ⅛ inch thick. Spread with apple mixture to within ¼ inch of edges of dough. Roll up as a jelly roll. Make slashes in top of each roll about 1½ inches apart. Whip egg whites slightly and brush over strudels. Place on lightly greased cookie sheets. Bake in 400° oven for 15 minutes; turn heat to 375° and bake 25-30 minutes, until lightly browned. (Freezes well.) Slice to serve.

Poppy Seed Filling:

After mixing poppy seeds and sugar with a little hot coffee to make a sticky paste, place a little at a time in a mortar and pestle and mash the poppy seeds. Place in a bowl and mix with rest of ingredients. Roll out as directed for apple filling and spread poppy seed mixture over, leaving a ¼ inch border of dough. Roll up as for jelly roll; make slashes, and brush with egg white. Bake as directed for Apple Strudel. (Freezes well.) Slice to serve.

Sour Cream Dough:

Make dough by cutting butter or margarine into flour as for pie dough. Mix egg yolk with sour cream, blending well, and add to flour mixture. Gather into a ball. Place dough in a bowl; cover with plastic wrap and refrigerate for 1 hour. Divide and roll out as directed under fillings. Bake as directed.

Almond Slices (Mandle Brout)

3 eggs
1 cup sugar
⅓ cup vegetable oil
1 teaspoon vanilla
1 teaspoon orange extract
1 tablespoon orange rind
3½ cups flour
3 teaspoons baking powder
¼ teaspoon salt
½ cup coarsely chopped
almonds
¼ teaspoon almond extract
2 tablespoons cocoa

Beat eggs, then add sugar and rest of ingredients (except cocoa), making a stiff dough. Roll half the dough into a flat cake about ¼ inch thick on a lightly floured surface. Add 2 tablespoons cocoa to rest of dough, working through thoroughly. Place chocolate dough, shaped like a thick sausage, down center of the flattened dough. Wrap flat piece around chocolate sausage and overlap. Cut in half and place each half on a greased cookie sheet, seam side down. Shape to 3 inches wide. Brush with water and sprinkle with sugar. Bake in 350° oven about 45 minutes, until lightly browned. Slice into ½ inch slices while still warm. Return slices to oven to crisp and lightly brown on both sides, about 15 minutes each side. (Keeps well but does freeze.)

Coffee Rolls (Rugelach)

3 cups flour
1 package dry yeast
½ pound butter or margarine
3 egg yolks
1 cup sour cream
1 teaspoon vanilla
Apricot preserves

Mix flour, dry yeast and butter like pie dough, cutting butter into dry ingredients to crumbly consistency. Add egg yolks, beaten with sour cream and vanilla, and mix well. Place in refrigerator overnight. Next morning, mix:

1 cup sugar   1 cup pecans, finely chopped
4 teaspoons cinnamon

Cut dough into 4 parts. Roll each piece of dough in sugar-nut mixture, rolling mixture well into dough. Roll out each part into circle and cut each circle into 16 parts; first cut in half, then in quarters, then in eighths and then in sixteenths. Roll up each single piece from wide part down to point. You will end up with a little horn-shaped pastry. Place on lightly greased cookie sheet and bake until light brown in 350° oven, approximately 20 minutes. Remove from pan at once and cool on rack. Keeps well for a few days. (Freezes well. May be spread with apricot preserves before cutting.

Little Cakes

1 package dry yeast
4 cups flour
2 teaspoons baking powder
4 tablespoons sugar
½ cup butter or margarine
⅔ cup sour cream or yogurt
⅔ cup milk
3 egg yolks

Add dry yeast to other dry ingredients and mix well. Cut in butter or margarine as for pie, until very crumbly. Combine sour cream or yogurt with milk and egg yolks, mixing well. Add to flour mixture and gather pastry into a ball. Divide pastry ball into 4 parts and wrap each in plastic wrap. Place in refrigerator for 1 hour. Take out dough and roll, 1 ball at a time, into a large oblong about ¼ inch thick on a well floured surface. Melt ¼ pound butter or margarine and brush over surface of rolled out dough. Fill.

Cocoa Filling: Cinnamon Filling:

¾ cup sugar   1 cup sugar
5-6 teaspoons cocoa   1 teaspoon cinnamon
3 egg whites, beaten stiff   Chopped pecans
                                 ¼ cup raisins (optional)

Mix ingredients for either filling and spread over buttered dough about ¼ inch thick. Roll up as for jelly roll and cut into 2-inch pieces. Pinch the cut ends of 1 side of dough together and place, with pinched side down, on a greased cookie sheet. Bake at 350° for 35-45 minutes. (Freezes well.)

Cottage Cheese Pie (Keeze Kuchen)

Crust:

4   tablespoons shortening
1   egg, beaten
5   tablespoons water
1   cup flour
1   teaspoon baking powder
½   teaspoon salt

Cream shortening and add beaten egg and water. Sift dry ingredients together and gradually add to other mixture, mixing until smooth. Line 11-inch or two 9-inch pie plates with dough, patting it in.

Filling:

2¼ cups cottage cheese, put through food mill or food processor
3   tablespoons sifted flour
½   teaspoon salt
3   tablespoons sour cream
4   eggs, separated
1⅓ cups sugar
1½ teaspoons cinnamon
1½ tablespoons melted butter
1½ teaspoons vanilla
⅓   cup raisins (optional)
⅓   cup chopped almonds (optional)

Mix cottage cheese with flour, salt and sour cream. Beat egg yolks and add sugar. Add to cheese mixture. Add cinnamon, melted butter, vanilla and stir in raisins and nuts, if you are using them. Beat egg whites until stiff and fold into cheese mixture. Pour into pie crust and bake in 325° oven for 1 hour and 15 minutes for 11-inch pie or 40 minutes for the two 9-inch pies or until firm. Cool and refrigerate. (Freezes well.)

Coffee Cake

1   cup sugar
1   cup butter
3   eggs, well beaten
1   cup sour cream
½   teaspoon baking soda
1½ teaspoons vanilla
3   cups flour
3   teaspoons baking powder
½   teaspoon salt

Streusel Mixture:

½   cup brown sugar
2   tablespoons flour
2   tablespoons melted butter
½   cup finely chopped nuts
2   teaspoons cinnamon

Mix the sugar and butter until soft cream; then add well beaten eggs. Mix sour cream, baking soda and vanilla and add to egg mixture, mixing well. Sift dry ingredients and add to other mixture, blending well, beating 5 minutes. Grease well a 10-inch tube pan. Make streusel and reserve 2 tablespoons. Pour half of cake batter into pan, then half of the rest of the Streusel mixture, sprinkling well over all. Add rest of cake batter and sprinkle top with remaining Streusel mixture. Bake in 375° oven for 35 minutes. Remove cake from oven and sprinkle reserved 2 tablespoons Streusel over cracks and rest of cake. Return to oven and bake 15-20 minutes, until cake tests done. Cool on rack before removing from pan. (Freezes well.)

Yeast Dough Coffee Cake (Babka)

½ cup warm milk
2 yeast cakes or packages
   of yeast
½ cup sugar
½ pound butter
3 eggs, separated
1 teaspoon vanilla
1 teaspoon almond extract
1 cup sour cream
4 cups flour
1 teaspoon baking powder
1 cup sugar
2 teaspoons cinnamon
   Raisins
1 (8 ounce) can crushed
   pineapple, drained

Stir yeast into warm milk; add 1 tablespoon of the sugar and set aside. Cream butter and rest of the half cup of sugar. Add egg yolks, vanilla, almond extract and sour cream, blending well. Add flour and baking powder mixed together alternately with the warm milk-yeast mixture and mix thoroughly. Cover and refrigerate overnight. Next morning, beat egg whites until stiff, gradually adding ½ cup of the sugar. Mix other ½ cup of sugar and cinnamon together. Roll out dough on lightly floured surface to ¼ inch thick in a large rectangle. Spread with beaten egg white and then sprinkle with sugar and cinnamon mixture; sprinkle with raisins and drained pineapple (if using) over all. Roll like jelly roll and cut into 6 pieces. Place pieces in 10-inch tube pan, cut side up. Cover and place in warm spot, free from drafts, and allow to rise for 1 hour. Bake in 350° oven for 1½ hours. Cool before removing from pan. (Freezes well.)

Honey Drops (Taglichs)

Syrup: (To be boiling while making dough.)

2½ cups honey
2½ cups sugar
½ teaspoon ginger

Put into largest size pot which has tight fitting cover. Bring to boil over medium heat, being careful not to scorch.

Dough:

9 eggs, beaten well
2 tablespoons oil
4 cups flour (more if needed)
⅛ teaspoon ginger
½ cup seeded raisins
   Nuts or coconut, finely
   ground (optional)

Beat eggs until very fluffy and add rest of ingredients to make a soft dough. Turn out on floured surface. Add a little flour if necessary as the dough should be stiff enough to be rolled between the floured palms of your hands. Pinch off walnut-size pieces of dough and roll into ropes about 3 inches long and ½ inch thick; loop and make a loose knot. Place an extra raisin in the center of the knot if desired. Set aside. Makes about 40-50. When all dough is formed, drop pieces into boiling syrup, one at a time, trying not to place one on top of another. Cover and lower heat to maintain a gentle boil. Boil for 40 minutes, being very careful not to burn. Shake pot gently occasionally. After 40 minutes remove cover and remove pot from heat. Immediately pour in 1½ cups boiling water. Allow Honey Drops to stay in syrup for 7-8 hours or overnight. Lift out and drain. Roll in finely ground nuts or coconut if desired or keep in a tightly covered jar with some of the syrup keeping them moist. Save remaining syrup for sweetening other foods, e.g. Carrot or Prune Tzimmes (see pages 146-147) or to make Honey Cake (see page 164).

Poppy Seed Triangles (Hats) (Hamantashen)

Filling:

1½ cups poppy seeds
3 tablespoons butter
¾ cup finely chopped nuts
¾ cup cut up raisins
1½ cups milk
3 tablespoons candied fruit, chopped
6 tablespoons honey
1½ teaspoons vanilla

Pour boiling water over poppy seeds to cover; allow to stand until cool. Drain off water and crush seeds in mortar with a pestle. Mix with the following 6 ingredients and simmer gently over low heat until very thick, stirring frequently. Cool and add vanilla.

Yeast Dough: (Baking Powder Dough follows. Use either.)

Make dough as for Yeast Dough Coffee Cake (see page 162), saving egg whites for other uses. Next morning, roll dough on lightly floured surface to about ⅛ inch thick. Cut into rounds about 3 inches in diameter. Wet edges of dough lightly with water. Place a tablespoon of filling on each round, spreading to ¼ inch from edges. Draw edges up on 3 sides to form an open triangle in the center of each, pinching ends of dough together. Place on lightly greased cookie sheets and brush with an egg beaten with 2 tablespoons cold water. Allow to rise in a warm place, without drafts, for 1 hour. Bake in 325° oven for 20-30 minutes, until cakes are rich, glossy, and golden brown. Cool on racks. (Freezes well.)

Baking Powder Dough:

2¼ cups flour
2 teaspoons baking powder
1 teaspoon salt
½ cup sugar
¼ cup melted butter
1 egg, beaten
¾ cup milk

Sift dry ingredients together. Make a well and put in liquids. Mix well and place on lightly floured surface; knead 3 minutes. Roll dough thin and cut in rounds about 3 inches in diameter. Place tablespoon of filling in center of each round. Wet edges of dough lightly with water. Draw edges up on 3 sides to form an open triangle in the center of each. Place on well greased cookie sheets and brush with egg and 2 tablespoons milk, beaten together. Bake in 375° oven to a rich, glossy and golden brown. Cool on racks. (Freezes well.)

Carrot Candy (Emberlarches) — Passover

3 pounds carrots, ground
3 pounds (6 cups) sugar
3 teaspoons ginger
1 cup chopped nuts

Grind carrots through meat grinder or food processor. Place in large pot with sugar and mix well. Put in 350° oven, stir occasionally; bake until very thick, about 2½-4 hours. Add ginger and nuts and mix well. Turn out on wet surface and spread to about ¾ inch thick. Allow to air dry for a day or two. Then cut as fudge into small squares.

Honey Cake

3 ½ cups flour
2 ½ teaspoons baking powder
1 teaspoon baking soda
½ teaspoon salt
1 teaspoon cinnamon
½ teaspoon ground cloves
¼ teaspoon ginger
1 cup sugar
3 eggs, separated
¼ cup oil
1 ⅓ cups honey, left from Honey Drops or pure honey
1 ⅓ cups warm black coffee
1 teaspoon vanilla
¼ teaspoon cream of tartar
Almonds for garnish

Mix dry ingredients and sift into mixing bowl. Make a well and add egg yolks, oil, honey, coffee and vanilla. Beat until blended and smooth. Add cream of tartar to egg whites and beat until stiff. Gently fold first mixture into egg whites, blending with a rubber spatula. Do not beat or stir. Pour batter into ungreased 10-inch tube pan and garnish with almonds. Bake in 350° oven for 50-60 minutes. Cake is done when it springs back when lightly touched with finger. Invert pan to cool. Remove after cooling. (Freezes well.)

Passover Sponge Cake (1)

8 eggs, separated
1 ½ cups sugar
⅓ cup orange juice
1 cup sifted Passover cake flour
⅛ teaspoon salt
1 teaspoon orange bits

Beat whites of eggs to very stiff, but not dry, add ¾ cup sugar very gradually, beating all the while and set aside. Beat egg yolks to lemon colored. Add ¾ cup sugar and beat to almost white. Add rest of ingredients, blending well, very thoroughly and gently. Fold in beaten whites, folding and lifting until all is blended thoroughly. Pour into 10-inch tube pan. Bake in 350° oven for 1 hour or until cake springs back when lightly touched with a finger. Invert to cool. (Freezes well.)

Passover Sponge Cake (2)

9 eggs, separated
1 ¾ cups sugar
1 cup less 1 ½ tablespoons potato starch
2 tablespoons lemon juice
3 teaspoons lemon rind

Separate white and yolks of eggs. Beat whites of the eggs very stiff; set aside. Beat the 9 egg yolks well; add sugar, lemon juice and rind, blending thoroughly. Add potato starch and beat again mixing through completely and gently. Fold in beaten whites carefully with a rubber spatula. Pour into 10-inch tube pan. Bake in 350° oven 40-50 minutes or until cake springs back when touched with finger. Invert and cool. (Freezes well.)

אל ישראל ישראל ישראל ישראל ישראל ישראל

Dessert Pancakes (Matzo Chrimsels) — Passover

4 matzos, soaked
3 tablespoons seeded raisins, chopped
3 tablespoons chopped almonds
4 eggs, separated
1 cup sugar
1¼ teaspoons vanilla

Prunes
Sugar
Orange juice

Crumble matzos and pour hot water to cover them. Allow to stand few minutes and then squeeze out excess moisture. Beat egg whites and set aside. Add rest of ingredients to soaked matzos. Fold in egg whites. Drop from tablespoon into hot butter and fry until golden on both sides. Place on large platter in slow oven to keep warm. Serve with Prune Sauce.

Prune Sauce:

Stew prunes with a little sugar and orange juice until tender. Cool to lukewarm and puree in blender. Taste and adjust flavor.

Beet Conserves (Aingermachs) — Passover

3 pounds beets or 4 (12 ounce) cans shoestring beets, drained
1 pound honey
1 pound sugar
¼ teaspoon ginger to taste
1 cup whole almonds

Cut beets into shoestring strips if using fresh; wash and cook in water to cover ½ hour. Drain beets; add honey; cook over low heat 10 minutes. Add sugar, ginger and almonds; mix well. Cook, stirring occasionally, until mixture is thick and beets are brown. Place in hot sterile jars. Serve as accompaniment to meat or serve for dessert with Sponge Cake (see page 164).

Butter Coffee Cakes (Putter Kuchen)

1 cup lukewarm milk
1 tablespoon salt
1 cup sugar
2 yeast cakes or packages of yeast
3 eggs, beaten
½ pound sweet butter, melted
⅞ cup sour cream
6-7 cups flour
Sugar, cinnamon, raisins and nuts or
Apricot jam

Mix together lukewarm milk, salt and sugar. Add yeast and stir until yeast is dissolved. Mix in eggs, melted butter and sour cream. (My cousin Constance adds a teaspoon of vanilla here.) First with a wooden spoon and then by hand add flour in two additions, adding enough to make a soft dough that is easy to handle. When mixed thoroughly, turn onto a lightly floured surface and knead until dough is smooth and elastic and doesn't stick to surface. Place in a lightly greased bowl, turning once to bring greased side up. Cover bowl first with plastic wrap and then with a towel. Let rise in warm place until double in size. Push down and roll out on either a floured or sugared surface. Brush with melted butter and sprinkle with sugar, cinnamon, raisins and nuts or apricot jam. Roll up as for a jelly roll. Cut in 2-inch pieces; place on a cookie sheet and cover lightly with a cloth for another 15 minutes. Bake in 350° oven until richly browned. (Freezes well.)

Passover Macaroons

1 cup egg whites, beaten stiff
2 cups sugar, added gradually
½ teaspoon salt
4 tablespoons matzo cake flour
¼ teaspoon almond flavoring
1 teaspoon vanilla extract
5 cups flaked coconut

Add sugar gradually to stiffly beaten egg whites, beating well. Fold in rest of ingredients. Drop by tablespoons on waxed paper-lined pans. Bake in 325° oven 15 minutes or until lightly colored. Remove with spatula and cool on racks.

Wine and Nut Cake — Passover

8 eggs, separated
1½ cups sugar
¼ cup orange juice
½ cup wine, red sweet
¾ cup sifted Passover cake flour
⅛ teaspoon salt
2 cups finely ground nuts

Separate eggs, and beat whites until stiff and glossy, gradually adding ¾ cups of sugar; set aside. Beat yolks and add ¾ cup sugar and the rest of the ingredients, beating well. Gently fold yolk mixture into beaten egg whites. Pour into 10-inch tube pan. Bake in 350° oven for 45-50 minutes or until cake springs back when touched with finger. Invert and cool. (Freezes well.)

Cream Puffs for Passover

1 cup water
½ cup butter or margarine
1 cup potato starch
½ teaspoon salt
4 eggs

Bring water and butter or margarine to a boil. Dump in potato starch and salt all at once; cook, stirring constantly, until dough leaves sides of pan. Remove from heat and add unbeaten eggs, one at a time, beating well after each addition. Drop by tablespoonful onto ungreased cookie sheets about 2½ inches apart. Bake in 450° oven for 20 minutes, lower heat to 325° and bake another 30 minutes. Cool; slit and fill either with flavored and sweetened whipped cream of custard filling.

Custard Filling:

1½ cups sugar
2 tablespoons potato flour or cornstarch
4 eggs, well beaten
Juice of 2 lemons
2 teaspoons butter or margarine
2 cups water

Mix sugar and potato flour or cornstarch; add to well beaten eggs, stirring constantly. Add lemon juice, butter and water and cook in top of double boiler, stirring occasionally, until thick. Cool before using. Makes 1 dozen Cream Puffs.

אלישראלישראלישראלישראלישראלישראלישראל

Italian

Antipasto

Greens
Thinly sliced red onions
Celery, thinly sliced
Fennel, julienned
Sliced tomatoes
Sliced radishes or fancy
    whole radishes
Olives, green or ripe
Salami
Prosciutto
Capicollo
Anchovies
Provolone
Tuna Fish
Mackerel in olive oil

Wash and dry greens on paper toweling. In a large bowl or on a large platter make a bed of the greens, tomatoes and radishes; cover with celery. Top with attractive groupings of olives, cubes of salami and/or prosciutto and/or capicollo, anchovies, cubes of provolone, tuna fish and/or mackerel. Dress with the following just before sering.

³⁄₄	cup olive oil	¼	teaspoon coarsely ground
¼	cup wine vinegar		black pepper
2-3	cloves garlic, crushed	½	teaspoon salt

Shake well; keep in tightly covered jar at room temperature.

Cheese Puffs (Bigne al Formaggio)

1   cup water
½   cup butter
½   teaspoon salt
1   cup flour
5   eggs
⅓   cup grated Parmesan cheese
⅓   cup minced prosciutto or
     capicollo
     Olive oil

Combine water, butter and salt in a saucepan; bring to a boil. Remove pan from heat and add flour all at one time; stir vigorously until dough is smooth. Return pan to fire and cook, stirring constantly, until dough leaves the side of pan and forms a ball. Remove from heat and add eggs, one at a time, mixing well after each is added. Blend in cheese and prosciutto and/or capicollo. Heat olive oil for deep frying to 375°. Drop by half teaspoonfuls into hot oil and fry until light brown. Drain on paper toweling. Serve hot or cold.

Anchovy Marinated Deviled Eggs

8   hard boiled eggs
2   (½ ounce) cans fillet of
     anchovies, chopped
1   clove garlic, crushed
¼   cup finely chopped
     parsley, flat leaf type
½   cup olive oil
¼   cup wine vinegar
     Dash of coarse ground
     pepper

Combine anchovies, garlic, parsley, oil, vinegar and pepper, making a thin sauce. Cut eggs lengthwise and place on serving dish; pour sauce over egg halves and allow to marinate at least half a day. May be made several days ahead and allowed to marinate.

Shrimp Scampi

2 pounds cleaned and de-
  veined large Shrimp
  Water to cover
1½ teaspoons salt
¾ cup olive oil
1 medium diced onion
7-8 cloves garlic, crushed
2 tablespoons chopped
  parsley
¾ teaspoon salt
¼ teaspoon pepper
½ teaspoon oregano
3 cloves garlic, crushed
¾ cup lemon juice

Cook shrimp in water to cover with 1½ teaspoons salt until shrimp are just tender, about 3 minutes. (Shrimp are of a better texture if they are heavily salted and allowed to stand in a colander for 20 minutes, then rinsed very well before cooking.) Drain shrimp after cooking and refrigerate until just before using as the time involved in preparing is just a few minutes. Heat olive oil to 350° in an electric frying pan and add diced onion and saute until golden. Add shrimp and 7-8 cloves crushed garlic, parsley, salt, pepper and oregano. Simmer, stirring constantly for about 3 minutes. Add the 3 cloves crushed garlic and lemon juice; cook, stirring constantly for 2-3 more seconds. Serve with sauce on little cocktail plates or with toothpicks to simplify eating.

Spaghetti Carbonara

6 strips sliced fresh or cured
  bacon, finely diced
4 eggs, well beaten
½ teaspoon salt
¼ teaspoon pepper
6 tablespoons grated
  Parmesan cheese
2 cloves garlic, crushed
2 tablespoons chopped
  parsley, flat leaf type
  if possible
2 tablespoons rendered
  bacon fat
12 cups water
1 tablespoon olive oil
1 pound spaghetti
4 tablespoons sweet butter,
  melted

Fry fresh or cured diced bacon in skillet, stirring until all is browned and crisp. Remove from heat and remove bacon with slotted spoon; drain on paper towel; cover with another paper towel and keep at room temperature. Break eggs into a medium size bowl; add next 6 ingredients, mixing well; refrigerate. Bring to room temperature while boiling spaghetti. Bring 12 cups water to a boil; add olive oil and spaghetti and boil uncovered, stirring occasionally for 8 minutes. Drain and place in a casserole, tossing with 4 tablespoons melted butter. To serve beat egg mixture thoroughly and toss with bacon bits through hot, drained spaghetti. Serve immediately allowing about 1 cup per portion.

Crisp Vegetables Dipped in Hot Spicy Sauce (Bagna Calda)

4   celery hearts, cut in half
      lengthwise
4   endive, cut in quarters
1   head cauliflower or
      broccoli, stalks and
      flowers cut into ½ inch
      strips
1   cup fennel, cut in julienne
4   large carrots, cut to match
      stick lengths
2   green peppers, cut in
      1-inch strips
1   package frozen artichoke
      hearts, cooked as directed,
      drained well or 1 can
      artichoke hearts, drained
      Italian breadsticks

Prepare fresh vegetables and refrigerate in ice water until just before serving time. Arrange attractively at serving time with bread sticks along side if desired.

Hot Spicy Sauce:

½   stick (¼ cup) butter, melted
6-8 cloves garlic, crushed
8   flat anchovies, chopped
¼   pound finely chopped
      fresh mushrooms
1   cup heavy cream, warmed
      Few grains red pepper
      Few dried basil leaves,
      crumbled

Simmer melted butter and crushed garlic for a few minutes and then strain. Return butter to pan and add rest of ingredients, stirring to blend well. Heat thoroughly but do not boil. Place hot sauce in a small chafing dish or fondue pot over low heat. Serve next to vegetables and bread sticks for dipping.

Rice and Tomato Soup

1   cup mashed potatoes
3   tablespoons butter
½   cup chopped onion
1   clove garlic, crushed
1   cup rice
1   pound can tomatoes
12 cups meat stock, hot
2   teaspoons salt
½   teaspoon white pepper
¼   teaspoon oregano
½   cup grated Parmesan cheese

Melt shortening and brown onion to golden. Add garlic and rice and simmer gently, stirring constantly, for 3 minutes. Add tomatoes and simmer for 10 minutes. Add hot stock; season and simmer gently for 1 hour. Taste and adjust seasonings. Skim off fat. Serve with grated Parmesan cheese.

Miniature Fresh Tomato Pizzas

1   package granulated yeast
      or yeast cake
¼   cup lukewarm water
4   cups flour
1   teaspoon salt
4   tablespoons shortening
2   eggs, well beaten
⅔   cup milk

Dissolve yeast in lukewarm water. Sift flour and salt together; cut in shortening to fine consistency. Make well and add yeast mixture, beaten eggs and milk. Mix well with hands, adding a little more flour if dough seems sticky. Turn out on lightly floured surface and allow to stand 10 minutes. Knead a few minutes and then place in a large greased bowl, turning dough so greased dough will be on top. Cover with plastic wrap and a towel and place in a warm spot. Allow to rise until dough is double in size, about 2 hours. Remove from bowl to lightly floured surface; knead down and roll out not more than ¼ inch thick. Cut dough into circles about 3 inches in diameter. Place circles on waxed paper and top with the following:

Olive oil	Mozzarella cheese
Ripe tomatoes, peeled, seeded and chopped	Pepperoni, anchovy fillets, mushrooms and sliced
Salt and pepper	onion
Oregano and sweet basil	Finely diced green pepper

Lightly brush top of each pizza with a little olive oil. Spread chopped tomatoes finely over oil. Salt and pepper and sprinkle with a little oregano and sweet basil. Place small pieces of cheese on pizza and then top with any of the following: pepperoni, anchovy fillets, mushrooms or sliced onions, and green pepper, as desired. Brush all lightly with a little more olive oil. Place on lightly greased baking pans and bake in 400° oven for 10-12 minutes or until cheese just melts and pizza dough is a light golden in color. Serve hot. (Freezes excellently. Cool to freeze; pack in airtight containers. Reheat frozen on lightly greased pans in 350° oven for 8-10 minutes.) Makes about 80.

Prosciutto and Melon

Melon
Prosciutto ham

Remove melon seeds; cut in small spears. Cut off peel and wrap each spear with a small thin slice of prosciutto, fastened with a pick.

Pasta with Basil Sauce (Pesto Genevise)

1 cup chopped fresh sweet basil or ½ cup home dried basil
2 cloves garlic
¼ cup pine nuts
4 tablespoons grated Parmesan cheese
1 cup olive oil
12 cups water
1 tablespoon olive oil
1 pound linguine
4 tablespoons melted sweet butter

Place basil, garlic, pine nuts, Parmesan cheese and olive oil in a blender and blend to make a thin paste. Keep in tightly covered jar at room temperature. Bring water to a boil and add the tablespoon of olive oil and the linguine. Boil, uncovered, stirring occasionally, for 8 minutes. Drain and place in a casserole with melted sweet butter. Before serving, toss pasta lightly, add ingredients from the jar and toss thoroughly. Serve immediately allowing about 1 cup per portion.

Stuffed Olives and Garlic

6 cloves garlic, sliced
1 jar stuffed olives

Place a half dozen cloves of garlic, sliced, in a jar of stuffed olives the day before using.

Linguine with White Clam Sauce (Linguine con Salsa alle Vongole)

3 dozen little neck clams
¾ cup olive oil
4 cloves garlic, finely chopped
¾ cup water
3 teaspoons chopped parsley, flat leaf type if possible
1 teaspoon salt
1 teaspoon oregano
¼ teaspoon white pepper

Brush clams with stiff brush under running water. Steam over ½ inch bubbling water, covered, until all clams open. Remove clams from shells, saving liquids, and chop clams coarsely. Add enough of the juices to chopped clams to make 3 cups chopped clams and juice. Heat oil and add garlic; cook 1 minute; add rest of ingredients including chopped clams and juice; heat through. May be made a day ahead and reheated to hot very gently just before using.

1 pound linguine
4 quarts boiling water
1 teaspoon olive oil
2 tablespoons butter

Linguine:
Break linguine in half and drop into boiling water and olive oil. Boil gently, uncovered, for 8 minutes or test doneness by scooping a piece of linguine on wooden spoon. If if sticks, linguine is done. Drain in colander and return to pot; stir through the butter and cover tightly. Toss hot sauce through linguine, mixing well. Serve about 1 cupful per person.

Snails alla Roma

48 large canned snails, rinsed and drained
3 tablespoons olive oil
4 cloves garlic, crushed
2 tablespoons chopped parsley, flat leaf type preferred
8 flat anchovies, chopped
4 tomatoes, peeled, seeded and chopped
1 canned or fresh yellow or red pepper, cut into dice
½ teaspoon salt
¼ teaspoon pepper
⅛ teaspoon crushed red pepper

Heat olive oil in skillet over medium heat and add garlic; cook until golden. Add next 4 ingredients and mix well. Add salt, pepper, and crushed red pepper; simmer gently 20 minutes. Add snails and stir thoroughly. Fill small snail shells, placing one snail in each shell and putting shell in snail plates. Place snail plates on cookie sheets and refrigerate or freeze. Place in 350° oven for 10-15 minutes if refrigerated or for 20-25 minutes if frozen, to heat to hot and bubbly. Do not overcook.

Mushrooms Parmesan (Funghi alla Parmigiana)

1½ pounds mushrooms, medium size
6 tablespoons olive oil
⅔ cup chopped onions
4 cloves garlic, crushed
2 tablespoons finely chopped parsley
⅔ cup Parmesan cheese
1 teaspoon salt
1 teaspoon oregano
Dash of red pepper
2 cups fine dried bread crumbs

Wash mushrooms; remove stems and drain caps on paper toweling. Finely chop stems and gently fry in olive oil for about 3 minutes. Add chopped onion and crushed garlic and cook slowly until onions are lightly browned. Add rest of ingredients, stirring lightly with a fork all the while. Remove from heat. Pile mixture lightly into mushroom caps, rounding tops rather highly. Place on cookie sheet which has been greased with olive oil. May be made to this point and refrigerated. Just before serving time, bake in 400° oven for 15-20 minutes, until lightly browned. (Finely chopped anchovies may be added to the stuffing if desired.)

Chicken and Spinach Egg Soup with Prosciutto

12 cups chicken broth
3 (10 ounce) packages
 spinach, cleaned, stems
 removed and coarsely
 chopped or 3 packages
 frozen chopped spinach
3 eggs
6 teaspoons flour
12 tablespoons grated
 Parmesan cheese
½ teaspoon salt
¼ teaspoon white pepper
⅓ pound prosciutto, cut
 in julienne

Simmer broth and spinach gently for 10 minutes. Beat eggs until thick and add flour, cheese, salt and pepper. Remove soup from heat and add 2 cups to egg mixture, blending well. Slowly pour egg mixture into broth, stirring constantly. Continue stirring and return to heat for 5 minutes. (Freezes very well; be sure to allow several inches of air space on top of container for expansion. Defrost and heat.) Garnish with stripes of prosciutto to serve.

Red Bean Soup with Cheese Puffs

1 pound red kidney beans,
 soaked overnight in cold
 water to cover
1 large onion
1 carrot
1 celery heart
1 bay leaf
½ teaspoon black peppercorns
¼ teaspoon marjoram
¼ teaspoon savory
2 large soup bones
12 cups water
1½ cups heavy cream

Drain beans and put on to simmer with next 9 ingredients. Simmer gently for 3-4 hours, stirring occasionally. Remove soup bones and put soup through food mill or food processor. Skim off fat and return soup to pot. Reheat and gradually add heavy cream, stirring all the time. Season highly with salt and pepper; remove from heat and keep tightly covered until time to serve. (May be frozen before adding cream. Defrost; heat; add cream and proceed.)

Cream Puffs:

½ cup water
½ cup butter
¼ teaspoon salt
½ cup flour
2 eggs
⅓ cup grated Parmesan cheese
¼ cup minced prosciutto ham

Bring water and butter to a boil; add salt and flour all at one time. Stir with a wooden spoon until mixture leaves sides of pan. Remove from heat and stir in eggs, one at a time. Add grated Parmesan cheese and minced ham, blending thoroughly. Drop by teaspoonfuls into olive oil heated to 375° and cook until golden. Drain and place on baking sheet lined with paper towels. Keep warm in 150° oven. (May be made day ahead and reheated in 250° oven for 15-20 minutes.)

Hot or Cold Vegetable Soup (Minestrone)

⅛ pound Canadian bacon, diced
⅛ pound prosciutto ham, sliced
⅛ pound Italian hot sausage, sliced
1 cup chopped onions
1 pound fresh tomatoes, chopped
1 cup red kidney beans, washed, soaked overnight and drained
1 celery heart, diced
1 large carrot, diced
2 potatoes, diced
1 small zucchini squash, diced
¼ cut ditalini or elbow macaroni
2 cloves garlic, crushed
8 cups meat broth
1 teaspoon salt
¼ teaspoon pepper
¼ teaspoon sage
½ teaspoon oregano
1 cup finely shredded cabbage
10 ounces spinach, stems removed, and chopped coarsely
½ cup grated Parmesan cheese
1 tablespoon chopped parsley, flat type if possible

Fry bacon, ham, sausage and onions together in a little olive oil until onions are lightly browned. Add tomatoes, beans, celery, carrot, potatoes, zucchini, garlic, ditalini or elbow macaroni and broth; simmer for 1 hour. Skim off fat and season with salt, pepper, sage and oregano. Add cabbage, spinach and parsley and simmer until vegetables are cooked. Stir through with cheese. Pass extra cheese for those who wish it.

Cold Fruit Soup

1   ripe cantaloupe or any type
      muskmelon, good size,
      peeled and seeded
1   red sweet apple, unpeeled
2   peaches, peeled or
      nectarines, unpeeled
1   orange, peeled
4-5 cups buttermilk
$^2/_3$ cup water
$^3/_4$-1 cup honey
1   teaspoon curry powder
$^1/_4$ teaspoon vanilla
$^1/_4$ teaspoon almond flavoring

Put fruits, half at a time, through food processor or blender, blending until heavy mush. Pour into a large bowl and mix with rest of ingredients, adding honey to taste. Taste and add more curry powder, if desired. Cover and refrigerate; serve cold in chilled bowls. Makes 12 servings.

Chicken Soup with Potato Dumplings

5-6 pound fowl, quartered
12 cups water
3   teaspoons salt
3   stalks celery or celery heart
2   carrots
1   large onion
2   large tomatoes, quartered
      or 1 cup canned tomatoes
$^1/_4$ teaspoon thyme
$^1/_8$ teaspoon sweet basil

Clean and wash fowl and combine with rest of ingredients. Cover and bring to a boil. Skim off top scum and continue simmering gently for 2-3 hours, until chicken is tender. Remove chicken from broth and strain. Cool and remove all fat. Skin and bone chicken; cut meat into small pieces and return to soup, if desired. Serve soup hot with the following dumplings.

Dumplings:

1   cup mashed potatoes
1½ tablespoons butter
1   egg yolk
2   tablespoons grated
      Parmesan cheese
$^1/_8$ teaspoon nutmeg
      Salt to taste

Combine mashed potatoes with all ingredients. Mix thoroughly and turn out on lightly floured board. Form into strip after rolling carefully in the flour; cut into ½ inch pieces and round into balls with palms of hands. Fry in deep hot olive oil until browned. Drain on paper toweling and serve in hot soup. (May be made ahead and reheated in 325° oven for 10-15 minutes.)

Lobster, Cod or Shrimp Marinara (Aragosta/Baccala all Marinara)

¼ cup olive oil
2 cloves garlic, crushed
1 green pepper, finely chopped
½ pound mushrooms, chopped
2 tablespoons chopped parsley
1½ teaspoons salt
¼ teaspoon pepper
⅛ teaspoon red pepper
3½ cups canned tomatoes

8 lobsters *or* 8 codfish steaks *or* 3 pounds shrimp

Sauce:

Combine all ingredients and simmer gently for 1 hour.

Prepare 8 lobsters, about 1 pound each; or 8 codfish steaks dipped in a beaten egg with 1 tablespoon olive oil, breaded with ½ cornmeal and ½ flour; or 3 pounds cleaned, deveined shrimp, breaded as codfish steaks. If lobsters are used, boil live until done; split down underside and clean out. Pour Marinara sauce over still warm lobsters and serve. If cod or shrimp is used, fry steaks or shrimp in hot olive oil until golden on both sides. Drain and place in a large baking dish. Pour sauce over fish or shrimp and top with fine dried bread crumbs, dotting with butter. Bake in 350° oven for 10-15 minutes.

Basic Italian Tomato Sauce (Salsa di Pomodoro)

½ cup olive oil
1 cup chopped onion
4 cloves garlic, crushed
2 (No.2) cans Bell tomatoes
2 (6 ounce) cans tomato paste
1 cup water
1 teaspoon sugar
½ teaspoon sweet basil
¼ teaspoon thyme
½ teaspoon oregano
¼ teaspoon celery salt
2 bay leaves
1½ teaspoons salt
½ teaspoon pepper
1 tablespoon mixed grated cheeses with spices (get at Italian grocery)

Heat olive oil in large skillet and saute onion and garlic until golden. Add next 11 ingredients; break up tomatoes into small pieces with a fork. Simmer, uncovered for 1½ hours. Add mixed grated cheese with spices and simmer, stirring, for 10 minutes.

No. 1 Shrimp in Foil (Shrimp Sarapico)

Per Serving

12 inch square aluminum foil
4 tablespoons diced
   Mozzarella cheese
4 tablespoons grated
   Parmesan cheese
¼ teaspoon oregano
¼ teaspoon pepper
1 teaspoon salt
1 tablespoon lemon juice
1 tablespoon pimiento, diced
6-8 shrimp

Place all ingredients in center of aluminum foil, topping with shrimp. Close aluminum foil bag by pinching top together. Bake 30 minutes in 400° oven. To serve Shimp Sarapico, place each hot foil bag on a plate and let each guest open his own.

No. 2 Shrimp in Foil (Shrimp Sarapico)

Per Serving

12 inch square aliminum foil
4 teaspoons olive oil
2 tablespoons diced onion
¼ teaspoon oregano
2 teaspoons lemon juice
½ cup diced fresh tomato
½ teaspoon salt
⅛ teaspoon pepper
1 tablespoon diced
   Mozzarella cheese
6-8 shrimp

Fry diced onion in olive oil until lightly golden. Remove from heat; drain off oil, and place with rest of ingredients in center of aluminum foil, topping with shrimp. Close aluminum foil bag by pinching top together. Bake 30 minutes in 400° oven. To serve Shrimp Sarapico, place each hot foil bag on a plate and let each guest open his own.

Meat Balls for Spaghetti

2 pounds ground beef
2 cloves garlic, crushed
2 eggs
2 cups soft white bread
   crumbs
2 teaspoons salt
½ teaspoon pepper
2 tablespoons chopped
   parsley
2 tablespoons grated
   Parmesan or Romano
   cheese

Mix all ingredients together well. Form into small balls and brown in hot olive oil. Proceed with recipe on page 178 for sauce, add meat balls together with the grated cheese and spices. Pour all over cooked, drained spaghetti (12 ounce package). Serve with grated cheese and crushed hot peppers.

Spaghetti Roma

¾ cup diced onion
3 tablespoons olive oil
1½ pounds ground beef
3 cloves garlic, crushed
2 (3 ounce) cans broiled
    sliced mushrooms or ⅓
    pound fresh ones, sauteed
6 cups tomatoes
3 cups tomato sauce
1 cup tomato paste
¼ cup chopped parsley
2 teaspoons oregano
1½ teaspoons salt
1 teaspoon Accent
½ teaspoon thyme
¼ teaspoon pepper
2 bay leaves
1½ cups water
8 hot sausages, fried rich
    brown, drained on paper
    towels, sliced
1 (12 ounce) package spa-
    ghetti, boiled and drained

In a large skillet, saute onion in hot oil until almost tender and lightly golden. Add ground beef and garlic; brown lightly. Add mushrooms with their liquid; stir in rest of ingredients, except spaghetti and sausages. Simmer gently, uncovered, for 2 or 3 hours, until thick. Remove bay leaves; add hot sausages and simmer 10 more minutes. Serve over hot spaghetti with Romano or Parmesan cheese, grated, and crushed red hot peppers.

Liver and Bell Pepper (Fegato con Peperoni)

2½ pounds baby beef
    liver, cut into thin
    slices, or chicken
    livers, halved
6 Bell peppers (green), diced
3 cloves garlic, sliced
1 large onion, diced finely
1½ teaspoons chopped
    parsley
1½ teaspoons salt
½ teaspoon pepper
1 large can Italian style
    peeled tomatoes

Dredge liver in flour. Put olive oil in large frying pan to ¼ inch deep and heat to piping hot. Fry liver, browning quickly on both sides. Add diced peppers, garlic, onion, parsley, salt and pepper and saute for about 5 minutes, until onions are lightly golden, stirring frequently. Add tomatoes and simmer about 20 minutes. Serve with Saffron Rice (see page 189).

Stuffed Beef Rolls in Tomato Sauce (Brociole)

8	slices top round steak, cut very thin
4	ounces salt pork
4	cloves garlic, crushed
½	cup celery tops
1	cup chopped parsley
1	cup fine dried bread crumbs
1	cup grated Parmesan cheese
1	teaspoon coarse black pepper
1	recipe Basic Italian Tomato Sauce (see page 178)
1½	cups macaroni

Put through grinder or food processor the salt pork, garlic and celery tops. Add next 3 ingredients and blend well. Spread each slice of steak thinly with salt pork mixture; roll up tightly; tie firmly with string. Sear in hot skillet in which you have placed olive oil to ⅛ inch depth and a clove of crushed garlic. Brown rolls on all sides. Add tomato sauce and simmer gently on top of stove for 1 hour or place in 325° oven for the same length of time. To serve, boil about 1½ cups macaroni until tender, about 20 minutes; drain and rinse in hot water. Place on platter with meat; sprinkle thickly with grated cheese and spread with tomato sauce from the meat. Serve with more cheese.

Chicken Florentine (Pollo alla Florentina)

2	frying chickens
4	tablespoons olive oil
6	tablespoons lemon juice
2	cloves garlic, crushed
2	teaspoons rosemary, crushed
1	cup flour
2	teaspoons salt
¼	teaspoon pepper
1	tablespoon parsley flakes
½	teaspoon dried sweet basil
1	cup olive oil
4	tablespoons olive oil
2	cloves garlic, sliced thinly
6	tablespoons Marsala dry wine
2	tablespoons chopped fresh parsley
1½	cups Basic Tomato Sauce (see page 178)

Place 2 frying chickens, cut in serving size pieces. Rinse and dry chicken pieces. In a plastic bag mix marinade and add chicken pieces. Seal tightly and allow to marinate at least four hours in refrigerator, turning bag occasionally.

In a plastic bag, mix flour, salt, pepper, parsley flakes and dried basil. Remove chicken from marinade and wipe gently with paper towels. Drop chicken pieces into flour mixture in plastic bag and coat evenly; shake off excess flour. Heat the cup of olive oil in a heavy skillet and gently fry chicken pieces, placing them skin down first, to a rich golden brown. When browned, place chicken one layer deep in a baking dish; set aside. Heat 4 tablespoons olive oil and fry garlic to a light brown. Remove from heat and stir in Marsala wine, parsley and tomato sauce. Spoon mixture over chicken in baking dish. Bake at 325° for about 45 minutes, covered, until thickest pieces of chicken are tender. Serve with fettucine with butter and anchovies. (Chicken freezes well. To reheat, place in 350° oven frozen for about 1 hour or until hot.)

Chicken Breasts Milanese

4   chicken breasts, boned
     and halved
2   eggs, beaten
¼   teaspoon salt
¼   teaspoon pepper
     Dried fine bread crumbs
1   cup olive oil
8   slices prosciutto or 8 slices
     Canadian bacon
8   slices Mozzarella cheese
16 tablespoons Basic Tomato
     Sauce (see page 178)

Beat eggs and add seasonings. Wipe chicken breasts and dip into beaten egg mixture and then coat with bread crumbs. Heat olive oil and fry chicken breasts gently and brown well on all sides. Drain on paper toweling. Place in greased baking pan. (Freeze at this point if desired; defrost and then proceed.) Top each piece with the prosciutto or Canadian bacon, then cover with a slice of Mozzarella cheese. Refrigerate until ready to bake. Bake in 350° oven for about 20 minutes or until cheese melts and is lightly golden. Serve topped with 2 tablespoons of hot Basic Tomato Sauce on each serving.

Kidney Beans, Macaroni and Sausage (Pasta e Fagioli)

1½ cups white kidney beans,
     soaked overnight in water
     to cover
8   Italian Hot Sausages, cut
     in quarters
1   medium onion, diced finely
3-4 cloves garlic, sliced finely
1   (16 ounce) can tomato
     paste
2½ cups water
2   tablespoons grated
     Parmesan cheese
1   teaspoon oregano
1   teaspoon salt
½   teaspoon black pepper
1   teaspoon fennel or anise
     seed
1   teaspoon celery seed
12 ounces small macaroni

Boil soaked beans until tender; drain, saving 1 cup of liquid. Place sausage in dry pan over medium heat. Cook, stirring occasionally until lightly browned all over and fat rendered. In sausage grease add onion and garlic and cook, stirring, until onions are lightly browned. Add tomato paste, water and rest of ingredients, except macaroni. Cook, covered, over low heat for one hour. Just before sauce is ready boil macaroni until done as you like it; drain. Add all to beans and cup of bean liquid and lightly mix together thoroughly. Serve hot and pass extra grated cheese for those who desire it. (Freezes well. Heat in covered casserole in 325° oven until hot.)

Veal Scaloppine with Marsala (Scaloppine di Vitello al Marsala)

2 pounds veal steak, ½ inch thick, cut in 3-inch pieces and flattened as much as possible
1 cup flour
1 teaspoon salt
¼ teaspoon pepper
¼ pound butter
½ pound mushrooms, quartered
½ cup (dry) Marsala wine

Put flour, salt and pepper in a bag. Toss in pieces of veal; shake and coat well. Melt butter in a large skillet and fry veal at 360° until golden brown, about 3 minutes each side. Add mushrooms and saute 2 minutes. Add Marsala and simmer for 2 more minutes. (Prepare just before serving.)

Veal Shanks (Ossobuco) Milanese

10 (2½ inch thick) slices of veal shank, with meat surrounding each bone
Flour
¼ pound sweet butter
3 tablespoons olive oil
1 teaspoon salt
¼ teaspoon pepper
1½ cups dry white wine
4 tablespoons butter
1 cup diced onion
½ cup diced carrots
½ cup diced celery
1 teaspoon sliced garlic
3½ cups chicken broth
2 cups peeled, seeded tomatoes
1 tablespoon chopped parsley
1 bay leaf
1 teaspoon thyme
½ cup chopped parsley
1 tablespoon minced garlic
Grated rind of 2 lemons

Rinse and wipe slices of veal shanks; tie securely and dust lightly with flour. Heat butter and olive oil in a large skillet until bubbly. Add shanks and fry slowly until brown on both sides. Sprinkle with salt and pepper. Remove to a large baking dish. Gradually add wine to skillet, scraping bottom to loosen all the particles; reduce to ½ cup and reserve. Fry the following 4 ingredients in 4 tablespoons butter until soft. Add to veal with the reduced wine mixture and chicken broth. Add peeled and seeded tomatoes, spreading over veal. Add the tablespoon chopped parsley, thyme and bay leaf. Simmer in 325° oven covered for 2 hours. Transfer veal to ovenproof serving dish, removing strings; keep warm. Strain pan juices and cook over high heat to reduce to about 2½ cups; pour over veal. Return veal to 325° oven for 10-20 minutes; sprinkle with chopped parsley, lemon rind and minced garlic; baste well; recover and bake another 5 minutes. Serve with Saffron Rice (see page 189). (If freezing, do so after baking for 2 hours. Cool completely before freezing. Defrost to reheat and proceed as above.) If you have the Bone Marrow Scoupers (Cuccio Per L'Ossobuco), by all means use them for eating the delicious marrow.

Veal Scaloppine in Tomato, Pepper and Mushroom Sauce
(Scaloppine di Vitello con Funghi e Peperoni)

2   pounds veal steak
½   cup olive oil
2   cloves garlic
3   cups sieved tomatoes
1   teaspoon salt
¼   teaspoon thyme
1   tablespoon chopped
     parsley
½   teaspoon oregano
¼   teaspoon pepper
6   tablespoons butter
2   green peppers, cut in
     1-inch squares
1   pound mushrooms, sliced
     in T's
¼   cup dry Marsala wine

Prepare meat for frying as in Scaloppine with Marsala (see page 183), flattening and flouring.

Heat olive oil with garlic in large skillet and brown veal on both sides. Combine next 6 ingredients and add to browned veal. Cover and simmer for 20 minutes. Meanwhile melt butter in another skillet and gently fry green peppers and mushrooms for 2 minutes, stirring frequently. Add to veal and sauce, stirring through gently; add Marsala and simmer for 2-3 minutes until hot.

Chicken Cacciatore

3-4 (1½-2 pound) broilers,
     split or cut for frying
     Flour, salt and pepper
6   tablespoons olive oil
1   large onion, diced
5   cloves garlic, crushed
1   large green pepper,
     chopped fine
1   teaspoon thyme
5   cups tomatoes
2   cans tomato paste
2   bay leaves
1   teaspoon oregano
1   teaspoon salt
1   cup water
4   tablespoons Marsala wine

Wash and wipe chicken. Put flour, salt and pepper in a paper bag and place chicken in a piece at a time. Shake until well coated. Brown chicken on both sides in hot olive oil. Add next 4 ingredients and fry, stirring frequently, until onions are golden. Add rest of ingredients and simmer 2 hours. As sauce cooks down, add just enough water to keep sauce at a thick consistency. (Serves 12.)

Veal with Tomato Sauce and Cheese (Veal Parmigiana)

Sauce:

6   cloves garlic, crushed
1   cup diced onion
6   tablespoons olive oil
2   (No. 2) cans tomatoes
2½   teaspoons salt
½   teaspoon pepper
2   (8 ounce) cans tomato sauce
½   teaspoon thyme
½   cup dry Marsala wine

Saute garlic and onion in olive oil until golden. Add tomatoes, salt and pepper and simmer 20 minutes. Add tomato sauce, thyme and Marsala and simmer 10 more minutes. Strain through food mill or mash in food processor.

Meat:

2   pounds veal steak, sliced
      very thin into 16 slices
2   eggs, well beaten
½   cup bread crumbs
½   cup fresh grated
      Parmesan or Romano
      cheese
6   tablespoons olive oil
¾   pound Mozzarella cheese,
      sliced

Mix bread crumbs and cheese together. Dip veal in beaten egg and then in crumb mixture. Fry to golden brown on both sides in hot olive oil. Set aside in large baking pan. Heat oven to 350°. Pour two-thirds of the sauce over veal. Slice Mozzarella cheese thinly and arrange on top of sauce. Sprinkle with another ½ cup Parmesan or Romano grated cheese. Cover with the rest of the sauce. Bake 30 minutes.

Steak Marino

4   (2 inch thick) filet
      mignon steaks or London
      broil
      Salt and pepper
½   teaspoon rosemary
4   teaspoons tarragon
2   tablespoons wine vinegar
2   tablespoons chopped
      parsley, flat type if
      possible
½   teaspoon crushed garlic
4   tablespoons chopped onion
2   teaspoons dry mustard
3   tablespoons butter
3   tablespoons olive oil
4   tablespoons tomato sauce

Wipe steaks and if using London broil use tenderizer as directed on product. Sprinkle filet mignon with salt and pepper or pepper only if using London broil. Mix rosemary, tarragon and wine vinegar together in a little bowl. Mix parsley, garlic, onion and mustard in another little bowl. Heat butter and olive oil in large skillet; add rosemary mixture. When bubbling, add the steaks and fry quickly until brown on one side. Turn steaks and then spoon over half the mixture from the second bowl onto steaks. Brown steaks on other side quickly. Remove pan from heat and placing steaks on cutting board slice for serving, against the grain, saving pan juices. Refrigerate meat but bring to room temperature before time to complete cooking. At time to complete cooking return pan to heat and stir until sauces are hot. Add steak slices, rest of mixture from second bowl and tomato sauce; cook, stirring until desired amount of doneness and steak is piping hot. Serve with sauces poured over steak slices on a heated platter.

Egg Noodles for Fettucine

4 cups flour
4 large eggs
3 tablespoons water
1½ teaspoons salt

Place flour in a large bowl. Make a well in center of flour. Mix eggs, water and salt, beating well. Slowly add to flour, about half at a time. Mix well and then add rest of liquid. Mix together and knead until dough is smooth, about 10 minutes. Cut dough in three pieces and roll out each piece on a floured surface until paper thin. Fold sheets of dough into rolls and cut crosswise into about ⅓ inch slices. Dry one hour, spreading apart. Cook al dente and drain.

With Cheese Sauce (Fettucine Parmesan):

½ pound sweet butter, melted slowly, to barely soft
1 egg yolk
1½ cups grated Parmesan

Prepare noodles as above. Put into hot pyrex bowl or crockery, not metal. Sprinkle quickly with the grated cheese and dot with slightly softened cheese and toss well mixing very lightly and serve as hot as possible.

With Anchovies Sause (Tagliatelle):

¾ cup sweet butter, melted slowly being careful not to brown
⅓ cup anchovy fillets, drained and washed
1¼ cups grated Parmesan cheese
¼ teaspoon white pepper

Prepare noodles as directed above. Placed cooked, drained noodles on a hot serving platter; sprinkle all over with one cup of the cheese which has been mixed with the white pepper. Mix together the melted butter and anchovies and pour the sauce over the noodles. Top with rest of cheese. Serve immediately.

Eggplant with Parmesan and Tomato Sauce (Melanzane alla Parmigiana)

2 medium eggplants
2 eggs, beaten
1 cup dried fine bread crumbs
Olive oil
1 teaspoon salt
¼ teaspoon pepper
¼ teaspoon crushed red pepper
1½ teaspoons oregano
3 tablespoons chopped parsley
½ cup grated Parmesan cheese
8 slices Mozzarella cheese
1½ cups tomato sauce (see page 178)

Peel eggplants and slice into ½ inch slices. Dip in beaten egg and then coat well with bread crumbs. Heat olive oil to ⅛ inch depth in large frying pan. Brown eggplant lightly in hot oil on both sides. Place browned slices in large baking dish, overlapping slices. Sprinkle with seasoning and grated cheese. Top with Mozzarella slices and pour tomato sauce over all. Bake in 350° oven for 30 minutes. (Freezes well. Bake only 15 minutes; cool and freeze. Reheat frozen in 350° oven for 40 minutes.)

Italian Sauce for Cooked Vegetables

¼ cup lemon juice
4 tablespoons olive oil
1 teaspoon salt
¼ teaspoon pepper
2 cloves garlic, crushed
⅛ teaspoon oregano

Mix well and set aside in warm place. Spoon over cooked, drained vegetables.

Italian Salad Dressing

¾ cup olive oil
¼ cup wine vinegar
⅛ cup water
½ teaspoon salt
¼ teaspoon pepper
4-5 cloves garlic, crushed

Combine all in tightly covered jar and shake well. Before using, shake again thoroughly. (This makes a large amount. Keeps well on cupboard shelf.)

Cornmeal with Tomato Sauce (Polenta)

2 cups yellow cornmeal
2 quarts boiling water
1 teaspoon salt
   Olive oil
2 cups diced onions
3 cups tomato puree
⅛ teaspoon sage
⅛ teaspoon thyme
½ cup chopped broiled
     mushrooms
¼ teaspoon pepper
½ teaspoon salt
2 cloves garlic, crushed
3 tablespoons minced
     parsley
1 cup grated Parmesan or
     Romano cheese

Add salt to boiling water in top of double boiler. Gradually add cornmeal, stirring constantly. Place on top of simmering water and cook about 40 minutes. Meanwhile, heat enough olive oil in frying pan to cover ⅛ inch depth. Add onions and saute, stirring until onions are golden brown. Add tomato puree, sage, thyme, mushrooms, pepper and salt, simmering gently for 35 minutes, stirring occasionally. Add crushed garlic and simmer 5 minutes more; add parsley and stir. When cornmeal is cooked, place half on a large platter; cover with half of sauce and sprinkle with half of cheese. Add rest of cornmeal and then remaining sauce and cheese.

Cheese Patties in Tomato Sauce (Gnocchi)

¾ cup water
2 tablespoons butter
1 cup flour
½ cup grated Parmesan or
  Romano cheese
½ teaspoon salt
¼ teaspoon paprika
2 unbeaten eggs

Bring water and butter to a boil. Lower heat and add flour, cheese, salt and paprika; mix together, stirring vigorously until mixture leaves sides of pan and forms ball of dough. Remove from heat and with a fork, beating vigorously, add eggs, one at a time; mix thoroughly. Flour hands well and take pieces of dough the size of a walnut and pat into thin cakes, about ⅛ inch thick. Chill. Brown each cake in hot oil on both sides. Drain on paper toweling and keep warm in low oven. Serve with following sauce and more grated cheese.

Sauce:

6 tablespoons butter
1 pound Italian hot
  sausage, diced
½ teaspoon sage
2 cups tomato paste
4 cups beef stock
½ teaspoon salt
¼ teaspoon pepper
1 cup Parmesan or Romano
  grated cheese

Fry sausage meat in melted butter, stirring occasionally, for about 10 minutes. Pour off excess fat. Add rest of ingredients, except grated cheese, and simmer for 30 minutes, stirring occasionally. Pour over Gnocchi and serve, passing grated cheese for each diner to add his own. (Sauce freezes well.)

Gnocchi alla Romana

4 cups milk
½ teaspoon salt
1 cup farina (cereal)
2 egg yolks
¼ pound sweet butter
1⅓ cups grated Parmesan
  cheese
½ teaspoon salt
¼ teaspoon M.S.G. (optional)
¼ teaspoon nutmeg

In a large Teflon or enamel pan, bring milk and salt to a boil. At boiling point, before milk overflows, add the farina slowly in the center, twirling with a wooden spoon, being careful not to form lumps. Stir continuously on medium heat until mixture is the consistency of mush, 5-10 minutes. Remove from heat. Add egg yolks, 6 tablespoons of the butter, Parmesan cheese, salt, M.S.G. and nutmeg, stirring until everything is well blended. While still hot, place mixture on lightly greased cookie sheets, smoothing it with a wet spatula until it is 1½ inches thick. Refrigerate until cold. With the spatula, cut parallel, horizontal and vertical lines forming small rectangles, about 3 x 2 inches. Turning them upside down, lay them in layers in a casserole, spreading each layer with cheese, forming a terraced tower, with a layer of only 1 at top, about 4-5 layers in all. Sprinkle each layer with more Parmesan cheese and dot it with remaining butter. Bake in 375° oven for 30-40 minutes, until golden and bubbling. Serve hot. (Freezes well. Defrost and bake for dinner time.)

188

Browned Potato Cake (Rosti)

4 cups grated cold boiled
    potatoes or raw potatoes
1¼ teaspoons salt
½ teaspoon pepper
1 tablespoon grated onion
4 tablespoons butter
1 tablespoon plus 1 tea-
    spoon bacon drippings

If using raw potatoes, grate and place immediately in cold water to cover. Drain and dry well to use. Add salt, pepper and onion to either potatoes and toss lightly. Melt butter and bacon drippings in heavy skillet. When hot, add potatoes and press down to make a smooth cake. Cover and cook over medium heat until heated through, about 10 minutes. Remove cover and cook 20-35 minutes, to form a thick brown crust. Place plate on top of skillet and turn out potato cake; slide back into skillet, brown side up, and cook to brown other side well. Slide onto hot plate and cut in wedges to serve.

Saffron Rice (Risotto all Milanese)

¾ cup butter
1 medium onion, diced
2 cups rice
⅓ cup pine nuts or sliced
    almonds (optional)
2 teaspoons salt
¼ teaspoon pepper
5 cups chicken broth
½ cup dry white wine
¼ teaspoon powdered saffron
    or 4 strands soaked in ¼
    cup warm water 10 min-
    utes, strained
1 cup grated Parmesan
    cheese (optional)

Melt half the butter in deep pan and fry onion to golden. Add rice, nuts, salt and pepper and cook, stirring constantly, for few minutes. Add wine and half of the broth. Cover and cook over low heat, adding more broth as it cooks away, until all broth is used. Add rest of butter and saffron water, stirring lightly with a fork. Cover and cook few more minutes. When ready to serve, sprinkle with grated cheese if desired. (May be made up to point of adding last of broth; reheat before serving time and finish cooking; shut off heat and do not uncover until ready to serve.)

Gorgonzola Dressed Romaine Salad

1-2 large heads romaine lettuce,
    washed, dried and torn
⅔ cup olive oil
3 tablespoons wine vinegar
2 teaspoons Dijon mustard
¼ teaspoon salt
¼ teaspoon white pepper
3-4 ounces Gorgonzola cheese
1 clove garlic

Prepare lettuce in the morning and place in a plastic bag in the vegetable drawer of refrigerator until time to dress. Mix next 5 ingredients in a jar with a tight cover and keep at room temperature. Crumble cheese and place in refrigerator. Clean clove of garlic, peel, wrap in plastic and put in refrigerator. At serving time, rub large salad bowl well with the clove of garlic. Dump in prepared lettuce and crumbled cheese. Pour enough dressing over all to coat lightly; toss.

189

Spinach Gnocchi

3   egg yolks
3   tablespoons grated
     Parmesan cheese
12 ounces cream cheese,
     room temperature
3   packages frozen chopped
     spinach, cooked and
     squeezed dry
     Flour
8   cups boiling water
1½ teaspoons salt
¼   pound lightly browned
     sweet butter
¾   teaspoon sage
6   tablespoons grated
     Parmesan cheese

Combine first 4 ingredients and refrigerate for several hours. Form into small Gnocchi, conical shaped about 1½ inches long with 2 inch base; roll in flour; refrigerate at least 1 hour. Drop into boiling water and salt and cook until Gnocchi comes to the top of the boiling water; remove with a slotted spoon to a buttered casserole. (Refrigerate at this point.) To finish, cover and place in 350° oven for 15 minutes. Pour over the lightly browned butter mixed with sage and Parmesan cheese; baste well. Cover and bake 5 more minutes or keep warm in 150° oven until serving time.

Green Noodles (Pasta Verde)

½   pound cleaned spinach,
     stems removed, or 1
     package frozen chopped
     spinach, cooked as
     directed and drained
8   cups boiling water
1   teaspoon salt
3   cups flour
½   teaspoon salt
3   eggs
1   cup grated Parmesan
     cheese
6   tablespoons butter
     Salt and pepper

Cook fresh spinach in boiling water with 1 teaspoon salt for 5 minutes. Drain and dry; cool and chop finely in blender; set aside. Place flour and salt in bowl and mix well; make a well in center of flour and add eggs, one at a time, mixing slightly after each addition. Add blended spinach and mix thoroughly to make a stiff dough. Turn dough onto a floured surface and knead for 3 minutes or until dough is no longer sticky. Cut dough in half. Roll out each half of dough very, very thinly, no more than ¹/₁₆ inch thick. Let stand covered for 1½ hours. Roll up each piece of dough lightly, like a loose jelly roll. Cut dough into strips about ½ inch wide. Unroll strips and arrange in single layers on waxed paper on a flat surface. Let stand until dry, all day or overnight. Store dried noodles in tightly closed containers. To serve, bring 12 cups water to a boil with ½ tablespoon salt. Gradually add noodles and boil about 10 minutes. Drain. Butter a 2-quart casserole and put in ⅓ of the noodles; sprinkle with ⅓ cup grated Parmesan cheese; dot with sweet butter and sprinkle with salt and pepper. Beginning with noodles, repeat layering, ending with Parmesan cheese and butter. Bake in 350° oven for 20-30 minutes, to hot and bubbly, covered. These may be fully prepared for baking the day before the dinner and baked prior to dinner time.

Fresh Mushroom Salad

1½ pounds fresh mushrooms, sliced in T's and refrigerated
6 teaspoons Dijon mustard
6 tablespoons red wine vinegar
¾ teaspoon salt
1 teaspoon oregano
½ teaspoon tarragon
¼ teaspoon pepper
1 cup olive oil
Shredded lettuce leaves or watercress

In a jar with a cover, combine the 7 ingredients listed under the mushrooms. Shake well and leave at room temperature. At serving time, toss mushrooms with dressing. Serve on individual salad plates on beds of shredded lettuce or watercress.

Bread Sticks (Grissini)

1 package dry yeast or yeast cake
¼ cup warm water
1½ cups warm water
¼ cup warm milk
2 teaspoons salt
5 cups flour
1 egg, beaten with 1 tablespoon milk

Add yeast to ¼ cup warm water and set aside for 10 minutes. Meanwhile, place 1½ cups warm water and milk in a large bowl. Add salt, 4 cups flour and then yeast mixture; blend, mixing well. Add the other cup of flour, kneading it in the bowl to make a smooth soft dough. Grease a large bowl lightly with oil and turn dough in bowl to bring greased surface to the top. Cover bowl with plastic wrap and towel. Allow to stand in a warm place until double in size, about 1½ -2 hours. Punch down dough and knead on a lightly floured surface a few minutes. Grease 3 large baking sheets. Lightly roll pieces of dough between palms of hands to make a rope about ¼ inch thick and 6 inches long. Place on baking sheets about 1 inch apart. Brush lightly with egg mixture; cover lightly with towels and place in a warm spot to allow to rise until about double in thickness. Brush with egg mixture again and sprinkle generously with coarse salt. Bake in 425° oven for 5 minutes; reduce heat to 300° and bake 5-10 minutes, until sticks are crisp and richly golden brown. Makes about 3 dozen bread sticks. (Freeze what you don't use right away. To reheat, defrost and wrap loosely in foil in 325° oven for 6-8 minutes.)

Stuffed Zucchini

8   small zucchini squash, boiled in water to cover for 15 minutes; drain, cool and cut in half lengthwise
1   large onion, diced
10   tablespoons sweet butter
4   tablespoons flour
1¼   cups milk
⅓   cup fine bread crumbs
3   tablespoons grated Parmesan cheese
¾   teaspoon salt
¼   teaspoon white pepper
6   tablespoons grated Parmesan cheese, blended with 3 tablespoons sweet butter, melted

Scoop out pulp from zucchini, leaving ¼ inch shell; chop pulp coarsely. Place pulp aside in bowl. Place zucchini shells in a baking pan, scooped side down and tilt pan to drain shells. Saute onion in 6 tablespoons butter until lightly golden. Squeeze out zucchini pulp and add to sauteed onion; simmer 5 minutes, stirring occasionally; set aside. In large skillet, melt 4 tablespoons butter; remove from heat and add flour, blending well. Gradually add milk, stirring to blend smooth, return to heat and cook, stirring until thickened. Remove from heat and add onion pulp mixture, dried bread crumbs, Parmesan cheese, salt and pepper; blend well. Wipe out zucchini shells with paper towels and stuff with mixture. Sprinkle generously with Parmesan cheese-butter mixture. Place in lightly greased baking dish. Refrigerate until baking time or freeze at this point. Defrost before putting in oven if frozen. Bring to room temperature and bake in 400° oven until hot and bubbly, 20-30 minutes. Keep warm in 150° oven. Serve hot.

Genoise Meringues

Using your favorite recipe, bake chiffon cake in jelly roll pans until just done. Cool.

Toppings:

Fruit brandy, rum, sweet Marsala
Apricot, cherry, pineapple or strawberry preserves
Meringue

Cut cake in 2-inch rounds. Brush with one of the liquors and top each in center with 1 teaspoon of the preserves. Put meringue in cookie press and form fancy swirl edgings around preserves. Place carefully on cookie sheets and bake 5-10 minutes in 300° oven or until lightly golden. Cool on racks. (These can be frozen, uncovered, on cookie sheet. Then place in covered container when frozen. Defrost and bring to room temperature to serve.)

Meringue:

2   egg whites, beaten stiff, but not dry
1⅓   cups sugar
¼   cup water
½   teaspoon vanilla

Place sugar, water and vanilla in saucepan and cook until mixture forms thread at the end of a spoon. Pour syrup gradually over beaten egg whites, beating constantly, until thick, spreading consistency.

Christmas Fruit Cookies (Piccoli Dolci)

2½ cups flour
2 teaspoons baking powder
½ teaspoon salt
¼ cup butter
1 cup sugar
1 egg yolk
1 teaspoon grated orange peel
½ cup light cream

1 egg white
1¾ cups confectioners sugar
1 teaspoon vanilla
¼ cup chopped nutmeats
¼ cup halved candied cherries
¼ cup mixed candied fruits

Sift first 3 ingredients. Cream butter and sugar; beat in egg yolks and the peel. Add cream with dry ingredients and gather together as for pie dough. Chill. Roll half of dough at a time into a rectangle ¼ inch thick. Spread with topping.

Topping:

Beat egg white until frothy. Beat in confectioners sugar and vanilla, beating until stiff. Spread on cookie dough. Sprinkle with chopped nuts, cherries and mix candied fruit. Cut with a sharp wet knife into 1 x 2 inch pieces. Place on lightly greased cookie sheet and bake in 375° oven for 10-12 minutes. Cool on racks. (Freezes well.)

Sweet Pastries (Ravioli Dolce)

1¾ cups flour
5 tablespoons shortening
½ teaspoon salt
Water

¼ pound Ricotta cheese
1 egg white
2 egg yolks
4 tablespoons sugar
½ teaspoon vanilla
Confectioners sugar

Mix flour, shortening and salt together with pastry blender or with fingers. Add enough cold water to make a stiff dough as for pie. Roll out very thin on lightly floured surface. Cut dough into 3-inch squares; top with filling and another pastry square; press together and seal.

Filling:

Mix all ingredients except confectioners sugar. Put 1 teaspoon of filling on center of a square of pastry; dampen the edges; cover with another square of pastry; seal tight with tines of fork. Repeat until all squares are used up. Fry in deep hot oil to golden brown. Drain on paper toweling. Keep hot in warm oven. Sprinkle with confectioners sugar and serve hot. (May be prepared for frying and refrigerated until just before dinner time.)

Frozen Chiffon Cupcakes (Biscuit Tortoni)

1 tablespoon gelatin
¼ cup water
1 cup milk, scalded
2 eggs, beaten
½ cup sugar
⅛ teaspoon salt
2 teaspoons almond extract or
   2 tablespoons Grand
   Marnier liqueur
1 cup cream, whipped
¼ cup macaroon crumbs
   Maraschino cherries

Soak gelatin in water and set aside. When gelatin is softened add hot milk; stir until gelatin is dissolved. Beat eggs in large bowl until thick and lemon colored, adding sugar gradually. Stir in milk mixture, salt and flavoring. Chill in bowl in refrigerator until thick and syrupy. Fold whipped cream into chilled mixture. Pour into 8-10 paper-lined cupcake holders or into freezing tray. Sprinkle tops with macaroon crumbs and top with maraschino cherries. (Freeze at least 3-4 hours until firm. Keeps in freezer up to 1 month.)

Macaroon and Chestnut Ice Cream (Amaretti con Morroni Gelato)

⅓ pound dried chestnut meats,
   enough water to cover
   Enough maraschino juice
   to soak shredded
   chestnuts
¾ cup grenadine
2 teaspoons almond extract
1 tablespoon vanilla extract
6 egg yolks
1½ cups sugar
⅓ cup water
1 quart heavy cream,
   whipped stiff
1 cup macaroon crumbs

Wash chestnuts and soak in water 3 inches above nuts overnight. Next day, boil in water to cover until chestnuts are soft; cool and shred through food mill or in food processor. Place in bowl and cover with maraschino juice, grenadine and extracts; soak for at least 3 hours. Beat egg yolks until lemon colored. Bring sugar and water to a boil using top of a large double boiler directly over heat. Remove from heat and very gradually, beating all the while, stir into egg yolk mixture. Return to pan and place over simmering water, stirring constantly; cook until mixture is thick. Remove from heat and beat until cold on slowest speed of electric mixer. Remove from mixer and fold in whipped cream, macaroon crumbs and shredded chestnut mixture. Turn into large freezer container or molds, cover tightly, and freeze. Serves 20.

Filled Rum Cake (Zuppa Inglese)

Using your favorite recipe, bake and cool one (10-inch) tube pan chiffon or sponge cake.

Filling:

½ cup sugar
¼ cup cornstarch
⅛ teaspoon salt
2½ cups milk
2 eggs, slightly beaten
1 tablespoon light rum or
    rum flavoring
1 teaspoon vanilla
1 tablespoon cocoa mixed
    with 1 tablespoon brandy
    or creme de cacao

Combine sugar, cornstarch and salt in top of double boiler. Add half cup of milk and stir until mixture is smooth. Add remaining milk and cook over simmering water, stirring constantly, until smooth and thickened. Pour small amount of hot mixture into beaten eggs; mix well and then stir into rest of hot mixture. Cook 5 minutes, stirring constantly. Strain and divide custard into 3 portions. Add the rum to 1 part, the vanilla to second part and cocoa brandy mixture to the third. Cool.

Prepare the following wine-rum mixture for use in frosting the cake.

½ cup light rum
3 tablespoons rum
    flavoring

½ cup sweet Marsala wine or
    grape wine

Frosting:

½ pint heavy cream, whipped
1 cup candied chopped
    mixed fruit

Cut cake into 4 equal layers. Place bottom layer on serving plate. Brush layer with ¼ of wine-rum mixture; spread with one of the light custards. Repeat second and third layers using wine-rum mixture on each layer and the other two fillings. Put final cake layer on top and pour remaining wine-rum mixture over it. Refrigerate overnight. Next morning, spread whipped cream over top and sides of cake. Sprinkle candied fruit all over top for attractive garnish. Serves 16.

Hot or Cold Zabaglione with Fruit

6 egg yolks, beaten (freeze
    whites for other use)
⅔ cup superfine sugar
1 cup sweet Marsala sherry
    wine
½ teaspoon vanilla
½ teaspoon orange bits
⅛ teaspoon cinnamon
1 cup heavy cream, whipped

Place egg yolks, sugar and Marsala in top of a double boiler over simmering water. Beat with a whisk, constantly scraping sides and bottom, until mixture mounds when whisk is lifted. If serving hot, add flavorings. Serve over cake or fruit. If serving cold, remove from heat and beat until thick with electric beater. When cooled, add vanilla, orange bits and cinnamon. Cover and refrigerate until cold. Whip cream stiff and fold into cold Zabaione, blending thoroughly. Serve in parfait glasses over fresh sugared fruit. Zabaglione will keep up to 3 weeks in refrigerator.

Cream Rolls (Cannoli)

Shells:

Make the shells the day before you plan to fill them.

Mix dry ingredients; cut in shortening as for pie. Add water, wine and orange bits and gather together as for pie dough. Roll on floured surface to about $^1/_{16}$ inch thick. Cut with cannoli cutter, if you have one, or cut a cardboard pattern of an oval about 4 x 5 $^1/_2$ inches and cut dough around this. Using about 6 cannoli aluminum tubes or cutting a broomstick or 1 or 1 $^1/_2$ inch diameter dowel into 6 lengths about 6 inches long and cleaning them well, wrap each oval loosely around each tube or stick. Beat an egg white until foamy and dampen overlapping edges with it, then press lightly to seal. Heat oil for deep frying at 400° and fry to golden brown, turning as they brown. Drain on paper toweling and allow to cool; slip shell off stick. When all are fried and cool, fill with the following.

4 cups flour
$^1/_2$ teaspoon salt
3 tablespoons sugar
6 tablespoons vegetable shortening
9 tablespoons water
9 tablespoons white dry wine
1 tablespoon orange bits
Egg white

Filling:

Boil water and sugar for 10 minutes; skim and cool. Beat in cheese for 2 minutes. Add rest of ingredients and mix well. Fill tubes carefully and dip filled tube ends in coarsely ground pistachio or walnut meats. (Freezes beautifully. Remove from freezer just before dinner guests arrive and arrange on serving plates. Allow to thaw to room temperature.) Makes about 5 dozen.

1 $^1/_2$ cups sugar
1 cup water
3 pounds Ricotta cheese
2 tablespoons chopped candied orange peel
$^1/_2$ cup grated sweet chocolate
1 teaspoon cinnamon
1 teaspoon orange bits
30 candied cherries, chopped
Pistachio or walnut meats, coarsely ground

Mexican

Mexican Bread — Tortillas

The following recipes for tortillas are not truly authentic because many of the ingredients are not readily available in the United States. The recipes, however, do produce excellent tortillas. Because tortillas freeze well, you can sometimes find the real thing in the freezer department of your supermarket.

Tortillas are always served hot. If they have been frozen or refrigerated bring them to room temperature before proceeding. To heat your tortillas sprinkle very lightly with a small amount of water on both sides; place them in a 350° oven for just a few minutes, turning to have them nice and warm but still soft.

Corn Tortillas—the Most Authentic

2	eggs
¼	teaspoon salt
5½	tablespoons white cornmeal
¾	cup cornstarch
½	cup milk, room temperature
2	tablespoons melted vegetable shortening or butter

Beat eggs and salt together; add the cornmeal and mix well. Combine the cornstarch and milk and form a smooth paste. Add the egg and cornmeal mixture and stir thoroughly until smooth. Add the melted shortening, stirring constantly. Grease a 7-inch skillet and heat it to medium hot. Pour a small amount, about a ¼ cup, of the batter on the whole skillet. When lightly brown, really just a dark golden, on one side, turn over and brown the other side in the same manner. Tortillas should be almost paper thin. Makes about 18 tortillas. Cool and wrap tightly in aluminum foil and place in the refrigerator or freezer until ready to use.

Flour Tortillas No. 1

2	cups all purpose flour
1	teaspoon salt
1	teaspoon baking powder
1	tablespoon shortening
½ -¾	cup lukewarm water

In a mixing bowl mix together flour, salt and baking powder. Cut in shortening as for pie. Add ½ cup lukewarm water and mix till dough can be gathered into a ball; if needed add more water, one tablespoon at a time. Let dough rest 15 minutes. Divide dough into 12 balls. On a lightly floured surface roll each ball into a 7-inch round. Trim uneven edges to make round tortillas. Cook on ungreased griddle over medium heat 1½ minutes per side or till lightly browned spots appear. Keep wrapped in refrigerator in aluminum foil after cooling. They do freeze well. To reheat use directions given above for Tortillas.

Flour Tortillas No. 2

4   cups flour
1½ teaspoons salt
¼   pound butter or margarine

Sift together the dry ingredients. Cut in the shortening as for pie. Add enough lukewarm water to form a soft dough. Turn onto a lightly floured surface and knead for 5 minutes. Divide the dough into 14 balls and cover with a cloth. Allow to rest for 30 minutes. Roll out each ball into a flat tortilla, trimming uneven edges to make round tortillas. Cook on an ungreased griddle over moderate heat. When showing a sprinkling of little brown spots turn and do other side in the same manner. Cool and wrap tightly in aluminum foil until ready to use; will keep in the refrigerator or freezer. Bring to room temperature and sprinkle with very little water; place in oven and serve warmed.

Salsas

Another staple served with every meal is salsa. This is a dipping sauce, usually very hot, but one may make it as mild as one wishes. Doritos or any corn chips are used for dipping. There are so many versions that I will give only four and you may try each until you find which suits your taste. Leave on table throughout the meal.

Red Salsa No. 1

6   large red tomatoes
2   jalapeno chilies, seeds removed and coarsely chopped *or* 1 small (7 ounce) can chopped chilies
2   tablespoons chopped onion
2   tablespoons vegetable oil
¼ cup chopped cilantro or parsley

Place the tomatoes in a baking dish in a 350° oven until the skins split. Remove from oven and when cool enough to handle remove skins and stems. Heat the oil to medium and add the chilies and onions. Cook gently until onions begin to be transparent; add the prepared tomatoes cut in eighths. Fry gently for a few minutes and when barely soft remove from heat. Put all through a blender or food processor for just a second or two. Remove and add chopped cilantro or parsley and salt to taste. Makes 3 cups.

Red Salsa No. 2

2   or more (to taste) canned
     pickled jalapeno chilies,
     minced
2   medium tomatoes, skinned,
     seeded and minced
1   small onion, grated
1-2 teaspoons minced fresh
     coriander or ½ teaspoon
     crushed dried coriander
1½ teaspoons salt

Remove stems from chilies. In small bowl mix all ingredients well. Allow to rest at least one hour before using; stir again. Use as dip for corn chips, tortillas or serve as a condiment for tacos, meat, poultry or eggs. Makes about 2 cups.

Green Salsa No. 1

20 small green husk tomatoes,
     halved
1-2 hot jalapeno chilies, diced
     or 1 small (7 ounce) can,
     minced
2   tablespoons vegetable oil
2   tablespoons chopped onion
¼   cup chopped cilantro or
     parsley

If fresh are not to be found, the green tomatoes are sometimes found canned in the Mexican section of supermarkets. Remove the husks and stems of fresh tomatoes. Cook the halved tomatoes and chilies in oil until tomatoes are tender. Add the onion and cook until just transparent. Remove from heat and put all through a blender or food processor for just a second or two. Remove and add chopped cilantro or parsley; salt to taste. Makes 3 cups.

Green Salsa No. 2

1   (12-13 ounce) can whole
     green Mexican tomatoes,
     or ½ pound fresh green
     husk tomatoes
2-4 fresh or canned pickled
     jalapeno or serrano chilies,
     to taste
1   tablespoon vegetable oil
1   small diced onion
1   clove garlic, cut up
½   cup cilantro or parsley
1   tablespoon coriander leaves
     or ¼ teaspoon ground
     coriander
½   teaspoon salt

Drain canned tomatoes or if using fresh remove stems and outer husks; rinse well. Remove stems from chilies as well as seeds. In a blender or food processor, blend until all ingredients are smooth.

In a saucepan over medium heat bring mixture to boiling. Reduce heat and simmer 10 minutes, stirring. Refrigerate. Good on meats and eggs, as well as dip. Makes 1½ cups.

Cheese and Smoked Oyster or Clam Log

1   (8 ounce) package cream
      cheese, room temperature
1   tablespoon Worcestershire
      sauce
6   drops Tabasco
½   teaspoon grated onion
1   tablespoon mayonnaise
1   can smoked oysters or clams
      Diced canned chilies
      Sliced stuffed olives

Mix first 5 ingredients together thoroughly. Drain smoked oyster or clams, but save the oil. Mash the oysters or clams smoothly with a fork. Using two pieces of waxed paper, each about 12 inches long, place one piece on a hard surface and spread cheese mixture into an oblong about 8 x 10 inches, spreading out smoothly. Down the center of the cheese place a 2 inch wide row of the mashed oysters or clams. Sprinkle with the saved oil and top with a scattering of diced chilies and a few sliced olives. Placing a long spatula under each side of remaining cheese flip over to cover filling, making cheese mixture overlap to cover filling. Place other piece of waxed paper on top of all, pressing around log, lightly roll together. Refrigerate at least 6 hours before using. Unroll from waxed paper. Place on serving dish. Serve with flat corn chips or crackers allowing each guest to spread his own.

Chilies con Queso

1   pound Monterey Jack with
      Jalapeno pepper cheese
2   tablespoons butter
2   cloves garlic, crushed
2   medium tomatoes,
      unpeeled, cut in small
      dice
½   cup milk
2   teaspoons cornstarch
1   tablespoon water
      Salt to taste

Coarsely grate the cheese. Heat butter in fondue pot and add garlic. Cook briefly and add the tomatoes. Stir and add the cheese and milk. Bring to a boil gradually, stirring. Blend cornstarch and water and add, stirring constantly. Add salt if desired. Place in fondue pot over heat to keep sauce warm. Serve with tostadas, fried tortillas, corn chips or French bread.

Creamy Guacamole

2   ripe avocados, peeled
      and chopped
1   tablespoon Tabasco sauce
2   tablespoons mayonnaise
1   tablespoon lemon or lime
      juice
½   teaspoon Worchestershire
      sauce
1   clove garlic, crushed

Combine all ingredients and blend in blender or food processor to smooth. Place pit of avocado in center of prepared guacamole; smooth over and spread lightly with more mayonnaise. Cover tightly with plastic wrap. Refrigerate until serving. Remove pit and blend in mayonnaise. Serve with corn chips. Makes about 1½ cups.

Guacamole with Cilantro

2   ripe avocados
1   tablespoon lemon juice
2   medium tomatoes, peeled,
     seeded and finely chopped
1   cup finely chopped onion
1   teaspoon salt
½   teaspoon garlic powder
¼   teaspoon pepper
1   tablespoon finely chopped
     cilantro

Mash the avocados with a fork. Add the lemon juice and blend well. Add rest of ingredients, combining thoroughly. Makes 3 cups. See preceding recipe for storing.

Ceviche

3   pound filet of sole or red
     snapper, cut bite-size
     Lime juice to cover fish
6-10 green olives
1   tablespoon vinegar
1   tablespoon salad oil
     Juice of 6 limes
4   red tomatoes, cut up finely
2   avocados, thinly sliced
5   teaspoons salt
1   onion, diced
½   cup cilantro, chopped
     Diced green chilies,
     fresh or canned

This is enough for a large gathering. Cut the proportions down to whatever you will be needing. Twenty-four hours before serving cover fish pieces with lime juice and refrigerate overnight. Later the next day rinse well and drain on paper toweling. Place in serving dish and add rest of ingredients plus the juice of approximately 6 more limes. Allow to marinate a few hours adding the sliced avocados last.

Jalapeno Bean Dip

2   cups refried beans (see
     page 220 or use canned)
1   cup sour cream
1   pickled jalapeno chili,
     minced

Combine ingredients; mix thoroughly and refrigerate. Use with corn chips, potato chips and/or crackers. Makes 1 ½ -2 cups.

Hot Bites

6	tablespoons butter
6	large flour tortillas
¾	cup grated Monterey Jack cheese
1	cup green chili salsa

Preheat oven to 200°. Melt 1 tablespoon of the butter in a large skillet over medium heat. Add 1 tortilla and fry on each side until lightly browned, about ½ minute. Place ⅛ cup of cheese in center length of tortilla and top with 1¼ tablespoons of the salsa. Fold sides of tortilla towards the center, overlapping slightly. Continue frying until tortilla is golden brown and cheese is melted, about 2-3 minutes. Transfer to platter and keep warm in oven. Repeat with remaining ingredients. Remove from oven and with a very sharp knife cut diagonally into bite-size pieces. (It is much easier to make them ahead of time and let them cool; refrigerate, then cut into bite-size pieces and reheat in a 375° oven for about 5 minutes.)

Tamale Balls

1	pound beef, lean, ground
1	pound ground pork
1	tablespoon chili powder
1½	cups white cornmeal
½	cup flour
1½	teaspoons salt
¾	cup tomato juice
4	large cloves garlic, crushed
	Sauce (recipe follows)

Mix beef and pork together; add all other ingredients. Mix well with hands and form into small balls the size of large marbles. Place in sauce and simmer about 2 hours. Keep hot in chafing dish. Serve on toothpicks or with small cocktail forks.

Tomato Sauce:

2	large cans tomatoes
1	teaspoon salt
1	tablespoon chili powder

Mash tomatoes with a fork. Add rest of ingredients and simmer 10 minutes to hot. Add little meat balls and simmer gently for 2 hours.

Mexican Fondue

1	pound Cheddar cheese, grated
1	pound Monterey Jack cheese, grated
¼	cup flour
2	teaspoons chili powder
½-1	clove garlic
1	(12 ounce) can beer
1	(4 ounce) can chopped green chilies

Mix the cheese, flour and chili powder. Rub inside of fondue pot with garlic. Add beer to fondue pot, heating slowly just until it stops foaming and begins to bubble. Gradually add cheese mixture a handful at a time, stirring constantly until melted and smooth. Add green chilies. Serve with vegetable strips, avocado pieces, French bread chunks, cherry tomatoes and corn chips. Pour hot fondue into chafing dish; keep hot while serving.

Pickled Jalapenos Stuffed with Cheese

25   chile jalapenos (pickled
       and canned)
½   cup cooking oil or
       margarine
1   cup grated Cheddar cheese
½   cup saltine cracker crumbs
½   cup flour
2   eggs, beaten
2   tablespoons milk

Cut a slit in jalapeno chilies; take seeds out and leave the stem. Rinse in cold water. Stuff chilies with grated cheese; set aside; make batter.

Batter:

Place cracker crumbs and flour on a large plate and mix thoroughly. Beat eggs with milk. Roll stuffed chilies in cracker crumb-flour mixture to cover completely. Remove and dip in egg-milk mixture and again roll in cracker crumbs and flour. Heat oil in a skillet and fry chilies until golden brown. Place on paper toweling and let cool and drain. Serve at room temperature.

Stuffed Mushroom Appetizers

36   large mushrooms
1   cup water
½   cup white cornmeal
¼   cup scallions, finely sliced
1 ½   teaspoons salt
½   teaspoon basil leaves,
       crushed
1   clove garlic, crushed
1   cup chopped pecans

Remove stems from mushrooms and finely chop 1 cup. In a saucepan combine water, white cornmeal, scallions, salt, basil and crushed garlic. Bring to a boil over medium heat, stirring constantly for about 2-3 minutes or until thickened. Add nuts and chopped mushrooms; mix well. Fill mushroom caps with cornmeal mixture and place on a jelly roll pan or baking sheet. Bake in a preheated 425° oven for 12-15 minutes. Serve hot. Makes 3 dozen stuffed mushrooms.

Cream Cheese and Chili Dip

1   small onion, grated
1   tablespoon butter
1   (7 ounce) can green chilies
4   ounces cream cheese
½   teaspoon salt
½   teaspoon white pepper
½   cup cream

Saute onion in butter until soft. Add chilies, salt and pepper. Simmer 10 minutes. Add cream cheese, stirring until melted. Stir in cream and remove from heat. Serve in a chafing dish or fondue pot to keep warm. Arrange raw vegetables and tortilla chips for dipping.

Nachos Casserole for Chips

Vegetable spray
2 tablespoons butter or margarine
1 clove garlic, crushed
1 cup finely chopped onion
1 (7 ounce) can chopped green chilies
1 large tomato, chopped
1 tablespoon fresh cilantro or 1 teaspoon dried cilantro (optional)
2 (1 pound) cans refried beans
½ pound Mozzarella cheese, diced
3 (7 ounce) packages cheese flavored tortilla chips
3 cups (¾ pound) shredded Cheddar cheese
7-8 jalapeno peppers, sliced into rings (optional)
Purple onion, sliced into rings (optional)
Creamy Guacamole (see page 202)

Spray a 3-quart, deep ceramic heat-proof casserole with vegetable spray. Melt butter in casserole; add garlic and saute until golden brown. Add onion, and saute until transparent. Add chilies, tomato and cilantro. Simmer until tender. Add refried beans, stirring until mixture is smooth. Stir in Mozzarella cheese; cook over low heat until cheese melts, stirring all the while, until mixture is bubbly. Cool. Cover with plastic wrap and refrigerate until ready to use.

Select unbroken chips and place on a cookie sheet or oven-proof platter. Top each with a generous teaspoonful of the bean mixture. Sprinkle with Cheddar cheese and top with a slice of the jalapeno pepper or a slice of the onion.

Broil 6 inches from broiler just until cheese melts. Top nachos with dollops of Creamy Guacamole. Makes about 12 dozen. (Bean mixture may be frozen. Defrost at room temperature and proceed.)

Cheese Soup (Caldo de Queso)

1 onion, medium, sliced
3 tablespoons butter
2 large potatoes, peeled and diced finely
1 large tomato
5 hot green chilies, peeled and seeded
6 cups chicken broth
¼ teaspoon salt
3 tablespoons milk
2 cups Monterey Jack cheese, cut into small dice

Fry in butter the onion and potatoes until the onions are lightly golden. Put the tomato in a blender or food processor until smooth. Strain the tomato and add to the onion and potatoes. Add sliced chilies and chicken broth; cook all until the potatoes are tender. Add salt. Just before serving reheat soup and add the milk, but do not let the broth come to a boil. When serving add all the cheese and serve immediately so hot soup just barely melts the cheese.

Pumpkin Soup (Sopa de Calabaza)

1 ½ pounds meaty beef short ribs
2 ½ quarts water
1   medium size fresh pumpkin
     or 3 cups canned
2   medium potatoes, peeled
     and quartered
2   large carrots, peeled and
     quartered
1   medium onion, quartered
1   long green chili pepper
4   tablespoons cilantro or
     1 teaspoon dried
2   teaspoons sugar
2   teaspoons salt
¼   teaspoon white pepper
½   cup light cream

In a large soup kettle brown the meat over low heat. Add water and bring to a boil; reduce heat. Cover and simmer 1 hour. Remove ribs from broth and allow to cool. In the meantime cook the fresh pumpkin until just barely tender, having removed the seeds and quartered it. When cool enough to handle remove the pulp from the skin and measure. Cut meat from the bones and return meat to broth. Discard bones. Add pumpkin to broth with the potatoes, carrots, onion, sugar, salt and pepper. Cover and simmer mixture over medium heat for 45 minutes. Pour half the mixture into a blender or food processor and blend until smooth. Repeat with rest of mixture. Return all to saucepan. Heat through; taste for salt and pepper. Pour soup into bowls and top each serving with a little of the cream, if desired. Do not stir after placing in serving bowls.

Mexican Gazpacho

3   cloves garlic
4   slices white bread
½   cup wine vinegar
2   pounds canned tomatoes
6   fresh tomatoes
1   cup cucumber, sliced
½   cup diced celery
1   cup sliced scallions
1   green pepper, finely sliced
4   cups tomato juice
2   cups water
     Garlic croutons

The day before: Use your largest bowl. Mince 3 cloves garlic and smash them against the bowl with the heel of a large spoon. Cut the crusts from 4 slices of white bread and add the slices to the bowl. Pour a half cup of wine vinegar over the bread and mash all together until it forms a paste. Stir in about 2 pounds mashed tomatoes and their juice. Add 6 peeled and chopped fresh tomatoes, 1 cup peeled, chopped and seeded cucumber, ½ cup diced celery, 1 cup finely sliced scallions and 1 seeded and finely diced green pepper. Add all to the prepared bowl along with 4 cups of tomato juice and 2 cups water. Refrigerate and taste for salt or pepper. Serve cold with garlic croutons on the side.

Chorizo (Mexican Sausage)

1   pound lean pork or beef,
     coarsely ground
1   teaspoon salt
2   tablespoons chili powder
1   large clove garlic, crushed
1   teaspoon oregano
2   tablespoons white vinegar

Mix all ingredients thoroughly. Store in refrigerator if going to to use within a week, otherwise freeze. (To use frozen cut off needed size piece and place back in freezer frozen.)

Tortilla Soup

4 cloves garlic, crushed
½ cup salad oil
8 large corn tortillas, cut into strips
1 large onion, sliced thin
½ cup diced celery
½ cup diced carrot
4 cups water
1 pound tomato sauce
2 bay leaves
2 teaspoons chili powder
2 (1 pound) cans red kidney beans
Crushed red pepper to taste

In a large soup kettle over medium heat, saute garlic in oil until lightly browned. Discard garlic. Fry tortilla strips in the oil until lightly browned and crisp. Drain on paper towels. In same oil saute onion, celery and carrot until onion is lightly browned, adding more oil if necessary. Stir in water, tomato sauce, bay leaves and chili powder. Simmer, uncovered, 15 minutes or until slightly thickened. Stir in beans. Simmer until vegetables are tender and all is heated. Discard bay leaves. To serve divide tortilla strips among 8 soup bowls, and add soup and sprinkle lightly with crushed red pepper or allow each guest to add his own amount of the crushed pepper.

Meat Ball Soup (Cocido)

¼ cup dried chick-peas
8 cups water
1 pound stewing beef
1 pound lamb cut for stewing
1 marrow bone
1 large onion, sliced
6 peppercorns
4 tablespoons tomato puree
3 carrots, sliced
3 potatoes, sliced
3 medium zucchini, sliced
4 medium turnips, sliced
1 clove garlic, crushed
Salt and pepper to taste
¼ teaspoon oregano, crushed
3 ears sweet corn, fresh or frozen, cut in 2-inch pieces

This soup is really a meal in itself and excellent for buffets. Serve with tortillas or hot rolls and Mexican beer (available in gourmet shops) and you really have a feast.

Soak the chick-peas in water to cover overnight. Drain and remove the skins of the chick-peas. Boil in 2 quarts of water together with the meat, marrow bone, onion and peppercorns. When meat is beginning to be tender, after about 2½ hours, add the puree, vegetables except the corn, and the seasoning. Simmer for a half hour or until vegetables and meat are tender. Add corn during the last 7-10 minutes of cooking. Serves 10.

Aztec Squash Blossom Soup (Sopa de Flor de Calabaza)

1   pound squash blossoms
4   tablespoons butter or
       margarine
1   small onion, finely chopped
8   cups chicken broth
½   teaspoon sesame seeds
       Salt and white pepper
       to taste

Remove the stems from the squash blossoms and chop the blossoms coarsely. Heat the butter and saute the onion until limp. Add the squash blossoms and saute for a few minutes. Heat the chicken broth with the sesame seeds. Add the squash blossoms and onion. Taste for seasonings. Cover and simmer gently for 5 minutes.

Asparagus and Filbert Soup (Sopa de Auvellanas y Esparragos)

½   cup filberts
1   tablespoon butter
1   medium onion, chopped
⅛   cup chopped boiled ham
8   cups chicken broth
¼   cup dry sherry
       Salt to taste
½   cup heavy cream
1¼ cups asparagus tips, cut
       into 1-inch pieces and
       cooked to tender

Cover filberts with boiling water and let stand for 10 minutes. Drain and remove the skins. Saute until golden in the butter. Lift out of butter with a slotted spoon and set aside. Saute the onion until golden in the remaining butter, adding a little more if necessary, until limp but not brown. Combine the nuts, onions and ham in the electric blender or food processor and blend to a smooth paste. Heat the broth; add sherry and the nut mixture, stirring to blend well. Taste for seasoning. Simmer 10-15 minutes. Remove from heat and beat in the cream. Add the asparagus tips. Reheat soup without allowing to boil.

Casserole of Shrimp (Camarones en Escabeche)

3½-4 pounds shrimp in shells
1½ cups salad oil
3   cups either cauliflower,
       peas, green beans, or
       combination of all
1   medium onion, diced
5   cloves garlic, thinly sliced
3   carrots, thinly sliced
¾   cup vinegar
2¾ tablespoons canned hot
       jalapeno chilies, or to taste
4   bay leaves
¼   teaspoon oregano
       Salt to taste

Peel and clean shrimp. Set aside. Cook until barely tender the cauliflower, peas, green beans or combination; drain and set aside. Saute the onion, garlic and carrots in oil until tender, stirring occasionally. Add vinegar and bay leaves. Add shrimp and allow to boil gently until shrimp are pink, about 3 minutes. Add previously cooked vegetables and chilies; turn off heat and cover. Cool and refrigerate. Taste for salt, and remove bay leaves. Serve cold. (Never cook in aluminum cookware; it changes the flavor.)

Aztec Chicken Casserole (Pastel Azteca)

30 corn tortillas, fried only
   20 seconds on each side,
   drained on paper toweling
3 large tomatoes
3 cloves garlic, cut up
1 medium onion
2 tablespoons cooking oil
1 (13 ounce) can evaporated
   milk
6 chicken breasts, steamed,
   cooled and cut in julienne
2 (4 ounce) cans diced hot
   chilies
2 cups shredded Monterey
   Jack cheese

Prepare tortillas (see page 199) and set aside, covered. Place the tomatoes, garlic and onion in a blender or food processor and puree. Put through strainer. Heat the oil to medium hot and add puree. Cook 2-3 minutes. Add the can of evaporated milk and turn off heat.

In a large casserole make a layer of tortillas. Scatter thickly some of the julienned chicken, diced chilies and cheese over some of the tortillas. Spoon over about ⅓ cup sauce. Repeat until all ingredients are used ending with a layer of the tortillas, sauce and about ¼ inch of the grated cheese. Bake, uncovered, until the cheese and sauce are bubbling in a 325° oven; do not allow to dry. (May be prepared early in the day and baked just before dinner time.)

Chicken Yucatan (Pollo Yucatan)

8 medium hot red or green
   peppers or jalapeno
   peppers
8 cloves garlic, unpeeled
1 large onion
⅔ cup whole blanched
   almonds
1½ teaspoons salt
1 teaspoon oregano
¼ teaspoon pepper
   Water
   White vinegar
2 (2½-3 pound) broilers,
   cut up
½ cup peanut or salad oil
   Romain lettuce leaves
2 tablespoons flour

Thread peppers and garlic cloves on a long metal skewer. Rotate skewer slowly over gas flame or electric element until outside of peppers and garlic are charred. Remove peppers and garlic from skewer. Remove peel from 1 garlic clove and set aside. Mince half of the onion and set aside. Cut remaining half into chunks. In blender or food processor blend almonds until finely ground. Add peeled garlic clove, onion chunks, salt, oregano, pepper, 4 tablespoons water and 2 teaspoons vinegar. Blend on medium speed until mixture is smooth. Spread mixture over chicken pieces to coat well.

In a large skillet over medium high heat, heat oil and cook chicken until browned on all sides. Remove chicken to a bowl and set aside.

In drippings cook minced onion until tender, stirring occasionally. Return chicken to skillet; add charred peppers, unpeeled garlic, 1¾ cups water and 2 teaspoons vinegar. Over high heat bring to boiling. Reduce heat to low; cover and simmer 30 minutes or until chicken is tender, stirring occasionally.

With slotted spoon, remove chicken, peppers and garlic to a platter that has a bed of romaine spread over the bottom. Skim off excess fat from liquid in skillet. In cup, mix flour and ½ cup water. Gradually stir flour mixture into liquid in skillet; cook over medium heat until slightly thickened, stirring constantly. Pour into gravy boat and serve with chicken.

Chicken Mole

4   chicken breasts
4   thigh and legs of chicken
10 dried red ancho chili peppers, cut in quarters soaked in 2 cups boiling water for 1 hour *or* 1 tablespoon chili powder
5   tablespoons almonds
2   onions, chopped
2   cloves garlic, crushed
3   tomatoes, peeled, seeded and chopped
½ cup raisins
1   corn tortilla, fried in oil and torn up in small pieces
½ teaspoon cinnamon
½ teaspoon ground cloves
¼ teaspoon ground coriander
2   tablespoons sesame seeds
½ teaspoon salt
4   tablespoons vegetable shortening
2   cups chicken broth
1½ ounces chocolate, cut into small pieces
    Toasted sesame seeds

Steam chicken until just under tender; save broth. Soak dried chilies, if using them, and save the liquid but discard the stems and seeds. Put through blender or food processor until fine. Add the almonds, onions, garlic, tomatoes, raisins, tortilla, cinnamon, cloves, coriander, salt, sesame seeds, salt and a few tablespoons of the water chilies were soaked in or water if using chili powder. Blend, adding liquid if needed, until paste is formed. Heat the vegetable shortening and add the chili paste. Cook, stirring 2-3 minutes. Add all the broth, stirring constantly. Add the chocolate and stir until melted. Sauce should be the consistency of heavy cream; add more liquid if needed. Spoon sauce over chicken in serving or baking dish in an attractive manner; cover with plenty of sauce. Bake, covered, basting once or twice with sauce, ½ hour in 350° oven until chicken is nice and tender. Sprinkle with toasted sesame seeds to make more attractive. (May be frozen ready to bake. Add ½ hour cooking time and put in frozen.)

Green Chicken (Pollo Verde)

1   large onion, quartered
2   cloves garlic, sliced
¾ cup fresh coriander or ½ teaspoon dried crushed coriander
1   (10 ounce) can green husk tomatoes
    Salt
½ teaspoon coarsely ground black pepper
2   (2-3 pound) broilers, cut up

Combine the first four ingredients, including the juice from the tomatoes, and place in blender or food processor. Blend to a coarse texture. Season to taste with salt and add pepper. Place the chicken pieces in a large casserole with a cover. Add the first mixture, cover, and cook over very low heat or in a 325° oven until the chicken is tender, basting occasionally, about 1 hour.

Turkey Mole

8 pound ready-to-cook
    turkey
1 onion, peeled
1 stalk celery, cut up
2 teaspoons salt
8 whole black peppercorns
2 (10½ ounce) cans con-
    densed chicken broth
¼ cup salad oil
2 cups sliced onion
1 clove garlic, crushed
2 tablespoons sugar
2 tablespoons flour
2 teaspoons salt
1 tablespoon chili powder
½ teaspoon ground cinnamon
1 teaspoon ground coriander
1 teaspoon ground cumin
1 teaspoon dried oregano
1 (1 ounce) square un-
    sweetened chocolate
1 pound can tomatoes,
    undrained
1 ripe banana
¼ cup sesame seeds, toasted

Place cleaned turkey, whole onion, celery, 2 teaspoons salt, black peppercorns, chicken broth and 3 cups of water in a large kettle. Bring to boiling; reduce heat and simmer, covered, 1 hour. Remove turkey and drain well. Boil broth, uncovered, until reduced to 2 cups. Strain and reserve.

In hot oil saute the sliced onion and garlic until golden, about 5 minutes, and remove from heat.

Stir sugar, flour, salt, chili powder, cinnamon, coriander, cumin and oregano into the onion and garlic mixture. Add the reserved broth, chocolate and tomatoes. Return pan to heat. Bring to a boil, stirring occasionally. Reduce heat and simmer, covered, stirring occasionally, 15 minutes. Pour half of the sauce into a blender along with half of a ripe banana, and blend to liquify. Process remainder of sauce and remaining half banana in similar manner.

Preheat oven to 375°. Place turkey in a roasting pan without a rack. Spoon sauce over turkey. (To freeze, carve turkey, assemble in an attractive casserole and cover with sauce.) Bake, covered, basting once or twice with the sauce for one hour or until turkey is tender. (If frozen add ½ hour cooking time.) To serve place whole turkey in a shallow serving dish or deep platter. Pour sauce over turkey. Sprinkle with toasted sesame seeds. (If obtainable, Mexican chocolate is the best.)

Tijuana London Broil for Grill

2 pound beef flank steak
½ cup dry red wine
½ cup tomato sauce
1 teaspoon chili powder
2 (6 ounce) rolls of cheese
    with pimiento and
    jalapeno pepper
½ cup butter or margarine,
    room temperature
2 tablespoons chopped
    parsley
⅛ tablespoon ground cumin

Score steak diagonally on both sides. Place steak in a plastic bag; and then place in a shallow pan. Combine wine, tomato sauce and chili powder, and pour into bag over steak and seal bag. Refrigerate for at least 2 hours, turning the meat occasionally to distribute marinade. In medium bowl combine the cheese, butter or margarine, parsley and cumin. Remove steak from bag and pat meat dry with paper toweling. Season with salt and pepper. Place steak on grill over medium coals; cover with aluminum foil tent or hood. Grill steak about 5 minutes; turn. Recover and grill 4 minutes more for rare, 6 minutes more for medium-rare. Spread cheese mixture over the top the last 2 minutes of cooking. Remove meat from grill and slice diagonally in very thin slices.

212

Grilled Country Ribs with Red Chili Sauce (Puerco en Adobo)

8   pounds pork loin country-
      style ribs, cut into serving
      size pieces
      Water
8   dried ancho chilies, stems
      removed *or* 1 tablespoon
      chili powder and 8 serrano
      chilies, stems removed,
      canned or fresh
2   (4 ounce) cans chopped
      green chilies, drained
2   cloves garlic, crushed
1½   cups vinegar
3   teaspoons salt
½   teaspoon ground cumin
½   teaspoon oregano
2   medium avocados, peeled
      and cut into wedges
1   large bunch radishes,
      sliced thickly

In a 5-quart Dutch oven or sauce pan, cover pork ribs with water. Over high heat bring to boiling. Reduce heat to low, cover, and simmer 1 hour or until ribs are tender. Meanwhile in a saucepan cover the ancho chilies with water. Over high heat bring to boiling. Reduce heat to low, cover, and simmer 5 minutes or until soft. Drain well. In blender or food processor, blend chilies or, if not using ancho chilies, chili powder with serano chilies and the next 6 ingredients until pureed.

Preheat broiler. Remove ribs from water; drain and arrange on rack in broiling pan. Broil 15-20 minutes, brushing with chili mixture occasionally and turning once. To serve arrange ribs on platter, and garnish with wedges of avocado and slices of radishes.

Pork in Tomatillo Sauce (Green Husk Tomato Sauce)

5   pound pork butt roast
2   bay leaves
3   cups water
3   (14 ounce) cans tomatillos,
      green husk tomatoes,
      drained
3   cloves garlic, sliced
3   tablespoons fresh *or* pickled
      serrano *or* jalapeno chilies,
      chopped *or* 7 ounce can
      diced green chilies
2   tablespoons capers
1   pound pitted ripe olives,
      drained

Remove bone and fat from the pork roast. Cut meat into 1 inch cubes. Place meat and bay leaves in a large kettle and add the water. Bring to a boil, lower heat, cover, and simmer until tender—about one hour. Skim off excess fat.

In blender or food processor place the tomatillos, garlic and chilies, and blend until smooth. Add to pork along with the capers and the ripe olives. Cook, uncovered, stirring occasionally, until the sauce thickens, about 35-45 minutes. Taste and add salt.

Wrap about 16 flour tortillas in foil and place in a 350° oven until hot, about 20 minutes. To serve allow each guest to spoon some of the pork filling into his tortilla and then serve sour cream, guacamole, and diced tomatoes to spread over filling. Roll or fold up to eat.

Mexican Pot Roast

4   pound beef chuck pot roast
4   tablespoons vegetable oil
1   (1 pound) can tomatoes, smashed
1   (7 ounce) can green chilies, drained, seeded and chopped
½   cup water
1   envelope (2 tablespoons) taco seasoning mix
4   teaspoons beef bouillon granules
1½   teaspoons sugar
½   cup cold water
4   tablespoons flour

In a heavy kettle brown meat on both sides in the hot oil. Combine undrained tomatoes, chilies, the first ½ cup water, dry taco seasoning mix, bouillon granules and sugar, and pour over meat. Simmer, covered, for 2-2½ hours or until meat is tender. Remove meat to a warm platter. Pour juices into a measuring cup and skim off fat. Add water, if necessary, to make 1½ cups liquid, and pour back into kettle. Blend the cold water into the flour to a smooth paste, and add to mixture in kettle. Cook, stirring, until thickened and bubbly. Slice meat, and serve with the taco gravy. If desired, serve with Avocado Salad (see page 223).

Mexican Drunken Chicken (Pollo Borracho)

3   tablespoons olive oil
3   tablespoons butter
4   breasts of chicken halves
4   chicken legs and backs
¼   pound cooked ham, coarsely chopped
1   cup seedless raisins
⅛   teaspoon ground cloves
⅛   teaspoon cinnamon
⅛   teaspoon ground coriander
⅛   teaspoon cumin
2   cloves garlic, crushed
2   cups dry white wine or sherry
   Salt and pepper
½   cup toasted slivered almonds
½   cup stuffed olives, halved
1   tablespoon capers

Heat olive oil and butter to 360° and brown chicken pieces on all sides. Add rest of ingredients except nuts, olives and capers. Mix well and cover. Simmer slowly until chicken is tender, about 45 minutes. Add rest of ingredients and cook, uncovered, 5 minutes. (Freezes well without the nuts, olives and capers. Defrost; reheat and add the nuts, olives, and capers.)

Mexican Filled Peppers (Chilies Poblanos)

1 cup sliced blanched
    almonds
1 tablespoon butter
3 cups cooked chicken, diced
½ cup raisins
    Chicken stock to moisten
2 eggs, beaten
    Salt
8 large green bell peppers
    Flour
1 egg, beaten

Heat butter and brown almonds until just golden. Remove from heat and add chicken and raisins. Moisten with chicken stock slightly and add beaten eggs. Taste and adjust seasonings with salt and pepper. Cut off tops of peppers, and remove seeds. Roast peppers on a rack in a 450° oven until skins crack, turning to do all sides. Remove peppers; place in a paper bag and put in refrigerator to cool. When cool, peel off skin under running water, and drain and dry on paper towels. Fill peppers with chicken mixture, but keep only about 1 inch thick. Dip peppers in flour and then in the 1 beaten egg. Fry in hot fat and serve with Tomato Sauce on page 204 under Tamale Balls.

Green Chilies Stuffed with Cheese (Chilies Rellenos)

8 large green chilies, roasted
    in 350° oven, dry, until
    skin splits; peel and cool
1 pound Monterey Jack
    cheese, cut into 2-inch
    strips
½ cup flour
½ teaspoon salt
3 eggs, separated
3 tablespoons flour
½ cup vegetable shortening

Mix the flour and salt together and set aside. Remove stems of chilies and seed after they are prepared as directed, and stuff with cheese. Prepare all chilies this way. Beat egg whites until stiff and slowly fold in flour mixture. Beat egg yolks lightly and fold into the egg white mixture. Roll the stuffed chilies in flour. Dip one at a time into the egg batter and quickly transfer the chilies to a skillet with medium hot melted shortening. Several chilies may be done at the same time. Brown on both sides and place on paper towels to drain. Keep warm in 200° oven. Garnish with favorite Salsa to serve (see pages 200-201).

Green Chili Casserole

12 large, whole green chilies,
    roasted in 350° oven, dry,
    until skin splits; seed,
    peel and cool
1 pound Monterey Jack
    cheese
6 eggs, beaten
6 tablespoons flour
½ tablespoon baking powder
1 teaspoon salt
4-8 tablespoons grated
    Parmesan or Romano
    cheese

Preheat oven to 350°. Cut the cheese into strips and stuff into prepared, seeded chile peppers and set aside. Beat eggs thoroughly and add flour, baking powder and salt, beating continually until smooth.

Lightly grease a 2-quart casserole with vegetable oil. Place a third of the stuffed chilies in the dish. Cover with a third of the egg batter. Continue layering the chilies and batter, covering the top layer of chilies completely with the batter. Sprinkle the grated cheese over top of all. Place in oven and bake uncovered 15-25 minutes or until crust is light brown and is firm enough to be shaken lightly without coming apart. Serve with your favorite tomato sauce.

Veal with Capers (Ternera con Alcaparras)

3½ pounds veal stew meat
    Salt
2   large onions, chopped
2   cloves garlic, sliced thinly
¼   cup capers, drained
6   canned large chilies
4   medium tomatoes, peeled,
      seeded and diced
½   teaspoon coarse ground
      black pepper
¼   teaspoon sugar
2   tablespoons vegetable
      shortening

Place the veal in a heavy kettle, and almost cover with water. Add salt and bring to a boil. Simmer, covered, until veal is tender when pierced with a fork, about 1½ hours. Skim regularly to remove any scum that forms. Strain and place the meat in a oven-proof casserole. Reserve the stock.

Combine the onion, garlic, all capers but 1 tablespoon, chilies, tomatoes and a little of the veal stock in an electric blender or food processor, a small quantity at a time, and blend in a smooth puree. Heat the vegetable shortening in a skillet, and add the puree and cook, stirring constantly, over a moderate heat for 3-4 minutes. Add enough veal stock to the sauce to make a medium thick gravy. Season with salt and pepper. Pour over the cooked veal and cover. Place in 350° oven for half an hour. Sprinkle with the reserved capers. Serve with beans and sauce.

Chicken Livers in Sauce (Salsa di Fegatini di Pollo)

1½ pounds fresh mushrooms,
      cut in T's
1½ pound can whole peeled
      tomatoes
½   cup butter or margarine
½   cup diced onion
2   cloves garlic, sliced thin
1   pound chicken livers, halved
½   cup sherry
2   tablespoons flour
2   teaspoons sage
1   teaspoon salt
¼   teaspoon coarse ground
      black pepper

Prepare mushrooms and set aside. Drain tomatoes, reserving juices; chop tomatoes, and set aside. In a large kettle, melt butter, and add onion and garlic. Saute until onions are golden. Add mushrooms and chicken livers, and saute until livers are browned, about 5 minutes. Add wine mixed with flour, sage, salt, pepper, tomatoes and reserved tomato juice. Simmer uncovered until hot, about 10 minutes, stirring occasionally. Serve over rice or pasta.

Beef Tongue Salad (Ensalada de Salpicon)

1   beef tongue, about
        2 pounds, washed
1   carrot
1   onion
1   stalk of celery
1   bay leaf
½   teaspoon marjoram
¼   teaspoon thyme
⅛   teaspoon cloves
¼   teaspoon chopped parsley
8-10 black peppercorns
1   tablespoon sesame seeds
1   teaspoon salt
2   medium size potatoes
1   pound can green beans,
        Frenched
1   medium onion, sliced
        thinly, and separated
        into rings
1   large tomato, sliced
        Romaine lettuce leaves

4   tablespoons vegetable oil
2   tablespoons water
½   cup vinegar
1   clove garlic, crushed
½   teaspoon oregano
1½   teaspoons salt
½   teaspoon coarse ground
        black pepper

Cook beef tongue in the next ten ingredients with water to cover. Bring to a boil and then simmer for about 2½-3 hours, until tender. Remove tongue from simmering water with a meat fork and hold under cold running water and peel off thick outer layer of skin. Cool and cut into thin slices. Cook potatoes; cool and slice medium thin and set aside. Drain green beans and season. Make following sauce.

Sauce:

Mix thoroughly and pour third of mixture over drained green beans and other third on onion rings. Marinate half hour and drain.

Arrange prepared ingredients in layers on large serving platter: Place lettuce leaves on serving platter, followed by a layer of the sliced potatoes, layer of green beans and layer of onion rings. Then top with a layer of the sliced beef tongue and garnish with the tomato slices. Pour remaining marinade over all.

Fish Veracruz (Pescado Veracruzana)

4   tablespoons olive oil
1   large onion, diced
2   cloves garlic, thinly sliced
6   medium tomatoes, diced
2   large fresh or canned
      pickled jalapeno chilies,
      minced
½   cup pitted small green
      olives, cut in halves
4   tablespoons capers
1   teaspoon salt
4-5 pound red snapper or sea
      bass, boned and cut into
      fillets

In a 10-inch skillet over medium heat warm olive oil to hot. Cook onion and garlic until lightly browned and tender, stirring occasionally. Stir in tomatoes and remaining ingredients, except fish, and heat to boiling. Reduce heat to low, and simmer, uncovered, 5 minutes. Add fish fillets to skillet and heat to boiling over high heat. Reduce heat to low, and cover and simmer until fish flakes easily when tested with a fork. Serve with rice.

Mexican Cornbread with Bacon

5   slices bacon, cooked crisp
      and crumbled
1   cup yellow cornmeal
1   teaspoon baking powder
1   (4 ounce) can chopped
      jalapeno chilies
3   cloves garlic, crushed
1   (17 ounce) can whole kernel
      corn, drained
1   cup milk
1½ cups grated Longhorn cheese

Reserve bacon grease. Mix together cornmeal, baking powder, chilies, garlic, corn, milk and crumbled bacon. Pour half of mixture into a bread pan with bacon grease smeared all around and excess left on bottom. Sprinkle ¾ cup of the cheese over top. Add remaining cornbread mixture. Top with remaining ¾ cup cheese. Bake at 350° for 30-40 minutes. Serve warm.

Squash with Cheese

5   medium zucchini squash,
      washed
½   cup vegetable oil
3   medium tomatoes, diced
3   green chilies, chopped
½   medium onion, coarsely
      chopped
    Salt and pepper
½   pound Monterey Jack
      cheese, diced

Cut squash in 2-inch chunks. Heat oil in a large skillet and add all ingredients except the cheese. Saute, stirring occasionally, until all vegetables are just tender. Add cheese and stir through hot vegetables. Remove from heat immediately and serve.

Green Rice

3 large green peppers
½ cup coarsely chopped
  cilantro
½ cup coarsely chopped
  parsley
½ cup coarsely chopped
  onion
1 clove garlic, crushed
2 teaspoons salt
¼ teaspoon black pepper
⅓ cup olive or salad oil
1½ cups raw long-grained rice
3 cups chicken broth

In blender or food processor combine one third of green pepper, cilantro, parsley and onion. Blend until very fine, and turn into bowl. Blend rest of the green pepper, cilantro, parsley and onion, half at a time. Add salt, pepper and crushed garlic to the vegetables in a bowl.

In hot oil in large skillet, saute rice, stirring constantly, 2 minutes, or until grains are golden brown. Add blended vegetable mixture, and simmer, stirring occasionally, 5 minutes. Meanwhile bring chicken broth to boiling in a saucepan, and pour over rice. Bring back to boiling. Reduce heat; simmer covered and without stirring, 13-15 minutes, or until rice is tender and all liquid absorbed. Fluff rice with a fork before serving. (This dish will freeze well and reheats in a microwave or standard oven beautifully.)

Saffron Rice

10 strands of saffron shreds,
  soaked in ⅔ cup hot
  water 15 minutes
1 tablespoon vegetable oil
2 tablespoons finely diced
  onion
1 clove garlic, crushed
2 cups short grain rice,
  cooked
4 tablespoons chopped mild
  chilies
4 tablespoons finely diced
  tomatoes, peeled and
  seeded
¼ teaspoon white pepper
  Salt to taste

Soak saffron shreds and after soaking drain, saving the water to use. Fry the finely diced onion in the heated oil until onion is golden, and drain off any oil. Combine all ingredients and toss together lightly while mixing through the saved saffron water. Taste for salt. Pour into a lightly greased casserole; cover, and bake in 325° oven for about 15 minutes, until liquid is absorbed and rice hot, being careful not to dry out too much.

Refried Beans (Frijoles Refritos)

2 cups red kidney beans,
   rinsed
Salt to taste
1 cup bacon drippings, heated
1 tablespoon minced onion

Soak the beans overnight in water to cover. In the morning add more water to make sure the beans are covered, as the beans absorb some of the water while soaking. Cook beans in a heavy skillet, covered, for 2-2½ hours until very tender. About 10 minutes before finishing cooking, fry the minced onion in ½ cup of the heated bacon drippings, and, stirring through thoroughly, add along with salt to taste. Mash the beans well and simmer until all the fat is absorbed, stirring constantly to prevent sticking or burning. Heat another ½ cup fat, lard or bacon drippings, and, stirring constantly, add and cook until mashed beans are completely dry.

Unmashed Flavored Beans

1 (7 ounce) can chilies,
   chopped
1 teaspoon oregano
½ cup grated Parmesan cheese
½ cup chorizo

Cook beans as directed in preceding recipe but add 1 (7-ounce) can minced or chopped chilies, 1 teaspoon oregano, ½ cup of grated Parmesan cheese and ½ cup chorizo that has been lightly fried, about half hour before all liquid is absorbed and beans are almost tender. Simmer gently until beans are soft and still in a little of the sauce. Taste for salt.

Mexican Beans and Chili (Frijoles con Chili)

3 cups Mexican beans (kidney
   beans), washed
Water to cover
3 tablespoons butter
1 onion
Salt and pepper

Wash beans and soak overnight in water to cover. Boil in same water, simmering gently, until tender. Add salt to taste and bring to a boil again; drain. Melt butter and fry onions until golden. Add beans; mix well and season to taste. Spread out on a large platter and cover with Chili Sauce.

Chili Sauce:

2 tablespoons oil
1½ cups chopped onion
¼ pound hamburg
1 teaspoon salt
¼ teaspoon pepper
½ teaspoon thyme
1 tablespoon chili powder
3 cloves garlic, crushed
1 pound can tomato sauce
2 cups stock or bouillon

Brown onion and hamburg in hot oil, stirring occasionally. Add rest of ingredients, mixing well. Simmer gently, stirring occasionally, until thickened. Taste and adjust seasoning.

Green Corn Tamales

Husk cement for sticking corn leaves together:

Mix all together by hand very well and set aside.

1   cup Masa Harine, if you can get it, or white corn meal
½   cup boiling water
¼   pound margarine
¼   teaspoon soda
½   teaspoon salt
4   ears of grated corn kernels

Filling:

12   ears corn
¾   pound margarine
1½   teaspoons salt
2   cups Ricotta or cottage cheese
2   cups grated Monterey Jack cheese
     Diced green chilies (optional)
     Sliced stuffed green olives (optional)
     White raisins (optional)

Cut off top and bottom of 12 ears of corn with their husks on, taking off about 1½-inch slice from each end and discard. Remove the tough outer leaves of the corn husks and discard. Soak in hot water, for at least a half hour, the leaves covering the inner husks, removing the corn silk. Shave off the kernels from the 12 ears with either a saw tooth or electric knife and put through a food processor to smooth.

Mix corn with next four ingredients very well, and set aside. Drain and dry the soaking corn husks. Place two or three of the dried corn husks together cementing with the mixture first given. Spread about 4-6 tablespoons, depending on the size of the corn husks, down the center about 2 inches thick, allowing enough husk on each side to fold over completely covering filling, and enough husk at each end to fold in to hold filling, topping the filling with any of the optional ingredients lightly, before folding. Fold one side of the corn husk over the filling and overlap it with the opposite side of corn husk. Finish by folding the pointed ends under the tamale. In a heavy kettle with a tight-fitting cover, rig up a steamer, either with a rack or by placing 4-5 custard cups on the bottom and covering them with a dinner plate. Stack the tamales one on top of the other, making sure the ends stay folded under. (The tamales may be frozen at this point, but will have to steam double the cooking time placed in kettle frozen.) To cook pour water only up to the steaming rack or plate; bring to a boil; cover tightly and steam for 45 minutes. To eat, unwrap the tamale on your dinner plate and eat only the filling. The sizes of the tamales depend on the size of the corn husks or personal taste.

Jalapeno Grits Souffle

1   cup uncooked grits
1   teaspoon salt
4   cups boiling water
½   cup chopped onion
1   clove garlic, crushed
2   tablespoons butter, melted
2   cups shredded sharp
     Cheddar cheese
½   cup diced jalapeno peppers
4   egg yolks
4   egg whites, stiffly beaten

Stir grits slowly into salted boiling water in a heavy saucepan. Cook over low heat about 5 minutes, stirring occasionally. Saute onion and garlic in the butter, and add with cheese and peppers to grits. Beat egg yolks until thick and lemon colored. Remove grits from heat and blend in yolks. Fold in beaten egg whites gently. Pour into greased 2-quart casserole or souffle dish. Bake in 350° oven for 1 hour.

Cottage Cheese Mold

¼   cup butter
¼   cup brown sugar
2   cups small curd cottage
     cheese
2   egg yolks
¾   cup raisins
¾   cup unblanched almonds,
     ground
¼   teaspoon vanilla

Cream butter and sugar very well. Add remaining ingredients and mix thoroughly. Turn mixture into a towel lined round mixing bowl, and refrigerate overnight. To serve, turn out onto a platter and surround with wedges of fruit in season and avocado.

Mexican Dinner Salad

2   medium heads butter
     lettuce
1½ large red or green bell
     peppers, slivered
½   cup cilantro sprigs or
     watercress
¾   cup sliced pitted black
     olives
¾   cup garbanzo beans, drained
8   ounces French dressing

Tear lettuce into bite-size pieces. Add all but dressing and toss lightly. Add dressing and toss to coat.

Avocado Salad (Guacamole Salad)

2 large ripe avocados, mashed coarsely
3 tablespoons chopped canned green chilies
1 tablespoon grated onion
1 clove garlic, crushed
1 large tomato, peeled, seeded, and diced
¼ cup finely chopped cilantro or parsley
¼ cup sour cream
3 tablespoons lime juice
¼ teaspoon Tabasco sauce
  Salt to taste

Add all ingredients, and mash lightly. Cover with plastic wrap tightly. Refrigerate about 1 hour to chill. Garnish with chopped pimientos, and serve individually mounded on lettuce leaves.

Mexican Corn Salad

3 cups fresh, frozen and thawed or 2 (12 ounce) cans whole kernel corn, uncooked, drained and chilled
1 medium red onion, chopped
½ cup diced green pepper
1 tablespoon finely chopped cilantro or parsley
¼ cup sour cream
¼ cup beef broth
2 tablespoons red wine vinegar
½ cup mayonnaise
  Salt and pepper to taste
1 tomato, peeled, seeded and diced
4 slices bacon, cooked crisp, drained and crumbled
  Thinly sliced scallions

In a large bowl mix prepared corn, red onion, green pepper, cilantro or parsley. In a small bowl whisk together sour cream and broth, and add vinegar; whisk to blend. Whisk in mayonnaise and beat until light and very smooth. Toss dressing over vegetables and taste for salt and pepper. Chill. When ready to serve, garnish with tomato, bacon and scallions.

Kahlua Almond Pie

Graham Cracker Crust:

1¼ cups graham cracker crumbs
¼ cup sugar
⅓ cup butter or margarine, softened

Preheat oven to 350°. Combine all ingredients and press into bottom and sides of a 9-inch pie plate. Bake 10 minutes. Cool.

Filling:

2 tablespoons sugar
1 tablespoon unflavored gelatin
1 cup Kahlua liqueur
1 cup milk
2 egg yolks, beaten
¼ teaspoon almond extract
2 egg whites
¼ cup sugar
Whipped cream
Toasted slivered almonds

Prepare graham cracker crust. Combine sugar and gelatin in a 2 quart saucepan and stir in the Kahlua and milk. Heat over medium heat, stirring constantly, until gelatin is dissolved. Stir small amount of Kahlua mixture into egg yolks. Return egg mixture to saucepan. Stir over low heat until thickened. Remove from heat, and stir in almond extract. Refrigerate until mixture mounds slightly when dropped from a spoon, 15-30 minutes. Beat egg whites until foamy, and beat in ¼ cup of sugar, 1 tablespoon at a time, beating until stiff and glossy. Fold gelatin mixture into egg whites, folding in carefully. Pour all into graham cracker crust. Refrigerate at least 3 hours. Garnish with whipped cream and toasted almonds.

Pastry Puffs (Sopaipillas)

2 cups flour
¼ cup vegetable shortening
1 tablespoon baking powder
1 teaspoon salt
⅔ cup milk
Salad oil
1 tablespoon confectioners sugar
½ teaspoon cinnamon
Honey

In a large bowl with a pastry blender mix flour, shortening, baking powder and salt as for pie. Add milk, stirring until dough holds together in a ball. Turn out dough onto a lightly floured surface and knead until smooth, about 3 minutes.

Roll half of the dough at a time into a 12 x 9 inch rectangle. Cut rectangular into twelve 3 x 3 inch squares. Repeat with remaining dough.

In a 3-quart saucepan over medium heat, heat 3½ inches of salad oil to 375° or use a deep fat fryer. Fry two dough squares at a time in hot oil, turning with a slotted spoon as soon as they rise to the surface and turning often until both sides are golden brown. (Dough will puff up.) Remove puffs to paper towels and drain thoroughly. Serve with a container of sugar and cinnamon mixed together and a bowl of honey and allow each diner to apply as much as he desires. Makes 24.

Vermicelli Soup (Sopa de Fideo)

1	pound vermicelli
½	cup shortening
½	cup tomato sauce
1	teaspoon salt
1	clove garlic, crushed
2	scallions, thinly sliced
5	cups chicken or beef broth, hot

In a wide skillet fry the vermicelli strands in the shortening, turning until golden on both sides. Transfer the prepared strands to a saucepan, and add broth and remaining ingredients. Cover and simmer over low heat for 20 minutes. Stir occasionally, separating strands with a long fork. Continue cooking, uncovered, until no longer watery. Flavor improves with reheating. Serve as a side dish instead of rice, beans or potatoes.

Kahlua Chocolate Cheesecake

1¼	cups chocolate cookie crumbs
¼	cup ground pecans
¼	cup butter or margarine, melted
¼	cup Kahlua liqueur
¼	cup water
1	tablespoon unflavored gelatin
1	(8 ounce) package cream cheese, room temperature
6	tablespoons mocha or chocolate flavored instant cocoa mix
⅓	cup sugar
¼	cup Kahlua liqueur
1	cup whipping cream
	Whipped cream
	Chocolate curls

Mix cookie crumbs, pecans and butter. Press mixture evenly in bottom of an 8-inch springform pan. Stir ¼ cup Kahlua liqueur, water and gelatin in a small saucepan over low heat until gelatin is dissolved, about 3 minutes. Cool. Beat cheese in small mixer bowl until fluffy. Beat in cocoa mix, sugar and ¼ cup Kahlua. Stir in gelatin mixture. Beat whipping cream in chilled bowl until stiff peaks form. Fold cheese mixture into whipped cream, and pour into crust. Refrigerate until set, about 4 hours. Remove rim of springform to serve. Garnish with whipped cream and chocolate.

Coffee with Milk (Cafe con Leche)

4	cups water
4	cups milk
8	tablespoons instant coffee
8	tablespoons sugar

About 10 minutes before serving, over medium high heat, heat water and milk until hot, but do not boil. Stir in coffee and sugar until dissolved.

Mexican Coffee

1 tablespoon Mexican coffee
1½ ounces either brandy or
    tequila
    Hot black coffee
    Whipped cream

For each serving mix the coffee and liquor in a large cup or glass. Fill with hot black coffee. Top with large dollop of whipped cream.

Little Nut Cookies

Cookies:

3¼ cups flour
1 cup chopped nuts
⅔ cup sugar
½ cup milk
⅓ cup butter or margarine,
    melted
1 egg beaten

Combine all ingredients and mix thoroughly. Form into 1-inch balls.

Sugar Coating:

3 tablespoons sugar
1 teaspoon cinnamon

Combine sugar and cinnamon and roll balls in it until well coated. Place about 2 inches apart on a lightly greased cookie sheet. Flatten with a fork to form a crisscross pattern. Bake in a preheated moderate oven, 375°, 12-15 minutes, until lightly browned. Makes about 4½ dozen cookies.

Custard Mold (Flan)

1 (14 ounce) can sweet
    condensed milk
1 (13 ounce) can evaporated
    milk
4 eggs, beaten
1 tablespoon vanilla
1 cup sugar

Beat first 4 ingredients well with electric mixer. Meanwhile in a 9-inch mold, heat the cup of sugar over medium high heat, stirring constantly, until sugar carmelizes into a dark brown. Remove from heat and pour in mixed ingredients. Place in a pressure cooker, covering the mold first tightly with aluminum foil and tying tightly with kitchen string. Add water to reach three-quarters of way up on mold. Place pressure cooker lid in place and when regulator starts to bounce lower heat and cook 15 minutes. Cool cooker; open it, and take mold out. When it cools a little turn the mold out on a serving platter. Refrigerate. (If you do not have a pressure cooker to accomodate the mold, place the mold in a larger pan that will go in the oven and hold water up to half way up on the mold. Bake, uncovered, at 350° about 1 hour or until knife comes out clean when tested. Cool and refrigerate 8 hours before unmolding.)

Gelatin Dessert (Almendrado)

2 packages plain gelatin
Dash salt
1 cup boiling water
6 egg whites
¾ cup sugar
2 teaspoons almond extract
Slivered almonds
Red and green food coloring

Dissolve gelatin, water and salt in small bowl. Set aside to cool. Beat egg whites until stiff and dry and gradually add sugar, 1 tablespoon at a time. Continue beating until stiff and glossy.

Add almond extract to cooled gelatin and mix thoroughly. Fold gently into beaten egg whites.

Divide egg whites into three equal parts. Add 20 drops of red coloring to one part, 20 drops of green coloring to another, and leave third portion clear.

Spoon green mixture into glass serving dish to make first layer; next, spoon in untinted gelatin mixture; third, spoon in red mixture. Cover with foil and refrigerate for about 3 hours. Serve slices of almendrado gelatin mold sprinkled with almonds and topped with sauce.

Sauce:

1 (13 ounce) can evaporated milk
1 can water
¾ cup sugar
6 egg yolks
1½ teaspoons almond extract

In a small saucepan combine milk, water and sugar. Beat ¼ cup of mixture into egg yolks, and set aside. Heat remaining milk mixture over medium heat until warm. Reduce heat and continue stirring and add egg yolks. Stir constantly until mixture thickens slightly, but is still runny, being careful the sauce does not curdle. It must be cooked very carefully and never allowed to come to a boil. Refrigerate until cold (will keep several days).

Frozen Margaritas Supreme

Lime wedge
Salt
1 (6 ounce) can frozen limeade concentrate, thawed and undiluted
¾ cup tequila
¼ cup Triple X Sec
Crushed ice
Lime slices (optional)

Rub rim of 4 cocktail glasses with the wedge of lime. Place coarse salt in a saucer and spin rim of each glass in the salt. Place prepared glasses in the freezer.

Combine limeade, tequila and Triple X Sec in container of electric blender and blend well. Add crushed ice to fill blender ¾ full and blend well. Pour drink into prepared glasses, garnish with a slice of lime if desired. Double or triple for amount desired.

South American

Shrimp Boats

Pastry: (Or buy Won Ton skins at store.)

Combine dry ingredients in bowl. Reserve 1 teaspoon beaten egg for sealing pastries or use ½ cup water mixed with 1 tablespoon cornstarch. Mix egg, ice water and sauterne and add to dry ingredients, forming pastry ball. Cover with a towel and allow to stand 10 minutes. Knead a few minutes until well blended. Divide dough into 4 pieces and roll each out on a lightly floured surface until very thin. Cut in 3-inch squares.

2   cups flour
1   teaspoon salt
1   egg, lightly beaten
½   cup minus 1 tablespoon ice water
1   tablespoon sauterne

Filling:

Heat oil until hot; add olives and onions; fry until onions are golden. Add tomato, green pepper, hearts of palm or bamboo shoots and the water. Cover and simmer a few minutes. Add parsley, salt, pepper and shrimp. Simmer gently, stirring, for a few minutes until shrimp are pink. Add flour by sprinkling over all, stirring all the while. Cook, stirring, for 2 minutes. Cool. Place about 1 teaspoon filling in the center of each pastry square. Dampen edges of dough. Fold, making opposite corners meet, then take each of the other corners and bring them to the point where corners have met; pinch edges together. Fry in hot fat at 375°, browning lightly on both sides. Drain on paper toweling and serve hot. (Freezes well and should be warmed in pan lined with paper toweling in 350° oven for about 20 minutes or until warm.)

2   tablespoons olive oil
3   tablespoons chopped stuffed green olives
4   tablespoons minced onion
½   cup minced fresh tomato
4   teaspoons chopped green pepper
½   cup diced hearts of palm or ½ cup diced bamboo shoots
¼   cup water
¼   cup chopped parsley
½   teaspoon salt
⅛   teaspoon pepper
1   cup chopped shrimp
1   tablespoon flour

Avocado Dip (Guacamole)

1   large avocado, soft and ripe
1   teaspoon lemon juice
3   drops Tabasco sauce
1   teaspoon minced onion
1-2   cloves garlic, crushed
1   tomato, minced (optional)
¼   teaspoon salt
¼   cup mayonnaise

Cut avocado in half, lengthwise, and scoop out the meat. Sprinkle shells with lemon juice. Mash pulp of avocado to a smooth spreading consistency, adding rest of ingredients. Return mixture to avocado shells; refrigerate for several hours before serving, coating tops with extra mayonnaise to keep them from discoloring. Blend in coating to serve. Makes an excellent dip and is especially delightful for dipping shrimp and/or Plantain Chips (see page 232).

South American Filled Pastries (Pastellitos)

Filling:

3 tablespoons butter
1 onion, diced
1 clove garlic, crushed
½ pound lean pork or
  chicken ground
1¼ teaspoons salt
2 tablespoons vinegar
1½ teaspoons tomato sauce
1 medium potato, cooked
  and chopped fine
3 hard boiled eggs, chopped
  fine
¼ cup chopped olives
1½ tablespoons capers
4 tablespoons raisins

Melt butter and fry onion and garlic over medium heat, until glazed. Add meat and cook, stirring until it is no longer pink. Remove from heat and add rest of ingredients, stirring lightly and mixing well. Cool.

Pastry:

3½ cups flour
1½ teaspoons salt
½ cup vegetable shortening
1 tablespoon butter
1 egg, beaten with ½ cup sour
  cream and ½ cup milk

Combine flour and salt in bowl. Cut in vegetable shortening and butter as for pie. Add rest of combined ingredients, gathering all together to form pastry ball. Divide dough in 3 pieces and roll out one at a time on well floured surface until very thin. Cut in 3-inch squares. Place about 1 teaspoon filling in the center of each pastry square. Fold dough making opposite corners meet, pinching edges together very well. Heat deep fat to 375° and fry until golden brown on 1 side; turn and fry other side. (Freezes well and should be warmed in pan lined with paper toweling in 350° oven for about 15 to 20 minutes or until thoroughly warmed.)

Plantain Chips

Green plantains
Salt
Hot oil for frying

Peel and slice plantain, slicing as thin as you possibly can. Drop into hot deep fat and fry to a light golden, being careful not to allow them to even begin to brown, as they burn quickly. Fry on both sides; drain on paper towels. Salt well and cool thoroughly. Store in a cover jar. Serve as you would potato chips or use for dips.

Cheese Crunchies

3 cups flour
1 teaspoon salt
½ teaspoon red pepper
½ pound butter
1 pound sharp cheese, grated

Sift dry ingredients. Cream butter and grated cheese together and add dry ingredients, working together thoroughly with hands. Form into long rolls, about 1½ inches in diameter. Wrap in waxed paper and place in refrigerator until ready to use, or put dough in freezer until 2 hours before ready to use. Slice thin and bake in 350° oven until crisp, about 10 minutes. Serve hot.

South American Hot Spicy Beef Tarts

Filling:

2 tablespoons vegetable oil
⅓ cup finely chopped scallions
½ pound lean beef, ground twice
½ cup finely chopped, peeled and seeded tomato
1½ teaspoons salt
2 cloves garlic, crushed
¾ teaspoon dry mustard
½ teaspoon red hot sauce
1 egg, slightly beaten
¼ teaspoon black pepper
⅛ teaspoon red pepper

Fry scallions in hot oil until limp. Add beef and fry, stirring until beef browns. Remove from heat and add rest of ingredients. Mix well. Return to heat for 1 minute and cook, stirring. Cool in refrigerator.

Pastry:

1½ cups flour
¾ teaspoon salt
⅛ teaspoon red pepper
½ cup butter or margarine
¼ cup ice water
Yolk of egg

Mix dry ingredients; add butter or margarine and cut in as for pie crust. Beat water and egg yolk together and add to mixture, gathering into a pastry ball. Roll pastry to ¹⁄₁₆ inch thickness; cut into 2½-3 inch rounds. Fill half of round with teaspoon of filling; fold over other half of pastry and press together with tines of fork. Prick tops and brush with leftover egg white, slightly beaten. Bake in 450° oven for 12 minutes. Serve hot. (Freezes beautifully; reheat in 350° oven for 8-10 minutes, placing in oven frozen.)

Cold Spanish Vegetable Soup (Gazpacho)

¼ cup wine vinegar or
   white wine
¼ cup olive oil
3-4 cups tomato juice
1½ cups chicken broth
1 medium green pepper, cut
   in large dice
1 cucumber, seeded and cut
   in large dice
½ cup chopped onion
3 tomatoes, peeled and
   seeded, cut in large dice
1½ teaspoons salt
½ teaspoon coarse black pepper
   Dash of cayenne
¼ teaspoon sweet basil
2 cloves garlic

Using blender, add half of wine vinegar or wine, half of olive oil, half of tomato juice and half of chicken broth together in container, then add half of all vegetables and 1 clove of garlic. Run the machine for about 2-3 seconds. Pour into large bowl used to assemble the whole. Now add other half of ingredients to container, plus the seasonings. Turn on machine for another 2-3 seconds. Pour into bowl; stir well and taste to adjust seasonings. Chill. To serve, chill soup well and also chill soup bowls, if you have room in refrigerator. Gazpacho should be served very, very cold. Offer an assortment of chopped fresh peeled and seeded tomatoes; chopped, seeded cucumbers; chopped green peppers; chopped parsley and toasted garlic croutons in separate bowls. Each person will help himself to whatever crunchy vegetable he likes and garnish with croutons. If you like a thinner consistency for your gazpacho, simply thin out with water, a little at a time, until as thin as you desire. Blend well. (Gazpacho freezes very well. Should the oil separate on standing in refrigerator or in defrosting, simply stir vigorously to blend.)

Cuban Black Bean Soup

1 pound black beans, washed
   and drained
10 cups water
2 tablespoons salt
1 tablespoon oil
5 cloves garlic
½ tablespoon cumin
½ tablespoon oregano
⅛ cup white vinegar
4 tablespoons olive oil
1¾ cups onions, sliced
   lengthwise
2 green peppers, diced fine
⅓ cup dry sherry
2 cups boiled rice
1 medium onion, very
   finely chopped
3 tablespoons olive oil
2 tablespoons white vinegar

Soak beans in water overnight. Add salt and oil to beans and water and cook until soft. Crush with mortar and pestle the garlic, cumin, oregano and vinegar. Heat oil in a large kettle; add sliced onions and green peppers and fry until onions are brown. Add crushed ingredients, frying slowly. Add cooked beans and broth to kettle and cook slowly until just before serving time. Add sherry and blend well; taste. To serve, mix the boiled rice, onion, olive oil and 2 tablespoons vinegar together. Place several tablespoons of the rice mixture in each soup plate and then add soup. Best if made the day before. (Freezes well.) May be put in blender or food processor and returned to soup pot before adding rice mixture, if smooth soup is preferred.

White Garlic Soup (Ajo Blanco)

2 eggs
4-6 cloves garlic
2 teaspoons salt
¼ cup olive oil
2 tablespoons wine vinegar
4 slices white bread, soaked
  in water and squeezed dry
3 cups water
7 cups clear chicken broth

Place half of all ingredients at a time in a blender. Blend thoroughly for about 1 minute. Place in bowl and do other half; combine. Taste and adjust seasonings. Serve hot or cold.

Almond Soup (Sopa de Almendras)

2 tablespoons butter
2 tablespoons flour
4 cups chicken broth
2 cups blanched almonds,
  ground
2 cloves
¼ teaspoon nutmeg
¼ teaspoon mace
⅛ teaspoon thyme
1 teaspoon salt
4 cups cream
½ cup slivered almonds
  Paprika

Melt butter in soup kettle. Add flour and blend until smooth. Gradually add chicken broth, stirring all the while. Add ground almonds and seasonings; taste and adjust for salt. Simmer gently for ½ hour. Strain and add cream; heat about 3 minutes. Garnish with slivered almonds and sprinkle with paprika. Serve hot or cold. (Freezes well.)

Chicken Soup (Sopa Canja)

1 fowl, cut up
2 cloves garlic
3 teaspoons salt
¼ teaspoon pepper
1 cup chopped onion
¼ cup water
½ cup rice
12 cups water
¼ teaspoon thyme
2 bay leaves
4 sprigs parsley

Fry the fat from the fowl with 2 cloves garlic to make 3 tablespoons rendered chicken fat. Season pieces of chicken well with salt and pepper and brown nicely in rendered chicken fat. Add onions and fry until golden. Add ¼ cup water and rice; cover and simmer gently until rice has absorbed all moisture, stirring occasionally so that rice doesn't stick. When rice has absorbed moisture, add 12 cups water and rest of ingredients. Simmer gently, covered, until chicken is tender enough to come off the bones. Bone chicken and cut in small pieces. Return to soup. Remove bay leaves; taste to adjust seasonings and simmer to reheat.

Cocido

1   ham bone of ¼ pound
    smoked ham, cut in large
    dice
1   pound can chick peas,
    drained
8   cups water
2   chicken breasts, boned and
    cut in large dice
3   tablespoons Spanish olive oil
1   large onion, diced
3   cloves garlic, crushed
2   tomatoes, skinned and
    seeded and cut in eighths
1   bay leaf
1   teaspoon thyme
¼   teaspoon cayenne
3   large potatoes, cut in
    large dice
1   Spanish sausage (Chorizo)
    or hot Italian sausage,
    sliced
½   pound summer squash, cut
    in large dice

Place ham, chick peas and water in a large kettle and simmer over medium heat. Heat oil and fry chicken pieces, onion and garlic until chicken is lightly browned. Add tomatoes, bay leaf, thyme and cayenne. Cook, stirring until tomatoes are soft. Add chicken mixture to simmering broth. Place sausage in dry pan and brown on both sides. Add sausage and potatoes to broth and simmer until soft and the chicken is tender. Season with salt and pepper to taste. Add squash and simmer 10 minutes. Serve with boiled rice if desired. (Freezes well and keeps up to 6 months.)

Vegetable Soup and Cheese (Pisto Sopa)

3   large ripe tomatoes, peeled
    and coarsely chopped
1½ pounds fresh green beans,
    cut in 1-inch lengths
4   medium potatoes, diced
    (4½ cups)
12 cups water
1½ teaspoons salt
¼   teaspoon pepper
⅓   pound vermicelli or soup
    pasta
1   cup coarsely chopped
    fresh basil or 3 table-
    spoons dried
4   cloves garlic, crushed
¼   cup olive oil
1   cup shredded cheese

Place tomatoes and their juices and green beans in a large deep kettle. Add potatoes, water, salt and pepper. Bring mixture to a boil; reduce heat; cover and simmer 1 hour. Add vermicelli and cook 15 minutes. Taste for seasonings. In medium size bowl mix basil, crushed garlic and ¼ cup olive oil. Stir so oil covers mixture well. Allow to stand for 1 hour. (This is the Pisto.) Stir about ½ cup of soup into the Pisto, then mix back into the kettle. Gradually add cheese, about 2 tablespoons at a time, stirring well after each addition. Blend in thoroughly and serve immediately. (Freeze before adding cheese. Defrost, reheat and blend in cheese as directed.)

Meat and Vegetable Soup (Sancocho)

2 tablespoons cooking oil
1 fowl, cut up
½ pound spareribs, cut in 1-inch pieces
1 ham bone
2 pounds potatoes, diced
½ pound longaniza, cut up if you can get it, or 5-6 hot Italian sausages, cut up
4 green plantains, sliced, if you can get them
3 ears corn, cut off the cob
½ pound yucca, if you can get it, chopped, or ½ pound sweet potato, chopped
¼ cup chopped parsley
1 green pepper, diced
1 cup chopped onion
Few coriander seeds
4 cloves garlic, crushed
1 tablespoon vinegar
16 cups water
Salt to taste

Saute chicken in oil to brown on all sides. Bring rest of ingredients to a boil and simmer gently for ½ hour. Add fried chicken and drippings; stir well and adjust seasonings. Simmer gently until chicken is tender. Serve in soup bowls plain as a hearty soup or over rice as a main dish. Serves 12.

Meat Chowder (Puchero)

½ fowl, cut up
2 pounds stewing beef, cut up
½ cup precooked beans
½ small head cabbage, shredded
4 medium potatoes, diced
4 sweet potatoes, diced
3 carrots, diced
½ pound squash, diced
2 leeks, diced or 1 large onion, diced
4 ears corn, cut off the cob
6 tablespoons rice
Salt and pepper to taste

Place all ingredients together in a large soup kettle. Cover with boiling water and simmer gently until meat and chicken are tender. Twenty minutes before serving, taste and adjust seasonings. Serve in deep bowls, steaming hot.

With Prunes (Potted):

1	eye of the round tenderized or tenderloin, cut through lengthwise 3 or 4 times to make holes for stuffing
28	pitted prunes, cut in half
18	(½-inch) pieces of bacon
4	tablespoons butter
½	slice bacon, diced
2	cups dry white wine
1	cup water
1	teaspoon salt
⅛	teaspoon pepper
3	tablespoons flour
3	tablespoons water
½	teaspoon salt
⅛	teaspoon pepper
4	tablespoons sugar

Push 8 halves of pitted prunes alternately with the pieces of bacon into each lengthwise cut, stuffing well. Melt butter and brown meat on all sides; remove from pan. Add half slice bacon, diced, to butter in pan and parcook. Replace meat in pan and scatter bacon on top of the roast. Add rest of pitted halves of prunes, wine and water. Cover and cook, simmering gently, 30 minutes for rare, 50 minutes for medium well. Blend water and flour; add salt, pepper and sugar and mix well. Add 1 cup liquid from around roast and return all to pan. Cook until gravy is thickened, stirring constantly. Remove meat, allow to rest 5 minutes and slice. Serve gravy separately.

With Pimiento Stuffed Olives (Roasted/Broiled):

1	eye of the round tenderized or tenderloin, cut through lengthwise 3 or 4 times to make holes for stuffing
2	tablespoons large capers
28	large pimiento stuffed olives
18	(½-inch) pieces of bacon
6-8	cloves garlic, crushed
2	tablespoons coarsely ground black pepper
2	teaspoons coarsely ground salt

Push some of capers, stuffed olives and pieces of bacon into each lengthwise cut, stuffing well. Set aside. Mix crushed garlic well with salt and pepper. Rub and pat into outside of meat all of the garlic mixture. Preheat broiler. Place meat on a broiler pan and put pan on the very bottom shelf in a large oven. Broil meat 20 minutes on one side; turn and broil 20 minutes on other side for medium rare or broil 25 minutes per side for medium, or roast in 200° oven 1 hour per pound. Allow to rest 5 minutes before slicing. Serve with rice and beans.

Pig's Feet or Short Ribs of Beef and Vegetables (Guezo)

8   pigs feet, scrubbed and boiled in salted water until tender with 3 cloves garlic or 16 short ribs of beef, very lean
1   tablespoon salt
1   teaspoon black pepper
1   tablespoon oregano, crushed fine
4   cloves garlic, crushed
2   tablespoons vinegar

4   tablespoons olive oil
2   tablespoons vinegar
4   large potatoes, diced
1¾   cups coarsely chopped celery
1¼   cups chopped onion
1   cup chopped green pepper
1   cup chopped tomatoes
1   teaspoon black pepper
1   teaspoon oregano
1   (8 ounce) can tomato sauce
1   (6 ounce) can tomato paste
2   teaspoons salt
2   (1 pound 4 ounce) cans drained chick peas
5   cups water

If using short ribs, make marinade from salt, pepper, oregano, garlic and vinegar. Rub into short ribs and allow to marinate for 20 minutes. Heat 3 tablespoons vegetable oil with ½ teaspoon sugar until oil is piping hot and sugar is melted and browned. Add pieces of meat and marinade; cover and cook on high heat, turning frequently, until meat is well browned on all sides. Lower heat and cook, turning occasionally, while making the following sauce.

Sauce:

Heat oil and vinegar and add vegetables, black pepper and oregano; cook 7 minutes, stirring frequently. Add tomato sauce and tomato paste; cook 5 minutes, stirring all the while. Add drained pig's feet or the short ribs and juices and the rest of the ingredients. Simmer gently for about 1 ½ -2 hours. (Some South Americans like to serve this in a soup dish over rice. We prefer it as is. Freezes well.)

Puerto Rican Roast Pork

5-6   pound pork roast
7   cloves garlic
2   teaspoons oregano
3   tablespoons coarse salt
¾   teaspoon peppercorns
2   tablespoons fresh orange juice
2   tablespoons fresh lime juice

Place garlic, oregano, salt and peppercorns in a mortar and crush smooth with the pestle. Add juices and mix well. Rub mixture into roast and marinate overnight. Roast in 325° oven until a meat thermometer stuck in the fleshy thick part of roast (not near bone) reads 185°, about 2½-3 hours.

Spanish Beef Stew (Guisado)

1   pound dried garbanzos
      (chick peas)
1   teaspoon salt
6   slices bacon
3-4   pounds stew beef
1   large onion, diced
1½   cups mushrooms, sliced
2   carrots, sliced
1   cup beef broth or bouillon
2   cups tomato sauce
2   cloves garlic, crushed
½   teaspoon oregano
¼   teaspoon thyme
1   bay leaf
½   teaspoon cumin
      Salt and pepper

Soak garbanzos overnight in water to cover 2 inches above the peas. Next morning, rinse and place in water to cover with 1 teaspoon salt and boil until soft, about 2-3 hours; drain. Fry bacon in largest size skillet until crisp and brown; remove and set aside. Dry stew beef well and brown in hot bacon grease. Add onion, sliced mushrooms and carrots; mix well and cook, stirring for 3 minutes. Add beef broth, tomato sauce, seasonings and garbanzos; mix well and cook, stirring occasionally, until beef is tender, about 45 minutes. Crumble bacon and add to stew, heating briefly. Serve with rice. (Freezes well.)

Spanish Paella

3   chicken breasts, cut in
      small chunks
¼   cup butter
1   clove garlic, crushed
1   Chorizo or Italian hot
      sausage, sliced
¼   cup diced onion
¼   cup diced green pepper
¼   teaspoon ground coriander
2   teaspoons capers
¼   teaspoon oregano
4   tablespoons tomato sauce
1   teaspoon vinegar
2   cups rice
4   cups chicken broth
1   teaspoon saffron shreds,
      soaked in warm water
16-24 shrimp
¾   pound lobster meat, cut in
      large dice
8   small clams, scrubbed
8   mussels, scrubbed
1   cup drained canned peas
1   pimiento, cut in julienne

Saute chicken pieces in ¼ cup butter with garlic until chicken is lightly browned. Add Chorizo or Italian sausage slices and fry, turning on both sides. Add onion, green pepper, coriander, capers, oregano, tomato sauce and vinegar and mix well. Add 2 cups rice and stir to coat all over. Add 4 cups chicken broth and saffron and water; cover; simmer for 15 minutes. Add shrimp and continue to cook about 5 minutes, covered, until rice is done and broth absorbed. Add lobster pieces and drained peas, tucking them into the rice. Garnish with pimiento julienne; cover and heat through gently. Meanwhile, steam clams and mussels over water until they open. Garnish Paella with clams and mussels; pour over 2 tablespoons of broth from clams; reheat gently. Serve promptly. (Can be made up to point of adding shrimp and refrigerated. Reheat and add shrimp; cook gently until heated through and shrimp are cooked and broth absorbed. Proceed from there to finish.)

Rice and Chicken (Arroz con Pollo)

½   cup olive oil
1   cup diced onion
1   cup diced green pepper
2   cloves, garlic, minced
½   pound mushrooms,
      quartered
3   tablespoons butter or
      margarine
1   pound can plum tomatoes
2   teaspoons salt
¼   teaspoon pepper
1   large bay leaf
2   chickens, cut into 16
      serving-size pieces; salt,
      pepper, paprika
1½ cups long-grain converted
      rice
4   tablespoons butter or
      margarine
2   cups chicken broth
1   package frozen LeSueur
      little peas
1   pound asparagus in long
      spears
1   pimiento, cut in julienne

Saute diced onion, diced green pepper and minced garlic in hot olive oil, stirring frequently, until onions are lightly brown. Meanwhile, saute quartered mushrooms in 3 tablespoons butter, stirring occasionally, for 3 minutes. Combine all cooked ingredients and add canned tomatoes, salt, pepper and bay leaf; mix well. Salt and pepper chicken pieces and roll each one in paprika. Place in sauce, spooning sauce over chicken. Cover and cook gently for 20 minutes. Meanwhile, heat other 4 tablespoons butter or margarine and when melted, remove from heat; add rice, stirring to coat well. Add coated rice to chicken with half of the chicken broth. Simmer, covered for 10 minutes, stir and add rest of broth to keep moist and simmer another 10 minutes. Test to see if all is done, testing chicken as well as rice to make sure all is tender. Taste and add salt if needed. Cook peas and asparagus with a minimum of liquid; drain and nicely garnish along with the pimiento. (Freezes well without garnishes. Defrost and reheat in 300° oven for 40 minutes and garnish.)

Dominican-Style Chicken

3   cut up frying chickens
2   teaspoons oregano
⅓   cup vinegar or lemon juice
⅔   cup oil
2   teaspoons salt
½   teaspoon black pepper
3-4 cloves garlic, crushed

Place oregano in a small frying pan and heat until warm. Rub oregano between palms of hands to a powder. Mix rest of the following ingredients with oregano and pour over chicken pieces, rubbing and coating them well. Cover and place in refrigerator for at least 1 hour or more. Broil chicken pieces until nicely browned on both sides, basting frequently with marinade. Turn heat to 350° and finish cooking until chicken is fork tender. May be barbecued on top of grill, wrapped with foil, for 45 minutes. Remove foil, finish barbecuing, basting frequently until nicely brown on both sides and tender. (Freezes well after broiling. Defrost and place in oven as directed above.)

Fried Tenderloin Steaks (Filete)

8 tenderloin steaks, cut 1¼ inches thick
1 teaspoon oregano
2 teaspoons vinegar
1½ teaspoons salt
2 cloves garlic, crushed
1 medium onion, chopped fine
2 tablespoons olive oil
8 slices bacon

Pound each slice of tenderloin to about ¾ inch thick. Place oregano in a small frying pan and heat until warm. Rub oregano between palms of hands to a powder. Mix with following 5 ingredients and spread over tenderloin slices. Cover and place in refrigerator for ½ hour or more. Circle each steak with a strip of bacon, securing with a toothpick. Grease the largest size skillet lightly and heat until hot. Sear tenderloin slices to brown quickly on each side. Cook to desired amount of doneness: for rare, 4 minutes one side and 3 minutes other side; for medium rare, 5 minutes on one side and 4 minutes on other side. Serve immediately.

Stuffed Baked Fish (Pescado Relleno)

2 whole fish for baking
Salt and pepper
1 lobster, boiled, cut meat in small chunks when cooled
2 (7½ ounce) cans crabmeat or frozen crab, cut in small chunks
1 cup fine dried bread crumbs
2 eggs, beaten
3 tablespoons melted butter
1 teaspoon salt
¼ teaspoon pepper
3 tablespoons lemon juice
¼ cup chopped ripe olives
¼ cup chopped green stuffed olives
1 teaspoon tarragon leaves
1 teaspoon dill weed
1 tablespoon minced onion
½ cup dried fine bread crumbs
¼ teaspoon nutmeg
½ teaspoon salt
¼ teaspoon pepper
2 tablespoons dried parsley flakes
1 cup dry white cooking wine
Melted butter

Wipe fish well and season with salt and pepper, inside and out. Mix the next 13 ingredients together well. Stuff fish and tie together or hold together with toothpicks. Mix other bread crumbs, nutmeg, salt, pepper and parsley flakes together well. Sprinkle a thin layer of this bread crumb mixture over bottom of a pan large enough to bake both fish, using about half of mixture. Place fish on this layer and pour wine over all, then sprinkle top of fish with remaining crumb mixture. Drizzle with melted butter. Cover pan loosely with aluminum foil. Bake in 350° oven for 30-40 minutes, removing foil for last 15 minutes of baking. Serve with Colombian Corn Pudding (see page 246). (Does not freeze well after cooking. Prepare for cooking early in the day and bake just before dinner time.)

Crustaceans in Wine and Tomato Sauce (Zarzuella)

1   cup dry white wine
1   (28 ounce) can peeled
     tomatoes
4-6 cloves garlic, crushed
4   scallions, whites only,
     chopped
¼   cup olive oil
1   tablespoon dried parsley
     flakes
1   teaspoon powdered mustard
1   teaspoon salt
1   teaspoon paprika
½   pound fish fillet (sole
     or seasonal)

Mix ingredients listed at the side together in a blender or food processor, blending well. Simmer about 1 hour until reduced and thickened.

1   (1½ pound) lobster,
     steamed or boiled
1   dozen large shrimp
1   squid, cleaned, if avail-
     able, cut into ½ inch
     circles
2   dozen little neck clams,
     washed under cold water
     with a brush
2   dozen mussels, washed
     under cold water with a
     brush (double clams if
     you do not care for
     mussels)

Cook lobster 10 minutes, until red, and shrimp for 3 minutes, until pink, separately. Cool and cut lobster and shrimp into ½ inch pieces. Refrigerate. Cook squid in 1 cup water and ½ cup white wine for 45 minutes, until tender; drain; refrigerate. Fifteen minutes before serving, steam the clams and mussels until they open; discard the ones that do not open. Remove half of the clams and/or mussels from shells and add to simmering sauce along with the prepared pieces of lobster, shrimp and squid. Add rest of clams and mussels in their shells. Bring all to a gentle boil. Remove from heat. Serve with small side dishes of rice. Serves 4 generously. Serve with garlic bread. (Does not freeze well. May be prepared ready to add the crustaceans when reheated.)

Pickled Lamb (Adobo de Cordero)

5   pound lamb shoulder, cut
     in ½ inch slices
5   onions, thinly sliced
3-4 cloves garlic, sliced thin
     Salt and pepper
     Juice of 3-4 lemons

Place a layer of sliced meat in a large deep baking dish. Spread a layer of sliced onions and garlic on top. Salt and pepper and sprinkle with lemon juice. Repeat layers until all ingredients have been used. Allow to marinate overnight in refrigerator. When ready to cook, place meat in a single layer on a large broiler pan, basting well with liquid. Broil about 6 inches from heat about 4 minutes each side, basting occasionally. Serve the juices over the broiled meat.

Shrimp Casserole (Camaraos)

3 pounds cooked, shelled, deveined shrimp
1½ tablespoons olive oil
1½ cups coarsely chopped celery
1½ cups coarsely chopped onion
1½ cups coarsely chopped green pepper
3-4 cloves garlic, crushed
3½ cups plum tomatoes, canned or fresh
1 pound can tomato puree
Salt and coarse ground black pepper to taste
2 whole cloves
2 whole allspice
3 bay leaves

Heat vegetable oil in a large heavy kettle and add celery, onion, and green pepper. Cook until onions are golden. Add garlic and simmer over low heat for a few minutes. Add tomatoes, tomato puree, salt and pepper to taste. Tie cloves, allspice and bay leaves in a small cheesecloth bag and add. Bring to a boil and then reduce heat and simmer; cook for 20 minutes, stirring occasionally. Add cooked shrimp and simmer for 3 minutes longer. Remove spice bag and place in large casserole. Place in 300° oven for 15 minutes. Serve hot with rice.

Spanish Vegetable Casserole (Pisto)

½ pound bacon, fry crisp, drain on paper towels, crumble; pour off all but 2 tablespoons drippings
2 eggplants, unpeeled, cut in ½ inch cubes; salt and drain with weight on them ½ hour
2 medium onions, sliced and circles separated
3-4 medium zucchini squash, prepare same as eggplant
1 green pepper, cut in circles
2 cloves garlic, crushed
1 pimiento, cut in julienne
1 cup tomatoes, peeled, quartered and seeded
1 can artichoke hearts, drained

Fry lightly the drained and wiped eggplant in the saved drippings. Remove from pan and place in deep serving casserole. Fry zucchini the same way, adding olive oil if you need more fat; add to eggplant. Fry onion, green pepper and garlic until onions are golden and soft. Add to casserole and salt and pepper lightly, mixing well. Garnish top of casserole with quartered tomatoes, pimiento and artichoke hearts. Top with crumbled bacon. Can be served hot or cold. Bake at 350° for 35-40 minutes and serve or allow to cool and serve. Best serve cold when serving with Paella, see page 240. (Freezes well before baking.)

Spanish Orange Salad

6   large navel oranges, peeled and sliced thickly
4   tablespoons olive oil
3   tablespoons lemon juice
1   clove garlic, crushed
    Lettuce leaves
    Oregano

Place oil, lemon juice and garlic in a small container with a cover and shake well. Put orange slices in a bowl and pour dressing over, tossing to cover well. Refrigerate until ½ hour before serving time. Allow to rest at room temperature. Make a bed of lettuce leaves on 8 plates; place about 3 slices of orange on each plate. Sprinkle lightly with oregano and serve.

Paraguayan Cornmeal

4   tablespoons butter
1   cup diced onion
¼   cup diced green pepper
1   large tomato, chopped
½   cup chicken broth or bouillon
1   teaspoon salt
1   teaspoon baking powder
1   cup milk
1   tablespoon melted butter
1   cup grated Cheddar cheese
2   cups cornmeal
4   tablespoons butter

Melt first 4 tablespoons butter and saute onion and green pepper, stirring, until onion is lightly browned. Add tomato and cook, stirring, until tomato is mushy. Add broth or bouillon, salt, baking powder and milk; bring to a boil stirring constantly. Add grated cheese and cornmeal, stirring constantly until well blended. Remove from heat. Melt other 4 tablespoons butter in a baking dish. Pour in cornmeal mixture and spoon some of the melted butter over top, coating well. Bake in 375° oven until nicely browned, about 30 minutes. Cut in thick slices to serve. (Does not freeze well.)

Brazilian Rice

2   tablespoons shortening
3   tablespoons diced onion
1   small clove garlic, crushed
2   teaspoons salt
2   cups long grain rice
1   tablespoon tomato paste
4   cups hot stock or bouillon

Heat shortening; add onion and saute, stirring constantly, until onion is lightly golden. Add rice and garlic; cook stirring, for about 1 minute. Remove from heat and add tomato paste; mix well. Add stock or bouillon; mix well and return to heat. Boil over high heat for 2 minutes; cover and reduce heat to simmer gently for 10 minutes or until rice is dry. (Freezes well. Reheat in covered casserole in 350° oven for 30 minutes.)

Rice and Beans (Arroz y Habichuellas)

1	pound South American red beans or 2 (15 ounce) cans red kidney beans, drained
1	slice bacon, diced
1	cup diced onion
2	tablespoons tomato paste
1	teaspoon sugar
1	cup stock or bouillon
2	cloves garlic, crushed
¼	teaspoon marjoram or cayenne
½	teaspoon salt
¼	teaspoon pepper
½	teaspoon paprika

If using South American red beans, cover with water after washing well and allow to soak overnight. Next day cook in same water until tender; drain. Fry bacon with onion until onion is golden. Add tomato paste, stock and seasonings, using cayenne if a hot sauce is desired. Cook, stirring occasionally, until sauce is creamy. Add beans and cook for 10 minutes over low heat, stirring occasionally. Serve over boiled or steamed rice. (Sauce and beans freeze well.)

Colombian Corn Pudding

6	ears fresh corn or 6 cups drained whole kernel corn
3	eggs, beaten
¾	cup milk
4	tablespoons melted butter
1	teaspoon paprika
	Salt and pepper
	Slices of Jack cheese

Cut corn off cob and place in bowl (or use canned corn). Mash corn with a wooden masher. Add remaining ingredients, except cheese, and mix well. Turn half of mixture into a buttered casserole; cover with slices of cheese. Pour on remaining corn mixture. Bake in 300° oven for 40 minutes, or until silver knife comes out clean from top layer of corn mixture. Unmold on heated platter and serve in wedges.

Casserole of Sweet Potatoes, Bartlett Pears and Pecans

8	sweet potatoes, slice ½ inch thick and cut in half circles
½	cup butter
1	large can Bartlett pears, drain and save juice
	Dry white wine to add to juice to make 2 cups
1	cup pecans

Melt butter in frying pan and fry sweet potato pieces until nicely golden on each side. Drain on paper towels. Place fried pieces in casserole; tuck Bartlett pears in between potato pieces and sprinkle pecans over all. Pour over wine and juice mixture. Bake covered in 350° oven for 30 minutes. Uncover; bake 20-30 minutes until only slightly moist.

Fried Plantains with Sauce (Platanos Fritos Salsa)

6   ripe plantains
¼ pound sweet butter
1   cup brown sugar
1   tablespoon lime juice
⅔ cup sherry (Spanish)
9   cloves
½ teaspoon cinnamon
1   teaspoon orange bits

Slice plantains lengthwise and then in half. Fry pieces in butter until golden brown. Add rest of ingredients and keep stirring until syrup is formed, spooning syrup over plantains. Cover and bake at 350° for 15 minutes. Serve in syrup as a side dish. (Freezes well.)

Condiment for Flavoring (Sofrito Cricillo)

May be purchased in many South American grocery stores. Makes a delicious flavoring to be added while cooking meats and vegetables. Recipe makes a large quantity, but it keeps well in refrigerator or may be frozen.

10 medium large onions
4   bulbs garlic
12 large green peppers
3   (4 ounce) jars pimientos
10 medium tomatoes
1   (10 ounce) jar mixed capers and olives (pit olives, reserve liquids and add)
2   pounds salt pork
2   tablespoons black pepper

Grind all ingredients in meat grinder, or put through food processor. Place in large kettle and boil, bubbling gently and stirring frequently, until all liquid is evaporated and just grease remains on top. Cool and fill jars; do not cap until grease is cold enough to mix through each jar thoroughly. Use 1 tablespoon sofrito to 1 pound hamburg with no other seasoning and prepare for a delectable surprise. Add 1 tablespoon sofrito to 2 packages buttered frozen cooked vegetables. Venture and try!

Coconut Custard Mold (Flan de Coco)

1   cup light brown sugar
¼ cup water
2   (14½ ounce) cans sweetened condensed milk
6   eggs
2   small coconuts, grated, or 1½ cans shredded coconut
2   (13 ounce) cans evaporated milk
2   teaspoons vanilla

Mix brown sugar with water and cook over medium heat, stirring constantly, until mixture is past syrup stage and becomes thick and puffy and a rich golden brown. Have ready a large casserole dish or mold. When brown sugar is ready, spread about ⅛ inch layer around bottom and slightly up the sides of the dish or mold; it will harden as it is spread. Meanwhile, in a large bowl add rest of ingredients and beat in an electric mixer at medium speed about 5 minutes. Pour on top of caramel. Bake in a large pan with boiling water at least half way up on casserole or mold. Bake in 350° oven for 1 hour or until silver knife comes out clean. Remove from pan of water, cool, and then refrigerate overnight or until ready to use; must be refrigerated at least 10 hours before unmolding. Unmold and serve garnished with more grated coconut. (Do not freeze.)

Spanish Custard (Flan)

1 jar cooked prunes, drained
1 cup light brown sugar
¼ cup water
8 eggs
¼ teaspoon salt
3 cups milk
½ cup sugar
1 teaspoon vanilla
1 tablespoon rum extract or cognac
½ teaspoon dried grated orange rind
⅛ teaspoon cinnamon
1 (14½ ounce) can sweetened condensed milk

Mix brown sugar and ¼ cup water in saucepan; cook over medium heat, stirring constantly, until mixture is past syrupy stage and becomes thick and puffy and a rich golden brown. Have ready large casserole dish or mold. When brown sugar is ready, spread in about ⅛ inch layer all around bottom and slightly up sides of dish, it will harden as it is spread. Place drained, cooked prunes on top of caramel equally spaced. In large bowl, break eggs, add salt, milk, sugar and flavorings. Beat at medium speed for about 5 minutes. Add the can of condensed milk and beat for 3 minutes. Pour into mold and place mold in a large pan with boiling water at least half way up on dish. Bake in 350° oven for 1 hour or until silver knife comes out clean. Remove from pan of water; cool and then refrigerate overnight; must be refrigerated at least 10 hours. Unmold to serve. Pass leftover prunes and syrup for extra sauce if desired. (Do not freeze.) Serves 12.

Orange Fruit Cake (Torta de Frutas con Naranja)

1 cup brown sugar
½ cup shortening
1 egg, beaten
1 cup sour milk
1 teaspoon soda
2 cups flour
½ teaspoon baking powder
½ teaspoon salt
1 cup raisins, chopped
1 large orange, ground with skin
½ cup shredded coconut
½ cup nuts, chopped fine
1 tablespoon rum or rum flavoring
2 tablespoons sugar
Juice of large orange

Cream butter and sugar and add beaten egg; mix well. Dissolve soda in sour milk. Sift flour, baking powder and salt. Add alternately the milk mixture and sifted dry ingredients to sugar mixture. Add chopped raisins, ground orange, shredded coconut, chopped nuts and rum or flavoring, beating well. Bake in a well greased and floured baking dish, 9 x 9 inches, in 350° oven for 45 minutes or until cake tests done. Mix 2 tablespoons sugar and juice of orange and pour all over cake. Return to oven and bake 5 more minutes. Do not frost as orange and sugar mixture will make a glaze. Cool on rack. (Freezes well.)

Coconut Ice Cream (Sorvete de Coco)

2	coconuts, shredded or 1½ cans shredded coconut
6	cups milk
2	tablespoons flour
⅛	teaspoon salt
1½	cups sugar
6	eggs, separated
2	teaspoons vanilla
1½	cups cream, whipped thick

Cook shredded coconut and milk together over medium heat for 10 minutes. Cool and strain through several thicknesses of cheesecloth or dish towel, wringing out every drop of milk. Put milk into double boiler; blend in flour, salt and sugar, which have been mixed together. Cook 12 minutes, stirring constantly. Pour little of mixture over beaten egg yolks and gradually add to double boiler mixture. Add flavoring and cook, stirring all the while, for 3 more minutes. Pour into refrigerator trays and freeze for 2 hours. Remove mixture from trays; fold in stiffly beaten egg whites and whipped cream, blending well. Return to trays and cover or place in container with cover and finish freezing. (Keeps up to 3 months.)

Sweet Caramel Sauce (Dulce de Leche)

2	quarts milk
3	cups sugar
1	vanilla bean or 2 teaspoons vanilla

Bring milk to a boil and skim off foam. Add sugar and vanilla bean and mix well; simmer gently, removing scum, for 2 hours and 20 minutes. Strain and add vanilla if not using bean and cool in refrigerator. Serve as topping for ice cream.

Spanish Castilian Liquor Cake (Bizcocho)

3	eggs, separated
2	whole eggs
1	cup sugar
¾	cup flour
½	teaspoon baking powder
½	teaspoon cinnamon
⅛	teaspoon salt

Beat egg yolks, whole eggs and sugar on high speed for 7 minutes. Sift together dry ingredients and gradually beat into first mixture; beat well. Beat egg whites until stiff and dry; stir 1 dollop of beaten whites into flour mixture, gradually folding this into remaining whites. Grease and line with aluminum foil a 12 x 9 inch baking pan; grease again before pouring in batter. Bake in 350° oven for 45-50 minutes, until top springs back at the touch of a finger. When cold, peel off foil and dress.

Dressing:

½	cup sweet Duff Gorden or Dry Sack sherry
¾	cup warmed and strained apricot preserves mixed with 2 teaspoons water
1	cup whipped, sweetened and flavored heavy cream

Spoon sherry over top of entire cake. Spoon over prepared apricot preserves and refrigerate. Spread with whipped cream just before serving if cake is made day ahead of planned serving time.

Orange Cream (Creme de Naranja)

1 cup sugar
½ cup water
6 eggs
  Juice of 2 large oranges
1 teaspoon orange bits or rind
⅛ teaspoon cinnamon

Boil sugar and water to soft ball stage; allow to cool. Beat eggs slightly and mix through orange juice. Strain through finest strainer or dish towel, twice, into top of double boiler. Add cooled syrup and orange bits or rind, mixing well. Cook over simmering water, stirring constantly, until slightly thickened, being careful not to cook over too hot water or to overcook as this will make it curdle. Pour into small dessert dishes and sprinkle with cinnamon. Refrigerate before serving.

Spanish Baba au Rhums

1 cup water
½ cup butter
1 cup flour
4 eggs

Bring water and butter to a boil. Add flour all at once and mix vigorously with a wooden spoon until flour leaves sides of pan. Remove from heat and cool slightly. Beat in eggs, 1 at a time, beating until smooth. Drop in hot oil by dessert spoonfuls and deep fry to a rich brown; drain on paper towels and cool. Pour over syrup to moisten; save extra syrup to spoon over just before serving.

Syrup:

½ cup sugar
¾ cup apricot juice
1 teaspoon lemon juice
2 tablespoons dark rum or 1 tablespoon rum flavoring

Boil sugar and apricot juice together 10 minutes. Add lemon juice and rum and mix together well. Spoon over fried pastries; allow to stand at least 2 hours before serving.

Nut Wafers

6 egg whites
¾ cup sugar
1 teaspoon vanilla
1 cup flour
½ pound sweet butter, melted and cooled
1 cup any kind of nut-meats, whole or halved

Beat whites until stiff. Add small amounts of sugar and the vanilla, beating constantly. Alternately add flour and melted butter, beating them in slowly and thoroughly. Add the nutmeats and mix thoroughly but lightly. Line a 9 x 13 inch jelly roll pan with aluminum foil and pour mixture into it. Bake in 350° oven about 45 minutes or until it tests done. Cool in foil on a rack. When completely cool, wrap in foil and place in freezer. When frozen, it is ready to use, but it will keep for months in the freezer.

To use, quarter the cake and, a quarter at a time, slice the pieces into thin strips, dip in sugar on both sides, and bake in a 350° oven until golden brown (about 10-12 minutes). Keeps several weeks in a dry, covered container.

Index